CONSTRUCTING AND DECONSTRUCTING POWER IN PSALMS 107-150

Society of Biblical Literature

Ancient Israel and Its Literature

Thomas C. Römer, General Editor

Editorial Board:
Suzanne Boorer
Mark G. Brett
Marc Brettler
Cynthia Edenburg
Victor H. Matthews
Gale A. Yee

Number 19

CONSTRUCTING AND DECONSTRUCTING POWER IN PSALMS 107-150

W. Dennis Tucker Jr.

SBL Press
Atlanta

Copyright © 2014 by SBL Press

All rights reserved. No part of this work may be reproduced or transmitted in any form or by any means, electronic or mechanical, including photocopying and recording, or by means of any information storage or retrieval system, except as may be expressly permitted by the 1976 Copyright Act or in writing from the publisher. Requests for permission should be addressed in writing to the Rights and Permissions Office, Society of Biblical Literature, 825 Houston Mill Road, Atlanta, GA 30329 USA.

Library of Congress Cataloging-in-Publication Data

Tucker, W. Dennis.
    Constructing and deconstructing power in Psalms 107-150 / by W. Dennis Tucker Jr.
        p. cm. — (Society of Biblical Literature ancient Israel and its literature ; number 19)
    Includes bibliographical references and index.
    ISBN 978-1-58983-972-4 (paper binding : alk. paper) — ISBN 978-1-58983-974-8 (electronic format) — ISBN 978-1-58983-973-1 (hardcover binding : alk. paper)
    1. Bible. Psalms CVII–CL—Criticism, interpretation, etc. 2. Power (Christian theology)—Biblical teaching. I. Title.
    BS1430.52.T83 2014
    223'.206—dc23
                                                 2014010039

Printed on acid-free, recycled paper conforming to
ANSI/NISO Z39.48-1992 (R1997) and ISO 9706:1994
standards for paper permanence.

Contents

Acknowledgments vii
Abbreviations ix

1. Book 5 in the Psalter: An Introduction 1
   1.0. Introduction to the Study   1
   1.1. Book 5 in Recent Scholarship   6
   1.2. Foreign Nations as the Enemies in the Psalter   12
   1.3. Summary   16

2. The Achaemenid Dynasty and Imperial Ideology..................................19
   2.0. Introduction   19
   2.1. Cyrus and the Origins of an Empire   22
   2.2. Timeless Attitudes in the Achaemenid Imperial Ideology   26
   2.3. The Dissemination of Imperial Ideology   42
   2.4. Conclusion   52

3. Constructing and Deconstructing Power: Part 1 55
   3.0. Introduction   55
   3.1. Psalm 107   59
   3.2. Psalms 108–110: The Opening Davidic Collection   68
   3.3. The Hallel Psalms   82
   3.4. Conclusion   93

4. Constructing and Deconstructing Power: Part 2 95
   4.0. Introduction   95
   4.1. The Psalms of Ascents   95
   4.2. Psalm 137: Recalling the Power of Empire   119
   4.3. Psalms within the Final Davidic Collection   124
   4.4. Conclusion   135

5. Reconstructing Power: Images of Yahweh in Book 5 139
   5.0. Introduction   139
   5.1. The Chief Tenets of Zion Theology and the Notion
       of Power   140
   5.2. Yahweh as the God of Heaven   142
   5.3. The Hand of Yahweh and the Nearness of God   149
   5.4. The Role of Zion in Book 5   153
   5.5. Psalm 145 and the Kingship of Yahweh   156
   5.6. Conclusion   161

6. The Identity of the People of God: Deconstructed and
   Constructed Power 165
   6.0. Introduction   165
   6.1. Rejection of Human Power as the Source of Deliverance   169
   6.2. A Theology of the Poor in Book 5   174
   6.3. Conclusion: The Poor Servant and Its Implications   184

7. Conclusion: Book 5 and Imperial Ideology 187
   7.0. Introduction   187
   7.1. Psalms 146–150: An Extension of Themes   190
   7.2. Conclusion   196

Bibliography 197
Index of Ancient Sources 217
Index of Modern Authors 225

Acknowledgments

There are many individuals who have played a direct or indirect role in the research, writing, and production of this volume. To these I owe a great debt of gratitude. I would like to thank in particular my dean, Dr. David Garland of the George W. Truett Theological Seminary and the administration at Baylor University for granting me a research leave for the fall 2012 semester. This release time from administrative and instructional duties provided the necessary space for research and writing. I am grateful and most fortunate for my dean's continued interest in my research and his constant encouragement and support in my scholarly endeavors. I am especially indebted to my good friend and colleague Dr. Andrew Arterbury for his willingness to assume the duties of Associate Dean for Academic Affairs during my absence. His capable leadership was appreciated by everyone at the Seminary, but by none more than me. My administrative assistant, Mrs. Nancy Floyd, has been invaluable to the completion of this project. She assumed a number of duties in an effort to provide me additional time for work on this book. Her generous spirit has not gone unnoticed nor unappreciated.

I am most fortunate to work at a university with other scholars in the field of Psalms scholarship. Our friendship and collegiality has certainly benefited my research. My colleagues at Baylor University, Drs. Steve Reid and Bill Bellinger, graciously read excerpts from my work and offered wise counsel during the process. I first shared the idea for this book with Bill at a cafe in Oxford while attending the Oxford Conference on the Psalms hosted by Sue Gillingham in 2010. His encouragement there provided much of the impetus to move forward with this work.

There are other Psalms scholars who have read portions of this work and offered feedback. I am grateful for Professor Frank Lothar Hossfeld from the University of Bonn and his doctoral students, Till Steiner and Johannes Bremer, who read portions of this work and freely shared their own research related to the Persian period and the theology of the Psalter. Their research shaped my own thought in a number of ways. I am also indebted to Professor Dirk Human from the University of Pretoria who read several of the initial chapters. His friendship and generous spirit have been a constant encouragement to me. As I was completing the final chapter in this book, my doctoral supervisor, Marvin E. Tate, passed away. Although I graduated nearly fifteen years ago, he and I had remained in close contact over the years, often sharing our research with one another. He was a *Doktorvater* in every sense of the word. I consulted with him on this project at numerous points and benefited greatly from his suggestions. From early on, he instilled in me a deep love for the Psalter. I pray I will do the same with my own students, and in so doing, honor his legacy.

I am grateful to Dr. Steven McKenzie, previous editor of the Ancient Israel and its Literature Series, and to Dr. Thomas Römer, current series editor, for their willingness to include this volume in this series. Bob Buller, Leigh Andersen, and the production staff at the Society of Biblical Literature were enthusiastic and able guides in bringing this volume to fruition. Their professionalism, thoughtfulness, and care for detail made this a much better work.

My wife, Tish, and our three daughters, Hannah, Sarah, and Hope, always make life so much richer. They graciously allowed me to slip away to our study in the evenings and to hide away early on Saturday mornings in order to see this work to completion.

This work is dedicated to my parents, Wade and Elizabeth Tucker. For nearly a half-century they have faithfully ministered to and with many congregations. Their commitment to the God who lifts up the needy from the dust heap (Ps 113:7) has left an indelible imprint upon my life. For that, I remain most grateful.

W. Dennis Tucker Jr.
Advent 2013

Abbreviations

A2Hc	Royal inscription attributed to Artaxerxes found in Hamadan
A?E	Royal inscription of either Artaxerxes II or III found at Elvend
A?P	Royal inscription of either Artaxerxes II or III found at Persepolis
AB	Anchor Bible
ABRL	Anchor Bible Reference Library
AcIr	Acta Iranica
AH	Achaemenid History
AJSL	*American Journal of Semitic Languages and Literature*
AMI	*Archäologische Mitteilungen aus Iran*
ANES	*Ancient Near Eastern Studies*
AOAT	Alter Orient und Altes Testament
ATANT	Abhandlungen zur Theologie des Alten und Neuen Testaments
AZERKAVO	Veröffentlichungen des Arbeitskreises zur Erforschung der Religions- und Kulturgeschichte des Antiken Vorderen Orients
BBB	Bonner biblische Beiträge
BBR	*Bulletin of Biblical Research*
BCOT	Baker Commentary on the Old Testament
BE	Biblical Encyclopedia/Biblische Enzyklopädie
BETL	Bibliotheca ephemeridum theologicarum lovaniensium
BHS	*Biblia Hebraica Stuttgartensia*. Edited by Karl Elliger and Wilhelm Rudolph. 5th ed. Stuttgart: Deutsche Bibelgesellschaft, 1997.
Bib	*Biblica*
BJSUCSD	Biblical and Judaic Studies University of California, San Diego

BN	*Biblische Notizen*
BTB	*Biblical Theology Bulletin*
BZ	*Biblische Zeitschrift*
BZAW	Beihefte zur Zeitschrift für die altestamentliche Wissenschaft
CahT	Cahiers Théologiques
CANE	*Civilizations of the Ancient Near East.* Edited by Jack M. Sasson. 2 vols. Peabody, Mass.: Hendrickson, 1995.
CBQ	*Catholic Biblical Quarterly*
CC	Continental Commentaries
CHJ	*Cambridge History of Judaism.* Edited by W. D. Davies and Louis Finkelstein. Cambridge: Cambridge University Press, 1984–2006.
ConBOT	Coniectanea biblica: Old Testament Series
COS	*The Context of Scripture.* Edited by William W. Hallo and K. Lawson Younger. 3 vols. Leiden: Brill, 1997-2002.
DB	Behistun Inscription of Darius I
DE	The Granj Nameh inscription of Darius I
DNa	Inscription at Darius I's burial tomb at Naqsh-i Rustam near Persepolis
DNb	Inscription at Darius I's burial tomb at Naqsh-i Rustam near Persepolis
DPd	Inscription of Darius I found at Persepolis
DPe	Inscription of Darius I found at Persepolis
DPg	Inscription of Darius I found at Persepolis
DPh	Trilingual text of Darius I from the apadana at Persepolis
DSab	Trilingual inscription on a statue of Darius I found at Susa
DSe	Inscription of Darius I found at Susa
DSf	A trilingual text of Darius I from Susa
DZc	Inscription of Darius I found at Suez
EvT	*Evangelische Theologie*
FAT	Forschungen zum Alten Testament
FOTL	Forms of the Old Testament Literature
HALOT	Koehler, Ludwig, Walter Baumgartner, and Johann Jakob Stamm. *The Hebrew and Aramaic Lexicon of the Old Testament.* Translated and edited by M. E. J. Richardson. 2 vols. Leiden: Brill, 2001.
HANES	History of the Ancient Near East Studies

HBM	Hebrew Bible Monographs
HBT	*Horizons in Biblical Theology*
HR	*History of Religions*
HTKAT	Herders theologischer Kommentar zum Alten Testament
HTR	*Harvard Theological Review*
ICC	International Critical Commentary
Int	*Interpretation*
JBL	*Journal of Biblical Literature*
JBT	*Jahrbuch für Biblische Theologie*
JNES	*Journal of Near Eastern Studies*
JSNT	*Journal for the Study of the New Testament*
JSOT	*Journal for the Study of the Old Testament*
JSOTSup	Journal for the Study of the Old Testament: Supplement Series
KAT	Kommentar zum Alten Testament
KHC	Kurzer Hand-Commentar zum Alten Testament
LHBOTS	Library of Hebrew Bible/Old Testament Study
LSTS	Library of Second Temple Studies
LXX	Septuagint
MLBS	Mercer Library of Biblical Studies
MT	Masoretic Text of the Hebrew Bible
NIB	*New Interpreter's Bible.* Edited by Leander Keck. 12 vols. Nashville: Abingdon, 1996–2004.
NIDOTTE	*New International Dictionary of Old Testament Theology and Exegesis.* Edited by Willem A. VanGemeren. 5 vols. Grand Rapids: Zondervan, 1997.
NRSV	New Revised Standard Version
OBO	Orbis biblicus et orientalis
OIP	Oriental Institute Publications
OP	Old Persian
OTE	*Old Testament Essays*
OTG	Old Testament Guides
OTL	Old Testament Library
OTS	Old Testament Studies
OtSt	Oudtestamentische Studiën
PIBA	Proceedings of the Irish Biblical Association
PRSt	*Perspectives in Religious Studies*
QD	Quaestiones disputatae
SB	Sources bibliques

SBB	Stuttgarter biblische Beiträge
SBLABS	Society of Biblical Literature Archaeology and Biblical Studies
SBLDS	Society of Biblical Literature Dissertation Series
SBLSymS	Society of Biblical Literature Symposium Series
SBM	Stuttgarter biblische Monographien
SBS	Stuttgarter Bibelstudien
SemeiaSt	Semeia Studies
SJOT	*Scandinavian Journal of the Old Testament*
SNTSMS	Society for New Testament Studies Monograph Series
STDJ	Studies on the Texts of the Desert of Judah
StIr	*Studia Iranica*
T&K	*Texte & Kontexte*
TgPss	*Aramaic Targums of the Psalms*
TLOT	*Theological Lexicon of the Old Testament*. Edited by Ernst Jenni, with the assistance of Claus Westermann. Translated by Mark E. Biddle. 3 vols. Peabody, Mass.: Hendrickson, 1997.
VT	*Vetus Testamentum*
VTSup	Supplements to Vetus Testamentum
WBC	Word Biblical Commentary
WMANT	Wissenschaftliche Monographien zum Alten und Neuen Testament
XPh	Daiva Text, a Persian text found at Persepolis attributed to Xerxes
XPl	Persian text found at Persepolis attributed to Xerxes
ZAW	*Zeitschrift für die Alttestamentliche Wissenschaft*
ZTK	*Zeitschrift für Theologie und Kirche*

1
BOOK 5 IN THE PSALTER: AN INTRODUCTION

1.0. INTRODUCTION TO THE STUDY

"Whoever is among you of all his people, may Yahweh his God be with him. Let him go up!" (NRSV, modified). These hopeful words conclude the book of 2 Chronicles. Coupled with a modified version of the Cyrus decree, the narrator places this generous invitation on the lips of Cyrus. With such an invitation, the writer of Chronicles appears to imply that the suffering of exile has ended and that the joyous, even celebratory, work of restoration lies just ahead. Likewise, Deutero-Isaiah announces such a theme in the salvation oracles found in that collection. These oracles portend a future in which the people of God will "go up" to enjoy a land prepared for the exiles. Deutero-Isaiah suggests, albeit it with more poetically persuasive imagery, that with the arrival of Cyrus, history will be righted and so will the people of God.

Historians have frequently labeled the period beginning with the edict of Cyrus, "the Restoration."[1] Perhaps like the narrator of 2 Chronicles, scholars have sought to paint this period as one fraught with hope, a period filled with restorative possibility. At times, the attention given to such possibilities may have overshadowed the larger socio-political dynamics asso-

---

1. See most notably, Peter R. Ackroyd, *Exile and Restoration: A Study of Hebrew Thought of the Sixth Century B.C.* (OTL; Philadelphia: Westminster, 1968). See also the works of John Bright, *A History of Israel* (4th ed.; Louisville: Westminster John Knox, 2000); Michael D. Coogan, *The Old Testament: A Historical and Literary Introduction to the Hebrew Scriptures* (2d ed.; Oxford: Oxford University Press, 2010). Norman K. Gottwald uses the term "restoration" but refers to this period more broadly as "Israel's Colonial Recovery," recognizing the socio-political implications of imperial rule for Yehud (*The Hebrew Bible: A Brief Socio-Literary Introduction* [abridged by Rebecca J. Kruger Gaudino; Minneapolis: Fortress, 2009], 235–336).

ciated with empire—dynamics that no doubt influenced the events that transpired in a small region of the Persian Empire called "Yehud."

Recent studies have attempted to rectify this deficiency by paying particular attention to the concept of empire more broadly, as well as its impact on the texts generated in this particular period.[2] As a result of such extensive work, Jon Berquist has even suggested that a paradigm shift of sorts has occurred in the nomenclature associated with that period, shifting from that of "exile and restoration" to that of "empire and colony."[3] This shift, according to Berquist, has provided a "different conceptual framework for understanding Jerusalem and its environs in the time of the Persian Empire."[4] Equally so, this "different conceptual framework" has opened up new avenues for reading and interpreting the literature generated under empire. For obvious reasons, research along these lines has focused primarily on narrative texts such as Chronicles, Ezra, and Nehemiah, and selected prophetic texts (e.g., Haggai, Zechariah, Malachi, and Trito-Isaiah). These studies have sought to discern the socio-political and

---

2. Examples of such work would include Jon L. Berquist, *Judaism in Persia's Shadow: A Social and Historical Approach* (Minneapolis: Fortress Press, 1995); "Constructions of Identity in Postcolonial Yehud," in *Judah and the Judeans in the Persian Period* (ed. Oded Lipschits and Manfred Oeming; Winona Lake, Ind.: Eisenbrauns, 2006), 53–66; Jeremiah W. Cataldo, *A Theocratic Yehud? Issues of Government in a Persian Province* (LHBOTS 498; New York: T&T Clark, 2009); Kenneth G. Hoglund, *Achaemenid Imperial Administration in Syria-Palestine and the Missions of Ezra and Nehemiah* (SBLDS 125; Atlanta: Scholars Press, 1992); John Kessler, *The Book of Haggai: Prophecy and Society in Early Persian Yehud* (VTSup 91; Leiden: Brill, 2002); Melody Knowles, *Centrality Practiced: Jerusalem in the Religious Practice of Yehud and the Diaspora in the Persian Period* (SBLABS 16; Atlanta: Society of Biblical Literature, 2006); Oded Lipschits and Manfred Oeming, eds., *Judah and the Judeans in the Persian Period* (Winona Lake, Ind.: Eisenbrauns, 2006); John W. Watts, ed., *Persia and Torah: The Theory of Imperial Authorization of the Pentateuch* (SBLSymS 17; Atlanta: Society of Biblical Literature, 2001).

3. Jon L. Berquist, "Approaching Yehud," in *Approaching Yehud: New Approaches to the Study of the Persian Period* (ed. Jon L. Berquist; SemeiaSt 50; Atlanta: Society of Biblical Literature, 2007), 2. See also the article by Julia O'Brien in the same volume. She dispenses with the label "exile and restoration," preferring instead "exile and empire," reflecting scholarship's relatively recent foray into the study of empire and its impact on biblical studies ("From Exile to Empire: A Response," in *Approaching Yehud*, 209–14).

4. Ibid., 2.

socio-theological dimensions of the text as it relates to empire and the role of empire in the construction of identity and ideology.

Largely absent from research on empire, and the Persian Empire in particular, however, has been the book of Psalms.[5] Although commentators have frequently assigned specific psalms (e.g., Pss 1; 9–10; 107; 137; 145) to the postexilic period based on form or theme, they have not necessarily sought to explore the connections between the psalms and the larger imperial context in which the psalms were allegedly written or collected. In "Psalms and the Construction of the Self," one of the few recent articles attempting to evaluate the psalms with reference to the notion of empire, Berquist offers a somewhat cursory analysis of the psalms read as Persian period literature.[6] He suggests that the psalms construct identities that both connect to and resist the empire. Although Berquist's attention to identity formation is an important conclusion, and one to which we shall return later, his overall approach in the article remains too general and lacks the kind of specific engagement with the biblical text found in previous studies devoted to the role of empire in narrative or prophetic texts.[7]

---

5. Gunther Wanke has attempted to identify the principal themes of the psalmists during the Persian period. Among those identified by Wanke include: (1) the focusing of Israel's hope on Zion-Jerusalem; (2) a stronger orientation towards Temple worship in Jerusalem as a result of the change from "nation to congregation;" (3) the prominent attention given to the law; (4) the addition of a "universal dimension" to the image of God, separating such a conception from its close ties with Palestine; and (5) the use of wisdom theology ("Prophecy and Psalms in the Persian Period," *CHJ* 1:162–88, esp. 183–84). Surprisingly, altogether absent in Wanke's treatment of the psalms in the Persian period is any discussion of the Persian Empire itself and the political impact of empire upon the theology of the Psalter.

6. Jon L. Berquist, "Psalms, Postcolonialism, and the Construction of the Self," in *Approaching Yehud*, 195–202. Berquist opines that "the psalms were part of the empire's control of the region through its ideological social control of persons and lives. Psalms offer words and social spaces that shape individual experiences and emotions into socially accepted expressions, which at least indirectly serve imperial interests" (196). In his earlier work, *Judaism in Persia's Shadow*, Berquist is less shrill in his assertion that the psalms functioned to serve "imperial interests," suggesting instead that "within the songs are traces of the Persian Empire's domination of individual lives" (193). The evidence within the psalms themselves seems to support Berquist's claim that the psalms reflect the domination of human life by those in power (cf. Pss 125; 129; 144).

7. For a similar critique of Berquist's article, see O'Brien, "From Exile to Empire: A Response," 212.

As a result, what remains needed is an extended reading of the Psalter, or some portion thereof, that offers evidence of such claims, or that extends the argument in new and important ways.

Erich Zenger provided a new reading of the Psalter in light of empire in a brief but provocatively entitled article, "Der jüdische Psalter—ein anti-imperiales Buch?" Zenger suggests that the Psalter in its final form might properly be labeled a *Kampfbuch* against imperial powers.[8] Read in this way, the Psalter "concerns the political relevance of religious traditions" and attempts to explore the relationship, if any, between *Gebet* and *Politik*.[9] The psalms, individually and collectively, portray Yahweh as a warrior for justice and righteousness, but they also portray Yahweh as a warrior who wars against chaos. Zenger qualifies such a statement, arguing that chaos is often portrayed in biblical texts by "political systems, and especially in the kings and princes of enemy nations."[10] The Psalter makes the same claim repeatedly "that the biblical God of power brings the enemy to an end, breaking the threatening, oppressive, and destructive power."[11] According to this line of reasoning, the "anti-imperial" bias in the Psalter would appear to be solely directed at those who lie beyond the borders of Israel. Yet Zenger does not reserve critique of imperial power to foreign nations alone but instead suggests that the identity of power *within* Israel itself is altered in the structure and theology of the Psalter. As Zenger explains, by the end of book 5 (Ps 144), David is defined as the "servant of Yahweh, clearly not a powerful, imperial king, but a weak figure who stands in need of deliverance by Yahweh."[12] Thus for Zenger, imperial power writ large, be it foreign or otherwise, falls under the castigating gaze of the psalmists. Ideologically, for some interpreters, this may be an attractive proposal because it deconstructs empires of all sorts. As attractive as the proposal

---

8. Erich Zenger, "Der jüdische Psalter—ein anti-imperiales Buch?" in *Religion und Gesellschaft: Studien zu ihrer Wechselbeziehung in den Kulturen des Antiken Vorderen Orients* (ed. Rainer Albertz; AZERKAVO 1/AOAT 248; Münster: Ugarit, 1997), 95–105.

9. Ibid., 95. All translations are the author's unless otherwise noted.

10. Ibid., 97. See also Bernd Janowski, "Dem Löwen gleich, gierig nach Raub: Zum Feindbild in den Psalmen," *EvT* 55 (1995): 155–73. See especially Janowski's treatment of Egyptian iconography as illustrative of the connection often made between mythic war and historical-political enemies (169–71).

11. Zenger, "Der jüdische Psalter," 96.

12. Ibid., 98. For further comments on the role of David in book 5, see §6.2.3 in the present study.

1. BOOK 5 IN THE PSALTER: AN INTRODUCTION

may seem, it is still found wanting. While the Psalter does pose a challenge to imperial power, against both those within Israel but especially beyond, Zenger fails to acknowledge the differentiation that exists in the critique of each. The critique of foreign powers remains much more acute and far more pointed than the critique of the Davidic monarchy.[13] The critique, if it can be called such, against the Davidic monarchy is far more nuanced. It is less about a critique, as seen in the prophetic corpus, and much more about the growing awareness of the complex social and political context following the exile.

Similar to Berquist, Zenger provides only a sketch of what such a thesis might mean for reading and interpreting the Psalter. He suggests that Pss 2–89 formed an initial collection, a "messianic Psalter," but one that actually "democratized" the messianic perspective to include the nation of Israel in this role (cf. Ps 89:51).[14] Psalms 90–150 shift to a "decidedly theocratic concept" announcing the universal reign of Yahweh. The bulk of Zenger's article, however, is focused on Pss 1–2 as the introduction to the full collection and Pss 146–150 as the conclusion, with attention to their respective contributions to an anti-imperial bias. Book 4 and book 5, comprising a sizable portion of the Psalter, are covered in only two short paragraphs, providing exceedingly broad generalizations about each collection.

---

13. David C. Mitchell has challenged the assertion that the Psalter stands against any form of Davidic rule. For Mitchell, even a psalm such as Ps 89 is not meant to signal the end of the Davidic monarchy but rather likely meant to refer to a "David scion not yet come" ("Lord, Remember David: G. H. Wilson and the Message of the Psalter," *VT* 56 [2006]: 526–48). See also Mitchell's earlier work, *The Message of the Psalter: An Eschatological Programme in the Book of Psalms* (JSOTSup 252; Sheffield: Sheffield Academic Press, 1997). Although he does not address book 5 as a formal unit, he does consider the role of the Songs of Ascents and selected psalms from book 5 in his attempt to uncover an eschatological predictive program in the Psalter, similar to the alleged program in Zech 9–14. Although an intriguing proposal, it has failed to garner considerable support in recent psalms's scholarship, due primarily to Mitchell's attempt to reconstruct some form of an enthronement festival.

14. Zenger, "Der jüdische Psalter," 98. For a similar conclusion, see W. Dennis Tucker Jr., "Democratization and the Language of the Poor in Psalms 2–89," *HBT* 25 (2003): 161–78. On Pss 2–89 as a messianic collection, see Christopher Rösel, *Die Messianische Redaktion des Psalters: Studien zu Entstehung und Theologie der Sammlung Psalm 2–89* (Stuttgart: Calwer, 1999). For a different assessment of the David figure in the Psalter, especially in books 4–5, see Jerome F. D. Creach's *The Destiny of the Righteous in the Psalms* (St. Louis: Chalice, 2008), 99–110.

The chief weakness in Zenger's thesis is his failure to identify the basis for an anti-imperial theology in the Psalter, in particular, as it relates to foreign threats. He does suggest that such a theological move is born out of an encounter with a "hostile, wicked and destructive world."[15] Within such a world, according to Zenger, political systems, particularly the kings and princes of foreign nations, threaten the existence of Israel.[16] Beyond these rather broad claims, however, Zenger offers little else by way of specificity.[17] Or put differently, despite Zenger's penchant for a diachronic reading of the Psalter elsewhere in his scholarship, he offers little historical or ideological evidence in which to root his initial claims. The absence of such specificity does not undermine the final claims of Zenger (i.e., the Psalter has an anti-imperial bent), but it does weaken the force of his overall argument.

1.1. Book 5 in Recent Scholarship

Within the last three decades, the role of book 5, as a discrete unit within the Psalter, has received minimal attention, with many studies on the Psalter preferring instead to focus specifically on books 1–3 or book 4, or perhaps the Psalter more generally, including a discussion of book 5.[18] Gerald Wilson's work provided the initial impetus for considering individual

---

15. Zenger, "Der jüdische Psalter," 96.

16. Ibid., 97.

17. Zenger does suggest that the Psalter likely reached its final form around 200 B.C.E., in a time laden with external political threats and internal fissures (ibid., 95). For a more detailed diachronic proposal concerning the formation of the Psalter, see Erich Zenger, "Das Buch der Psalmen," in *Einleitung in das Alte Testament* (ed. Erich Zenger; 6th ed.; Stuttgart: Kohlhammer, 2006), 363–65.

18. For a review of contemporary scholarship on books 1–3, see Martin Leuenberger, *Konzeptionen des Königtums Gottes im Psalter: Untersuchungen zu Komposition und Redaktion der theokratischen Bücher IV–V im Psalter* (ATANT 83; Zürich: Theologischer, 2004), 93–123; for book 4, see 125–32. The recent volume in the Hermeneia series by Frank Lothar Hossfeld and Eric Zenger provides an exhaustive treatment of the individual psalms in book 5 as well as brief excursuses on the smaller compositional units within the collection (*Psalms 3: A Commentary on Psalms 101–150* [ed. Klaus Baltzer; trans. Linda Maloney; Hermeneia; Minneapolis: Fortress Press, 2011]). Although Hossfeld and Zenger give attention to the social and political themes in each psalm, the nature of the commentary format itself precludes them from providing a general assessment of issues related to empire in book 5. Their comments do, however, inform the treatment of the selected psalms in §3 and §4 of this study.

books and their significance to the Psalter as a whole, but as explained below, his treatment of book 5 proved lacking in many ways related to the present study. More recently, however, the works of Martin Leuenberger and Egbert Ballhorn have sought to explicate more fully the compositional and redactional history of book 5, while correspondingly, to identify thematic strands. The role of enemies and empires in the collection of psalms in book 5, however, receives minor attention in the works of Wilson and Leuenberger, while receiving more attention in the work of Ballhorn, as explained below.

1.1.1. Gerald Wilson and *The Editing of the Hebrew Psalter*

Gerald Wilson's groundbreaking work, *The Editing of the Hebrew Psalter*, signaled a significant methodological shift in Psalms research, one that has exerted considerable influence in the research on the Psalter for the last three decades.[19] Wilson explored the organizational strategy of the Psalter, and where possible, examined possible vestiges of editorial work. Although interested in the final form of the Psalter, Wilson's methodology derived in part from the apparent editorial techniques observed in Sumerian temple hymns and Mesopotamian hymnic incipits, with attention to their possible implications for a similar analysis of the Hebrew Psalter. Based upon the editorial positioning of royal psalms in books 1–3 (Pss 2, 72, and 89), Wilson surmised that the first three books were an exilic response to the loss of the Davidic monarchy and represented the community's desire for deliverance and even restoration.[20] At the conclusion of book 3, this desire is couched as a rebuke of God for his apparent

---

19. Gerald H. Wilson, *The Editing of the Hebrew Psalter* (SBLDS 76; Chico, Calif.: Scholars Press, 1985). Following his initial volume, Wilson refined his views in "The Use of Royal Psalms in the 'Seams' of the Hebrew Psalter," *JSOT* 35 (1986): 85–94; "The Shape of the Book of Psalms," *Int* 46 (1992): 129–42; "Shaping the Psalter: A Consideration of Editorial Linkage in the Book of Psalms," in *The Shape and Shaping of the Psalter* (ed. J. Clinton McCann Jr.; JSOTSup 159; Sheffield: JSOT Press, 1993), 72–82; "The Structure of the Psalter," in *Interpreting the Psalms: Issues and Approaches* (ed. David Firth and Philip S. Johnston; Downers Grove, Ill.: InterVarsity Press, 2005), 229–46; "King, Messiah, and the Reign of God," in *The Book of Psalms: Composition and Reception* (ed. Peter W. Flint and Patrick D. Miller Jr.; VTSUP 99; Leiden: Brill, 2005), 391–406.

20. This position was argued more forcefully in one of Wilson's final pieces, "King, Messiah, and the Reign of God," 391–406.

"hiddenness" in the midst of great national tragedy (89:46–51). Books 4 and 5 (Pss 90–150), according to Wilson, represent the response of the sages to the questions and dilemmas raised in the first three books. In support of this, Wilson stresses the location of wisdom psalms or those clearly influenced by the wisdom tradition (90, 107, and 145) at strategic points in both collections, in effect, influencing the tenor of both books. In summary, Wilson's volume provided the first extended treatment of the individual books within the Psalter, while also proposing a possible editorial strategy for its present arrangement.

In his analysis of book 5, however, Wilson surmised that a "detailed analysis of the editorial organization of the fifth book" proves difficult due to its unwieldy size (forty-four psalms) and the appearance of previous collections within book 5 which, he suggests, would appear to limit "the amount of editorial manipulation possible."[21] Despite these initial disclaimers, Wilson does proffer a number of suggestions related to the editorial structure of book 5 and its implications for considering the dominant thematic threads in that collection. He noted that there are two groups of Davidic psalms (Pss 108–110, 138–145) preserved in book 5 and their placement at the beginning and end of the collection may suggest the primary, and perhaps only, form of editorial intentionality within that book. Wilson avers that "While it is difficult to trace any clear strategy of editorial juxtaposition threading its way through the individual [psalms] ... the groups as a whole seem to intend to set up David as a model in response to the concerns of the [psalms] which precede them."[22] Despite the allusions to David, he correctly notes that the emphasis in book 5 shifts away from human kingship, at least as Israel's hope, and instead places its focus on Yahweh as the enthroned king (Ps 145). Book 5, according to Wilson, was meant to generate an attitude of trust and reliance upon Yahweh, as modeled in the life of David. Generally absent, however, from his discussion of the book as a whole are the threats posed by the political foes.[23] He does suggest that book 5 challenges the community to "trust in Yahweh as king rather than in fragile and failing human princes," but even here, the threat

---

21. Wilson, *The Editing of the Hebrew Bible*, 220. He notes that the large number of consecutive, untitled psalms within books 4 and 5 also present challenges in identifying an editorial strategy (177).

22. Ibid., 221.

23. Ibid., 227.

posed by such figures appears minimized and does not figure prominently in the analysis provided.[24]

1.1.2. Martin Leuenberger: A Theocratic Book 5

In *Konzeptionen des Königtums Gottes im Psalter: Untersuchungen zu Komposition und Redaktion der theokratischen Bücher IV–V im Psalter*, Martin Leuenberger makes a significant contribution to the analysis of the second half of the Psalter and the development of the "kingdom of God" theology which dominates it. In many ways, Leuenberger follows the consensus views established by Wilson and others concerning books 1–3, although he arrives at his conclusions in a way that differs methodologically from Wilson and much of the earlier North American work on the first three books in the Psalter.[25] According to Leuenberger the concept of a "messianic king" dominates Pss 2–89, and like Rösel and others, he suggests that the collection functioned independently as a "messianic Psalter." Leuenberger contends that Pss 90–106, containing the recurring language of יהוה מלך and the larger domain of associated images, were added to this earlier collection. The addition of these psalms consequently shifted the entire collection (Pss 2–106) to a theocratic Psalter.[26] Book 5 was a later addition, sharing the theocratic perspective of book 4, but developed and appended to the collection in three stages: 107–118; 119–136; and 137–150. Within each collection, important themes were advanced that support the larger claim of the kingship of Yahweh. Psalms 107–118 highlight, for the first time, the international experience of deliverance, while Pss 119–136 situate this experience of deliverance within the perspectives of creation and history. Psalms 136–150 adopt these themes in principle and develop, in Ps 145, a synthesis of the collection's theology. According

---

24. Wilson, "King, Messiah, and the Reign of God," 393.
25. Leuenberger, *Konzeptionen des Königtums Gottes im Psalter*, 85–92. Leuenberger's approach is two-pronged, analyzing the text diachronically through redaction history but also analyzing the text synchronically by considering the primary conceptual "horizon markers" (*Leithorizont*), in an effort to identify the fundamental claims through the collection (25). Wilson's approach would be considered largely synchronic.
26. Ibid., 92.

to Leuenberger, "the conceptual basis of book 5" exists in Ps 145, and particularly in verses 10–13.²⁷

> All your works shall give thanks to you, O Lord,
>   and all your faithful ones shall bless you.
> They shall speak of the glory of your kingdom
>   and tell of your power,
> To make known to all people your mighty deeds,
>   and the glorious splendor of your kingdom.
> Your kingdom is an everlasting kingdom
>   and your dominion endures throughout all generations. (NRSV)

This language, coupled with the יהוה מלך psalms in book 4 and the language employed in Pss 146–150, suggests that the "Psalter is a song of praise concerning the universal reign of God."²⁸

The specific presuppositions and conclusions of Leuenberger's compositional history are not of primary concern for this study. The chief concern relates to his view of the enemy in book 5 and its significance for understanding the collection. While the kingdom of God represents the primary theme of books 4 and 5 for Leuenberger (and most scholars), he does concede that a number of secondary themes are present. Among them is the opposition between the just and the wicked or the enemy, and frequently this opposition is manifested in some type of perceived threat. Within book 5, this threat to the just can be and is often extended to the international horizon (*Völkerhorizont*).²⁹ For example, in Pss 107–110 Leuenberger contends that the threat of the enemy outlined in Ps 107 is extended in Pss 108–110, with Ps 108 highlighting the international aspect of the threat through the listing of numerous enemy neighbors which function as a cipher for the nations writ large.³⁰ Likewise, the threat posed by an enemy nation in Ps 137 serves to introduce the final collection of book 5 (Pss 138–145). Leuenberger argues that the chief theme in that collection remains the kingdom of God, but it must be understood in light of the threat posed by the nations.³¹ He offers a more extended assessment of the enemy nations than that of Wilson, but fails in part to consider

---

27. Ibid., 387.
28. Ibid. See also Zenger, "Das Buch der Psalmen," 249.
29. Leuenberger, *Konzeptionen des Königtums Gottes im Psalter*, 383.
30. On the role of the nations in Ps 108, see §3.2.1 in this study.
31. Leuenberger, *Konzeptionen des Königtums Gottes im Psalter*, 320–45.

whether such rhetoric contributes to any form of an anti-imperial ideology in the collection.

1.1.3. Egbert Ballhorn: Book 5 in Light of a Proper *Leserichtung*

Leuenberger sought to provide a diachronic rendering of books 4 and 5 in the Psalter, suggesting that the dominant theme that bound the collections together was the kingdom of God. Egbert Ballhorn, in *Zum Telos des Psalters: der Textzusammenhang des Vierten und Fünften Psalmenbuches*, considers the same section of the Psalter as Leuenberger, but differs in approach methodologically.[32] His book begins with the question "Why should one read the Psalter *as a book*?" and continues by suggesting that one only understands the Psalter in all of its complexity in light of a proper *Leserichtung*, "reading direction."[33] As one reads from the beginning, various collections are identified throughout the Psalter. The synchronic approach employed by Ballhorn, however, "in no way can or must mean an eschewal of the diachronic analysis" of the text.[34] Diachronically Ballhorn, similar to Leuenberger, attempts to track the "formation" of the discrete units found within book 5, but he does so with a particular sensitivity to a proper *Leserichtung*. As he explains, "What stands at the end, has a greater weight. Whatever has the last word dominates" the entire collection.[35] Although the focus of his work is on books 4 and 5, he does locate these books within the larger "narrative structure" of the entire Psalter.[36] The differing collections and themes represented in the Psalter stand in "mutual dialogue." By that, he means that "these collections however are not in enclosed units, but exist in varying connections with one another" and the words and themes that unite these collections are what remains of primary importance.[37] Thus, the appropriate "reading direction" ensures that the reader recognizes how these themes have been "initiated, superimposed, transformed, negated, and carried forward."[38]

---

32. Egbert Ballhorn, *Zum Telos des Psalters: Der Textzusammenhang des Vierten und Fünften Psalmenbuches* (BBB 138; Berlin: Philo, 2004).
33. Ibid., 11, emphasis original.
34. Ibid., 28.
35. Ibid., 27.
36. Ibid., 32–33.
37. Ibid., 361.
38. Ibid.

Ballhorn identifies five themes in books 4 and 5 of the Psalter: the concept of Israel; the Torah; Israel and the nations; the changing character (*Gestaltwandlung*) of the Temple; and the Davidic King and the Kingdom of God. As noted above, according to Ballhorn, all five themes stand in a mutual dialogue across the various collections. The role of the nations in the final two books appears to shift somewhat from collection to collection, making it difficult to harmonize the various statements and their portrayal of the nations. In some texts such as Ps 96 or Ps 100, the psalmists offer a more sympathetic rendering of the nations and their participation in the kingdom of God. Other psalms (Pss 108–110; 144) offer a much more negative appraisal of the nations. Yet the apparent discrepancy in perspective may be better understood when nuanced correctly. He notes the subtleties in both lines of thought, explaining "Every form of human rule will be wiped out by God, but all humans will take part in the universal, eschatological praise of God (Ps 150)."[39] Thus, book 5 serves as an indictment against all forms of foreign power but not necessarily a castigation of all foreign people. In short, when understood properly, according to Ballhorn, the psalms found in book 5 possess an anti-imperial bent similar to the position outlined by Zenger.

1.2. Foreign Nations as the Enemies in the Psalter

Wilson, Leuenberger, and Ballhorn have recognized, in varying degrees, the presence of enemies in book 5. As will be made evident below (§§3–4), Leuenberger and Ballhorn, in particular, imply that the threat posed by the enemies may best be understood in many psalms in book 5 as a political threat, one associated with another nation or people group.[40] Neither

---

39. Ibid., 377.

40. The literature on the enemy in the psalms is extensive. For a general overview of selected positions in scholarship, see Hans Joachim Kraus, *Theology of the Psalms* (trans. Keith Crim; CC; Minneapolis: Fortress Press, 1992), 125–36; Steven J. L. Croft, *The Identity of the Individual in the Psalms* (JSOTSup 44; Sheffield: JSOT Press, 1987), 15–48; T. R. Hobbs and P. K. Jackson, "The Enemy in the Psalms," *BTB* 21 (1991): 22–29; Gerald Sheppard, "'Enemies' and the Politics of Prayer in the Book of Psalms," in *The Bible and the Politics of Exegesis: Essays in Honor of Norman K. Gottwald on his Sixty-Fifth Birthday* (ed. David Jobling, Peggy Day, and Gerald Sheppard; Cleveland, Ohio: Pilgrim Press, 1991), 61–82. See also the influential positions outlined in Harris Birkeland, *The Evildoers in the Book of Psalms* (Oslo: Dybwad, 1955); Sigmund Mowinckel, *The Psalms in Israel's Worship* (2 vols.; Oxford: Blackwell, 1962), 1:195–

scholar, however, provides a sustained analysis of the role of enemies and empires within the collection.[41] The identification of the enemy as a nation or foreign power has a long history within psalms scholarship and was championed most forcefully by Harris Birkeland in his monograph, *Die Feinde des Individuums in der israelitischen Psalmenliteratur*, and later in a subsequent revision of the thesis, *The Evildoers in the Book of Psalms*.[42] Although the identification of the enemy in communal laments as a foreign power (Pss 74; 79) was not disputed, the identity of the enemy in the individual psalms remained, and remains, a point of debate in psalms scholarship. As noted below, Birkeland sought to champion the claim that in many of the individual psalms the enemy was likely that of a foreign nation and that the "I" in the psalm either represented Israel or its designee (i.e., the king).

His initial work appeared nearly three-quarters of a century before the emergence of postcolonial criticism, yet in many ways, the two share common concerns, albeit through differing methodologies.[43] For example, Birkeland noted the frequency with which the Psalter spoke of the

---

219; and Othmar Keel, *Feinde und Gottesleugner: Studien zum Image der Widersacher in den Individualpsalmen* (SBM 7; Stuttgart: Katholisches Bibelwerk, 1969). A number of more recent studies have explored the metaphorical rendering of the enemy in the Psalter: Amy C. Cottrill, *Language, Power, and Identity in the Lament Psalms of the Individual* (LHBOTS 493; New York: T&T Clark, 2008); Dharmakkan Dhanaraj, *Theological Significance of the Motif of Enemies in Selected Psalms of Individual Lament* (Glückstadt: Augustin, 1992), 38–53; Bernd Janowski, "Dem Löwen gleich, gierig nach Raub," 155–173; Peter Riede, *Im Netz des Jägers: Studien zur Feindmetaphorik der Individualpsalmen* (WMANT 85; Neukirchener-Vluyn: Neukirchen, 2000).

41. Ballhorn does highlight the role of the enemy in selected psalms throughout his monograph and concludes with a very short summary of the relationship between Israel and the nations based on a proper *Leserichtung*. His summary, however, remains too general to offer much help in analyzing the role of empire within the collection (*Zum Telos des Psalters*, 376–77).

42. Harris Birkeland, *Die Feinde des Individuums in der israelitischen Psalmenliteratur: Ein Beitrag zur Kenntnis der semitischen Literatur- und Religionsgeschichte* (Oslo: Grøndahl, 1933); *The Evildoers in the Book of Psalms*.

43. See especially Jon L. Berquist, "Postcolonialism and Imperial Motives," *Semeia* 75 (1996): 15–35. See also Fernando Segovia, *Decolonizing Biblical Studies: A View from the Margins* (Maryknoll, N.Y.: Orbis Books, 2000); Rasaiah S. Sugirtharajah, *Postcolonial Criticism and Biblical Interpretation* (Oxford: Oxford University Press, 2002) and his more recent work, *Exploring Postcolonial Biblical Criticism: History, Method, Practice* (Malden, Mass.: Wiley-Blackwell, 2012).

enemies of the nation and the enemies of the "I", thereby creating "an outstanding feature in the ideology of the Book of Psalms."[44] This focus on an "ideology" of power that threatened Israel not only served his thesis well, it has also remained a central point of investigation and analysis in postcolonial criticism. For Birkeland, the continual threat of war and the persistent presence of imperial powers no doubt informed Israel's ideology of power. He states

> Wars occurred during the greater part of the history of Israel, and many [individual psalms] and [national psalms] are based on situations created by these wars. But Israel also suffered from gentiles when there was no war, viz. when gentiles ruled the country. As a matter of fact, Israel had to suffer from foreign occupation and domination in Assyrian, in Babylonian, in Persian, and in Greek and in Roman times ... Gentiles, thus, are found both within and without the Israelite society.[45]

The considerable work in biblical studies over the last three decades has explored the impact of the Persian Empire, in particular, on Yehud.[46] These studies have recast Persia and Persia's influence on the region in language that is similar to that of Birkeland's ("to suffer from foreign occupation and domination").

In an attempt to identify the impact of empire upon the theology of isolated psalms more generally, and the impact of the empire related to the identity of the enemy more particularly, Birkeland set out to redefine scholarship's approach to the question. Prior to his work on the subject, the enemy in the individual psalms was construed as either a group that stood in opposition to the "pious circles" of the "I" or, following Mowinckel's claim, the enemy was associated with sorcerers who allegedly plagued the psalmist with sickness.[47] Perceiving both options as unsatisfactory, Birkeland pursued a different path of investigation. According to his findings, there were twenty psalms that clearly identified the enemy as a foreign nation. In these psalms he noted patterns of language that remained consistent throughout this subset. For Birkeland, the term "pattern" func-

---

44. Birkeland, *The Evildoers in the Book of Psalms*, 7.
45. Ibid., 25.
46. See above, note 1.
47. See Sigmund Mowinckel, "'Āwen and the Psalms of Individual Lament," in *Psalm Studies* (trans. Mark E. Biddle; 2 vols.; Atlanta: Society of Biblical Literature, 2014).

tioned sociologically, "signifying a complex of traditionally combined manifestations of human behavior or ideology."[48] Thus, he alleged that the pattern used to describe the enemy as a foreign power in these twenty psalms included references to malicious speech by the enemy, treacherous behavior, hubris, and "absolute godlessness."[49] In many of the remaining individual psalms, he suggested that similar patterns of language appear in reference to the enemy, likely implying that these references should be construed as foreign powers, or their designees, as well. His approach proves suggestive in its attempt to identify a "pattern" or an "ideology" in the Psalter. He sought to identify an ideology of the enemy in the individual laments, and in some ways he succeeded in identifying such language and its contribution to such a sustained ideology. The presence of enemies, and in particular political enemies, formed the foundation of such an ideology and intersects in part with the present study. Whereas Birkeland sought to uncover patterns of language that would identify convincingly the enemy in individual psalms as a national political threat, this study will consider the language and patterns present in book 5 that suggest the Psalter contains an ideology that stands in response to power, and political power more particularly. In his postcolonial analysis on the book of Jeremiah, Steed Davidson suggests that a postcolonial perspective may refer to a "close reading of texts *qua* text to discover embedded codes of resistance or otherwise, to explore rhetorical shapes, and to examine literary constructions … it sees the Bible as subsumed within the rhetorics of resistance to colonial and hegemonic power."[50] Through a close reading of selected psalms, this study will consider the manner in which human power is envisioned and note the way in which a certain "rhetoric of resistance" emerges. This rhetoric generates an ideology that remains firmly anti-imperial in orientation. It is an ideology that at once seeks both to deconstruct and construct power.

---

48. Birkeland, *The Evildoers in the Book of Psalms*, 17.
49. Ibid.
50. Steed V. Davidson, *Empire and Exile: Postcolonial Readings of the Book of Jeremiah* (LHBOTS 542; New York: T&T Clark, 2011), 43. Postcolonial readings of biblical texts may also pay attention to the manner in which the text supports and promulgates the agendas of those in power. While such a reading may be justified in some biblical books, the psalms in book 5 do nothing to legitimate those who hold power, as will be suggested in the following chapters.

1.3. Summary

This study builds off the works of Wilson, Leuenberger, and Ballhorn, as well as that of Birkeland in an effort to extend Zenger's thesis regarding an anti-imperial tendency in the Psalter. Wilson, Leuenberger, Ballhorn, and Birkeland acknowledge, in varying degrees, the role of the enemy as political threat within book 5, yet none provides a thorough analysis of how the varying psalmists construct the image of the threat, much less, deconstruct it. While I am not seeking to reinvoke Birkeland's unequivocal claim related to the enemy in the individual psalms, I do propose that his *methodological approach* may be instructive to some degree. Methodologically, Birkeland remained focused on identifying the constitutive elements within an "ideology" focused on the enemy. In modern parlance, he used cultural criticism in an effort to identify the role of the enemy within selected psalms.

Within book 5, there is considerable attention given to the role of empire and political power within Israel's past and present circumstances. Using an approach similar to Birkeland's, one that gives attention to the sociocultural context of the text, I would argue that book 5 seeks to construct a subtle anti-imperial ideology in response to the threats imposed from all empires both past and present, but in particular the Persian Empire.[51] Julia O'Brien has argued that "Persian-period texts cannot be read apart from the ideological and material dimensions of the empire in which they were created."[52] The Persian period proved formative in the creation of texts and, like much of biblical literature, would likely have had a similar influence on the Psalter. Although some psalms certainly had their origins in the preexilic period, the Psalter as a whole began to take shape under Persian rule. Consequently, the present study attempts

---

51. Although David Carr explores the role of Scripture within a Hellenistic world, he is right in his insistence that texts function as "a phenomenon of cultural resistance. Like most forms of cultural resistance, it is integrally bound up with the elements and forms of the culture it resists" (*Writing on the Tablet of the Heart: Origins of Scripture and Literature* [Oxford: Oxford University Press, 2005], 274). See also Greg Carey's similar assessment on the appropriation of imperial language in the ideology of the book of Revelation ("Book of Revelation as Counter-Imperial Script," in *In the Shadow of Empire: Reclaiming the Bible as a History of Faithful Resistance* [ed. Richard A. Horsley; Louisville: Westminster John Knox, 2008], 157–76). See also the discussion on figured worlds and identity formation in §6 of the present study.

52. O'Brien, "From Exile to Empire: A Response," 214.

to locate much of the ideology of power found in Pss 107–145 within the stream of imperial ideology emanating from Persia.

The imperial ideology, which began in earnest under Darius I, dominated throughout the history of the Achaemenid dynasty, and likely would have influenced the ideologies and identity of those living in Yehud. Book 5 in the Psalter contains a strong critique of power, particularly that of foreign empires, and may best be understood as a response to the type of worldview generated and promulgated by the Persian Empire, a view that extended in many ways even into the reign of the early Hellenists, in particular Alexander.[53] For the community in Yehud after Darius I, their only frame of reference for imperial rule would have been that of the Persian Empire. Any attempt by those in Yehud to construct their own identity in response to such an ideology, much less any form of ideological resistance, would have required them to draw heavily from the ideology inculcated during that period. This is not to suggest that all of book 5 was formed during the period of Persian rule, although some surely was, only that the Persian imperial ideology served to foment a type of cynicism towards all human power.

In the following chapter, the chief tenets of Persian imperial ideology are identified, with particular attention given to the royal inscriptions and the accompanying iconography. The chapter will also explore how such an ideology may have been disseminated across an empire as massive as that of the Achaemenid's. Chapters 3 and 4 will consider a number of psalms in book 5 in an attempt to identify an anti-imperial ideology that appears throughout the collection. The ideology constructed in these psalms stands in stark contrast to the ideology of empire generated by the Persians and, in many ways, undercuts the depiction of power, subjugation, and cosmic order communicated through the propaganda of the Achaemenid dynasty. At no point in book 5 does a psalmist provide a thoroughgoing endorsement of the Persians or any other imperial power. Rather, as Ballhorn has noted correctly, the psalmists distinguish between the nations as political power, which will ultimately be destroyed, and "all flesh" (145:21), which will be invited to participate in the kingdom of Yahweh.

In addition to deconstructing the images of human power, the psalmists in book 5 also constructed an image of Yahweh as the sole source of

---

53. On the appropriation of Achaemenid imperial ideology by Alexander, see Pierre Briant, *From Cyrus to Alexander* (trans. Peter T. Daniels; Winona Lake, Ind.: Eisenbrauns, 2002), 873–76.

power. The psalms in book 5, in particular, emphasize that Yahweh is the God of the heavens, and as such, usurps any authority or power assigned to the deities of the other nations. This notion of Yahweh as the God of heaven and the implications for the construction and deconstruction of power will be considered in chapter 5. The psalms in book 5 constructed a particular identity for the people of God, one that stressed the inefficacy of human strength in the face of imperial power and called for utter reliance upon the Divine King. Chapter 6 will explore the manner in which various psalms advocate for such an identity

As Berquist has suggested, "an understanding of psalms within a historical context of the Second Temple must begin with the imperial context of the Persian Empire."[54] It is that to which we now turn.

---

54. Berquist, "Psalms, Postcolonialism, and the Construction of the Self," 195.

2
The Achaemenid Dynasty and Imperial Ideology

2.0. Introduction

In many ways, the empire created by Cyrus and the Achaemenid dynasty was unmatched by earlier iterations in Assyria and Babylon. In size alone, the enormity of the Persian Empire is without question. The empire stretched from the Indus to the Hellespont, and to the initial cataracts of the Nile, covering an area of nearly six million square miles.[1] Based on such proportions, Amélie Kuhrt claims in the opening line of her book that "the Achaemenid empire is the earliest and largest of the known empires."[2] The somewhat equivocal use of the term "empire" in scholarship often does little to clarify what constitutes an empire, much less, which one was first.[3]

---

1. Erhard Gerstenberger, *Israel in the Persian Period: The Fifth and Fourth Centuries B.C.E.* (trans. Siegfried Schatzmann; BE 8; Atlanta: Society of Biblical Literature, 2011), 45–67.

2. Amélie Kuhrt, *The Persian Empire: A Corpus of Sources from the Achaemenid Empire* (London: Routledge, 2007), 1; Jon L. Berquist, *Judaism in Persia's Shadow: A Social and Historical Approach* (Minneapolis: Fortress Press, 1995), 23.

3. Mario Liverani contends that the Akkad dynasty represents the first true empire ("Akkad: An Introduction," in *Akkad: The First World Empire: Structure, Ideology, Traditions* [ed. Mario Liverani; HANES 5; Padova: Sargon, 1993], 9). Chronologically, the Akkad dynasty predates the Achaemenid dynasty by nearly a millennium and a half, warranting the claim of Liverani. Contrary to Liverani's contention that Akkad was the first empire, William Schniedewind suggests instead that Assyria was the first "in a series of expanding empires" (*How the Bible Became a Book: The Textualization of Ancient Israel* [Cambridge: Cambridge University Press, 2004], 65). On the notion of empire itself, Julia O'Brien cautions that "the concept of empire itself runs the risk of being broad, generic, and ideologically driven. Once invoked, the label 'empire' can become a buzzword, a posture. The Achaemenid regime and the Yehud that it controlled can loose their particularities, giving up their distinctive voices to mouth the scripted lines of the grand imperial narrative" ("From Exile to Empire: A Response,"

Liverani suggests an alternative approach to the study of empire, one that is central to the methodological approach of this study. Rather than focusing on spatial questions ("Which empire was the largest?") or temporal questions ("Which empire was first?"), Liverani lays out a different methodology, explaining

> that the very term "empire" is too often employed in a simplistic manner, without clarifying its specific meaning, as if it designated something obvious, unequivocal, and almost physical in nature. On the contrary, the concept has quite different applications through time and space ... A more recent (and mostly implicit) proposal is to shift the stress from political structure to *political ideology*.[4]

In such an investigation, the historical machinations of the empire are critical to the analysis, but even more so, are the somewhat static, ideological claims that served to frame the identity of an empire, its subjects, and the world over which it ruled. As Briant has averred, "Power and the King were represented in timeless attitudes, not a particular king in a historical situation."[5] These ideological claims were "written in the immovable and infinite time of the King." Regardless of who occupied the throne, these claims defined the Achaemenid dynasty and the perception it sought to present to the world. The historical particularities of each king's reign and the larger narrative history of the Achaemenid dynasty would be left for others to write.[6]

The "timeless attitudes" mentioned by Briant are found primarily in the iconography and inscriptions of the Achaemenid empire. These images and inscriptions provide critical insights into the political ideology of their creators. Although speaking only about iconography and sculpture from the Achaemenid period, Margaret Root's overall observation concerning the aim of such works remains valid. She concludes that "neither the Achaemenid nor the traditional Near Eastern way of representing the imperial hierarchy and power relationships attempts to

---

in *Approaching Yehud: New Approaches to the Study of the Persian Period* [ed. Jon L. Berquist; SemeiaSt 50; Atlanta: Society of Biblical Literature, 2007], 210).

4. Liverani, "Akkad: An Introduction," 3–4, emphasis added.

5. Pierre Briant, *From Cyrus to Alexander: A History of the Persian Empire* (trans. Peter T. Daniels; Winona Lake, Ind.: Eisenbrauns, 2002), 7.

6. Ibid. See, for example, Herodotus, *The Histories* (trans. R. Waterfield; ed. Carolyn Dewald; Oxford World Classics; Oxford: Oxford University Press, 1998).

portray the actual complexities of the imperial situation. In each case, we are dealing with art, and art designed to portray kingship as the king wished it to be viewed."[7] In short, the ideology conveyed in the inscriptions, iconography, and sculpture of the Achaemenid dynasty served to promulgate a particular view of empire to the world, a view less concerned with realism and more interested in political persuasion.[8]

The rise of the Persians and the corresponding defeat of neighboring empires has been the subject of significant scholarly work in recent years.[9] The historical particularities of the Persian period, and further, the debates that exist in the secondary literature, are left to another study. This chapter will, however, consider broadly the Achaemenid dynasty and its creation of an imperial ideology that sustained an empire for over two centuries. The texts associated with Cyrus's victory over the Medes and the Neo-Babylonians will be considered first in an effort to establish the *initial* ideological claims associated with the Achaemenid dynasty.

---

7. Margaret C. Root, *The King and Kingship in Achaemenid Art: Essays on the Creation of an Iconography of Empire* (AcIr 19; Leiden: Brill, 1979), 131.

8. In defining the power of ideology in the hands of an empire, Liverani suggests that imperial "ideology has the function of presenting exploitation in a favourable light to the exploited, as advantageous to the disadvantaged ... it makes one act against one's own actual interests, for the sake of fictitious interests" (Mario Liverani, "The Ideology of the Assyrian Empire," in *Power and Propaganda: A Symposium on Ancient Empires* [ed. Mogen Trolle Larsen; Mesopotamia: Copenhagen Studies in Assyriology 7; Copenhagen: Academisk, 1979], 298).

9. The bibliography of secondary literature on the Persian Empire is considerable. Several volumes, however, have attempted to synthesize scholarship in an effort to present a more holistic rendering of the period. On the history of the Persian Empire, see Briant, *From Cyrus to Alexander*; Muhammed A. Dandamaev, *A Political History of the Achaemenid Empire* (trans. Willem J. Vogelsang; Leiden: Brill, 1989); Peter Frei and Klaus Koch, *Reichsidee und Reichsorganisation im Perserreich* (2nd ed.; OBO 55; Göttingen: Vandenhoeck & Ruprecht, 1996); Richard N. Frye, *The History of Ancient Iran* (Münich: Beck, 1984); and Kuhrt, *The Persian Empire: A Corpus of Sources from the Achaemenid Empire*. Treatments on the rise of the Persian Empire and its influence within the more narrowly confined context of Yehud are likewise extensive. Representative examples include: Berquist, *Judaism in Persia's Shadow*, 3–127; Lester L. Grabbe, *Yehud: A History of the Persian Province of Judah* (vol. 1 of *A History of the Jews and Judaism in the Second Temple Period*; LSTS 41:1; New York: T&T Clark, 2004), 263–349; and Erhard Gerstenberger, *Israel in the Persian Period*, 45–76. See also the collections of essays in Oded Lipschits and Manfred Oeming, eds., *Judah and the Judeans in the Persian Period* (Winona Lake, Ind.: Eisenbrauns, 2006); and Berquist, *Approaching Yehud*.

These ideological claims are expanded and, in many ways codified, under Darius I and subsequent Achaemenid rulers. The iconography and inscriptions created under these rulers provide evidence of a sustained ideology of empire.

2.1. Cyrus and the Origins of an Empire

In 559 B.C.E., Cyrus II rose to power as "king of Anšan," an Elamite city. Nearly a decade later (550 B.C.E.), the Medes led by Astyages attacked the forces of Cyrus II in response to an alleged rebellion. Herodotus acknowledges Cyrus's role in a possible revolt: "There are many tribes of Persians. The ones whom Cyrus got together and persuaded to rebel against the Medes were the ones on whom all other Persians depended" (Herodotus 1.125).[10] The precise reason, however, for such a rebellion against the Medes remains unknown. Kuhrt hypothesizes that "it is possible that the Medes exercised, or claimed to exercise, some kind of suzerainty over Anshan which the Persians challenged."[11] Alternatively, she suggests that the expansionist moves made by the Persians during that time may have provoked the aggression of Astyages. In the oldest recorded account of the incident, the Nabonidus Chronicle, the text hints at neither explanation and simply recounts the event as follows:

> (Astyages) mustered (his army) and marched against Cyrus, king of Anshan for conquest […] The army rebelled against Astyages and he was taken prisoner. They handed him over to Cyrus […] Cyrus marched to Ecbatana, the royal city. The silver, gold, goods, property […] which he carried off as booty (from) Ecbatana he took to Anshan.[12]

Given the paucity of explanatory information in this text, the subsequent legacy of Cyrus could have been that of a rebel or an usurper of the throne, yet it appears that early on, the ideology of the king as "liberator" was

---

10. On the use of Greek sources in the reconstruction of Persian history, see Briant, *From Cyrus to Alexander*, 1–10. Herodotus, according to Briant, holds pride of place among the ancient sources because, unlike his contemporaries, he shows no evidence of "systematic hostility to the Persians" (7). See also Kuhrt, *The Persian Empire*, 6–14.

11. Kuhrt, *The Persian Empire*, 48. See also Briant, *From Cyrus to Alexander*, 32–33.

12. "The Nabonidus Chronicle," 2.1–4 (Kuhrt, *The Persian Empire*, 50).

assigned to Cyrus instead. In his attempt to paint Cyrus as a liberator, Herodotus recounts that "the Persians were delighted to free themselves because they had long resented being ruled by the Medes" (Herodotus, 1.127). Further in the same text, Herodotus refers more explicitly to the cruelty of Astyages during his thirty-five year reign (Herodotus, 1.130). Likewise other Greek writers sought to portray Cyrus as a liberator who was benevolent and just in his dealings with conquered regions. In his recounting of the fate of Astyages, Justin notes that Cyrus captured him "and refrained from doing anything [to Astyages] except taking the kingship away from him" (Justin, 1.6.16). Justin notes, interestingly, that Cyrus behaved "more like a grandson than a victor," again rejecting any notion of Cyrus as tyrant or militaristic overlord.

The notion of Cyrus as a liberator becomes even more apparent in texts associated with his victory over the Neo-Babylonian Empire.[13] The Cyrus Cylinder recounts the fall of Nabonidus and Babylon to Cyrus, attributing the change in power to Marduk's displeasure with Nabonidus's cultic failures (5–7) and oppressive rule. The cylinder records that Nabonidus "repeatedly did that which was bad for his city. Daily […] he destroyed all his [subjects] with an unending yoke."[14] In the Verse Account of Nabonidus, the charges against King Nabonidus are even more damning. He is said to have put nobles to the sword, stolen the property of the people, and scattered their possessions. In a further attempt to capture the brutal rule of Nabonidus, the inhabitants of Sumer and Akkad were compared to corpses.[15] Kuhrt likens this notion of "corpse" in the cylinder to that of "prisoners."[16] Clearly the writers of the cuneiform texts had an anti-Nabonidus bias, but such a bias was in part due to their desire to portray Cyrus as the liberator. In the midst of such a bleak context, the cylinder records that Marduk searched for a "just ruler." Selecting Cyrus, Marduk took him by the hand and "like a friend and a companion he went by his

---

13. See David Vanderhooft, "Cyrus II, Liberator or Conquerer?" in *Judah and the Judeans in the Persian Period* (ed. Oded Lipschits and Manfred Oeming; Winona Lake, Ind.: Eisenbrauns, 2006), 351–72.
14. "The Cyrus Cylinder," 8 (Kuhrt, *The Persian Empire*, 71).
15. "The Cyrus Cylinder," 11 (Kuhrt, *The Persian Empire*, 71).
16. Kuhrt connects the notion of corpse with that of political prisoner in both "The Verse Account of Nabonidus" (6.26) and Isaiah 42:17. See Kuhrt, *The Persian Empire*, 73n6; "The Verse Account of Nabonidus" (Kuhrt, *The Persian Empire*, 75–79).

side" as Cyrus overtook Babylon. In summary fashion, the writer of the cylinder concludes, "[Cyrus] saved Babylon from its oppression."[17]

The Greek writers, in their attempts to recount the fall of Babylon, either knew or created traditions that were at odds with the cuneiform traditions.[18] Both Herodotus and Xenophon indicate that Cyrus was able to capture Babylon by diverting the flow of the Euphrates River, thereby allowing his troops to enter through the river channel. Vanderhooft provides an extended analysis of this explanation and the historical circumstances that might have warranted such a conclusion by the Greek historians. The physical geography, the seasonal timing, the defensive architecture and installations around Babylon, as well as its liturgical calendar, make the account plausible. As opposed to asking which account is to be preferred (the cuneiform or the Greek historians), Vanderhooft deftly remarks that

> Herodotus's narrative is largely shorn of theological considerations and avoids commentary on the competing religious claims for royal legitimacy that animate the cuneiform tradition. … [Herodotus] provides what might cautiously be called a rationalization for the more religio-political perspectives in the cuneiform tradition.[19]

In short, those who composed the cylinder were rooted in the theological and ideological claims associated with royal legitimacy and sought to construct an ideology of kingship rooted in the notion of the king as peaceful liberator.

Additional ideological claims concerning kingship appear in the cylinder. As Briant has argued, the cylinder does more than simply reflect the views of the Babylonian elites; it also "transmits the imperial program of Cyrus," albeit in a rather truncated form.[20] In line 19 of the cylinder, the text shifts from third to first person with Cyrus offering a series of announcements, in effect, setting forth an imperial ideology. Cyrus proclaims himself "king of the universe" and "king of the four quarters," a

---

17. "The Cyrus Cylinder," 15, 17 (Kuhrt, *The Persian Empire*, 71). See also Briant, *From Cyrus to Alexander*, 40–44.

18. Vanderhooft, "Cyrus II, Liberator or Conquerer," 354–62. As noted above, Herodotus does allude to the liberating rule of Cyrus in the Persians's defeat of the Medes, yet in his account of the fall of Babylon, such an attribution is altogether absent.

19. Ibid., 360.

20. Briant, *From Cyrus to Alexander*, 44.

concept with its roots in Mesopotamian royal ideology.²¹ In considering the ideology of universal rule found in the earlier Mesopotamian literature, Gerstenberger suggests

> that much of the energy of dominating all the earth, already present in these ancient rulers, was clad in mythopoetic concepts of winning and maintaining control within a larger part of that world, comprising Mesopotamia and some of its territories to the east, north, and west, e.g, Elam, Mari, Ebla, etc. The rest of the world, which certainly was known to exist beyond the neighboring states, did not matter too much yet, being included in a vague way ('four corners,' 'all foreign nations,' etc.).²²

As king of the four quarters, Cyrus explains that "all kings, who sit on thrones, from all parts of the world … brought their heavy tribute to me and kissed my feet."²³ Subsequent Achaemenid kings will self-describe in similar—if not exactly the same—terms, as will be observed below.

The cylinder also reflects other aspects of royal ideology. Having conquered Babylon, Cyrus proclaims that he has ordered society and put away those who might create trouble in the land. In lines 22 and 24, Cyrus reminds the reader that he entered Babylon peacefully, no doubt an allusion to the gods's involvement in his victory, but also an acknowledgment of his liberating work on their behalf to create an ordered cosmos. The notion of an ordered world will play an even greater role in the ideological claims of Darius and Xerxes.

With his defeat of Astyages in 559 B.C.E. and of Nabonidus in 550 B.C.E., Cyrus created an empire that would last nearly 220 years and, through expansion under subsequent kings, become the largest empire in history. Although the iconographic and textual witnesses under Cyrus are sparse at best, they nonetheless establish the framework for a political

---

21. Cyrus makes similar claims about himself on inscribed bricks that were found in an enclosure wall of Egishnugal in Ur; he makes the same claim on another clay cylinder found at Ur (Kuhrt, *The Persian Empire*, 75). The notion of king as ruler over the world has its roots in Mesopotamian royal ideology. See Grabbe, *Yehud: A History of the Persian Province of Judah*, 266–67; Liverani, "Akkad: An Introduction," 1–10; Sabine Franke, *Königsinschriften und Königsideologie: die Könige von Akkade zwischen Tradition und Neuerung* (Altorientalistik 1; München: LIT, 1995); Erhard Gerstenberger, "'World Dominion' in Yahweh-Kingship Psalms," *HBT* 23 (2001): 192–210.

22. Gerstenberger, "'World Dominion' in Yahweh-Kingship Psalms," 201–2.

23. "The Cyrus Cylinder," 28–29 (Kuhrt, *The Persian Empire*, 71–72).

ideology that will be developed more fully under subsequent kings, and one that will be implicitly challenged by subsequent subjects.[24]

2.2. Timeless Attitudes in the Achaemenid Imperial Ideology

Beginning with Darius, the Achaemenid dynasty shifted from a period primarily of conquest and expansion to one of internal consolidation.[25] The significance of such a shift under Darius should not be minimized, however. Central to this consolidation was a well-constructed and well-articulated imperial ideology. As Kuhrt has noted, it is only with Darius that the empire "stabilizes and begins to acquire its mature form" and only with Darius "that the concepts and ideals of Persian kingship and imperial rule receive their definitive, lasting shape."[26] While such concepts were alluded to in the Cyrus Cylinder and the Verse Account of Nabonidus and no doubt influenced Cambyses in his imperial conquests in Egypt and elsewhere, these ideas were developed more fully and with greater frequency in the iconography and inscriptions associated with Darius and Xerxes in particular, but seen also in the textual evidence associated with subsequent Persian kings. Briant argues that while Darius continued the work of Cyrus and Cambyses, "beginning with Darius, one may speak of an imperial enterprise in the fullest sense of the word."[27] In particular, for Briant, Darius's "imperial enterprise" was rooted in his capacity to create an empire that maintained a strongly unified identity amid the diversity of

---

24. Berquist stresses the importance of an imperial ideology, suggesting that "empires dominate not only by military and economic means, but also through ideology. The very idea of an empire is a belief that one power is virtually unstoppable and nearly omnipresent. The empire propagates this belief system and people accept it as part of imperial domination" (Jon L. Berquist, "Resistance and Accommodation in the Persian Empire," in *In the Shadow of the Empire: Reclaiming the Bible as a History of Faithful Resistance* [ed. Richard A. Horsley; Louisville: Westminster John Knox, 2008], 44).

25. Heleen Sancisi-Weerdenburg, "Darius I and the Persian Empire," *CANE* 2:1039. Sancisi-Weerdenburg contends that under Cyrus and Cambyses, the Persian Empire remained "loosely knitted together," but that under Darius, the internal structure of the empire and the political ideology that supported it were formalized. On the Egyptian expansion of the empire under Cambyses, see Briant, *From Cyrus to Alexander*, 49–61; Berquist, *Judaism in Persia's Shadow*, 45–50.

26. Kuhrt, *The Persian Empire*, 135.

27. Briant, *From Cyrus to Alexander*, 507.

its conquered people groups. Arguably this can be attributed to the imperial ideology that permeated all elements of the empire, both at the center and the periphery. The ideological claims promulgated repeatedly under Darius and Xerxes center around three important themes: the worldwide scope of the empire; the joyous participation of subjects in the empire; and the cosmic order created by the empire.

2.2.1. The Worldwide Scope of the Empire

As noted above, the Achaemenian dynasty established the largest empire in the world. The expanse of such an empire was not lost on the Achaemenian rulers, nor the power associated with such a claim. Consequently, as Darius and subsequent kings sought to create an entrenched ideology of empire, the notion of its worldwide reach was a central component. The Achaemenian dynasty, particularly beginning with Darius, attempted to root the political ideology of a worldwide empire in the creation narrative involving Ahuramazda. As Gerstenberger notes, "Given the wealth of religious statements of power and the missionary zeal of the Darius inscriptions, it is pointless to ask whether belief in Ahuramazda played a part in the politics of the state among the Achaemenids."[28] It did. Religion served to authorize, validate, and legitimize the imperial ideology established by Darius.

The creation narrative repeatedly used by the Persians is quite succinct in nature, particularly when compared with other ancient Near Eastern texts such as the *Enuma Elish* or even the accounts recorded in Genesis 1 and 2. The inscription at Darius's burial tomb at Naqsh-i Rustam begins

> A great god is Ahuramazda, who created this earth, who created yonder heaven, who created man, who created happiness for man, who made Darius king, one king of many, one lord of many.[29]

Although the creation narrative rehearsed by the Achaemenians is relatively brief, it does appear with considerable regularity. Chief among the elements mentioned in other Old Persian inscriptions is the claim that Ahuramazda alone is responsible for creating or making Darius king.[30] Of

---

28. Gerstenberger, *Israel in the Persian Period*, 51.
29. DNa §1 (Kuhrt, *The Persian Empire*, 502).
30. The repeated divine validation of Darius is likely in response to the somewhat

all the post-Behistun inscriptions that are over three paragraphs, nearly seventy-five percent contain wording and imagery similar to the inscription at Naqsh-i Rustam, with the most frequently repeated element being reference to Darius's ascension to imperial ruler as the will and work of the god Ahuramazda.[31] An inscription found at Persepolis (DPd) makes the connection explicit: "Great is Ahuramazda, greatest of the gods—he made Darius king, he bestowed kingship upon him; by the favor of Ahuramazda, Darius is king."[32] The frequent use of creation imagery creates what Bruce Lincoln calls a "cosmic consciousness," a term he employs to mean "a concern for how the creator conceived the world and what he intended for it."[33] The language in the Old Persian inscriptions is clear: the intent of Ahuramazda was that Darius would rule over the empire and further, that such a desire was coupled with the creative design of the world.

The connection between the reign of Darius and the creation of the world also reinforced in subtle ways the notion of a worldwide empire.[34] In the Naqsh-i Rustam inscription above, the earth (*būmi*) appears first in the sequence of created objects, followed by the heavens, then humanity, and ends with Darius as king. Such an order differs in part from other ancient Near Eastern texts. Typically in ancient Near Eastern cosmogonies, the heavens are mentioned prior to the mention of earth. In every instance but one, the Achaemenids place earth first in the list of creations. While the altered order could be passed off as insignificant, the fact that such an order is retained in virtually all of the texts suggests that the order may in fact be intentional.

The Old Persian term *būmi* can simply imply "earth" or "soil," but interestingly, the term also carries with it the connotation of empire. In eighteen inscriptions the term appears in cosmogonic accounts referring to the cre-

---

questionable story of Darius's rise to power. See below for a more detailed analysis of the Behistun inscription and its function as political propaganda.

31. Bruce Lincoln, *Religion, Empire, and Torture: The Case of Achaemenian Persia with a Postscript on Abu Ghraib* (Chicago: University of Chicago Press, 2007), 51. See, for example, the Granj Nameh inscription (DE) or the trilingual text from Susa (DSf) for inscriptions that reflect language similar to that present in DNa.

32. Kuhrt, *The Persian Empire*, 487.

33. Ibid., 52.

34. Lincoln notes that "in his own propaganda, Darius does not appear as an ambitious and competent man in search of power, but as the world's savior, who will reestablish the original divine order" (*'Happiness for Mankind': Achaemenian Religion and the Imperial Project* [AcIr 53; Leuven: Peeters, 2012], 16).

ation of the earth. Thirty-eight times, however, the term appears to allude to a sociopolitical reality (e.g., "the king in this empire [*būmiyā*]"). Thus the term may have functioned as a double entendre of sorts. To return to the Naqsh-i Rustam inscription, the first two paragraphs read

> A great god is Ahuramazda, who created this earth (*būmi*), who created yonder heaven, who created man, who created happiness for man, who made Darius king, one king of many, one lord of many;
> I am Darius the great king, kings of kings, king of countries containing kinds of men, king of this great earth/empire (*būmi*) far and wide.[35]

Texts such as Naqsh-i Rustam and others suggest that central to the belief of Achaemenian imperial ideology was the belief that the god they served was not only responsible for all of creation, but that from creation, Ahuramazda somehow knew and intended "that Darius, and his Achaemenian heirs, should, at some later time, become king over this *earth-cum-empire*."[36] Thus worldwide imperial rule, ideologically speaking, was not the result of military might, per se, but the culminating event in Ahuramazda's work in the world. In short, the world that was created by Ahuramazda was the same world meant to be governed ultimately by the Achaemenians. All subjects within the empire must likewise acknowledge that the Achaemenians operate based on a divine mandate to govern the world in which they live.[37]

---

35. DNa §1–2 (Kuhrt, *The Persian Empire*, 502). Identical language is found on other inscriptions. See, for example, the trilingual inscription that appears on a statute of Darius I found at Susa (DSab) or the trilingual text from the apadana at Persepolis (DPh). Such language is not limited just to texts associated with Darius. See also the royal inscription attributed to Artaxerxes found in Hamadan, A2Hc (Roland G. Kent, *Old Persian: Grammar, Texts, Lexicon* [New Haven, Conn.: American Oriental Society, 1953], 155).

36. Clarisse Herrenschmidt, "Désignation de l'empire et concepts politiques de Darius 1er d'après ses inscriptions en vieux perse," *StIr* 6 (1976): 17–58.

37. Sancisi-Weerdenburg noted that "obeying the king is equivalent to the worship of Ahuramazda, the king's god" ("Darius I and the Persian Empire," 2:1049). Although there are no signs that the Ahuramazda cult was imposed on the conquered nations, there was no tolerance for rejection of the king's authority. To reject the king's authority would in fact be to reject the claim that Ahuramazda had established the Achaemenian kingdom from the beginning of creation. Those who did in fact revolt had their cities destroyed and their temples burned to the ground—see, for example, the events surrounding the revolt of Miletus (Herodotus 6.18–22 [Kuhrt, *The Per-*

In practical terms, the association of a worldwide empire with the will of Ahuramazda did function as a mandate for militaristic conquest. As noted above, at its zenith, the Persian Empire was the largest empire to date, suggesting that significant military campaigns were waged in establishing such an empire. The military might of Persia and its reach was not lost on those who preserved its history in both inscriptions and iconography. At Naqsh-i Rustam on the tomb of Darius, the inscription speaks of Darius's military ventures, noting that "the spear of the Persian man has gone forth far" and that the "Persian man has delivered battle far indeed from Persia."[38] Numerous texts list the nations or people groups subjugated to Achaemenid imperial rule.[39] Even the Greek historians sought to portray the extent of the Achaemenid reach. In his *Histories*, Herodotus recounts the scene when Xerxes explains to Persian nobles his intent to invade Greece (ca. 483 B.C.E.):

> If we subdue them and their neighbors ... we will produce a Persian earth bordering on Zeus's heaven, for the sun will look down on no land that is neighbor to ours. Rather, having marched through all Europe together with you, I will make them all one land. For I learn thus: no city of men nor race of people will be left to oppose us in battle when those of whom I spoke have been removed. (*Histories* 7.8)

As Herodotus notes, the Persian campaigns are meant not only to subdue the Greeks and the other nations, but more broadly, to create a "Persian earth," a worldwide empire. Clearly the language placed in Xerxes mouth highlights the unifying force of a Persian imperial rule, "I will make them all one land," but such language also reinforces the magnitude of such an empire. It will be a "Persian earth" that matches in size Zeus's heaven.[40]

---

sian Empire, 226]). See also the assessment of Grabbe concerning religion and Persian policy (*Yehud: A History of the Persian Province of Judah*, 215–16).

38. DNa §4 (Kuhrt, *The Persian Empire*, 503). On the idea of the king as the epitome of the "Persian man" see Root, *The King and Kingship in Achaemenid Art*, 182–84.

39. For example, see the following royal inscriptions: DSab, DPg, A?E, DPe, DNa, and DSe. See below regarding the iconography accompanying such lists and the implications.

40. Lincoln, *Religion, Empire, and Torture*, 69–70.

2. THE ACHAEMENID DYNASTY AND IMPERIAL IDEOLOGY   31

2.2.2. The Joyous Participation of Subjects in the Empire

In the iconography and texts created by the Achaemenian dynasty, the kings portrayed their rule over the worldwide empire in a way that broke significantly with ancient Near Eastern prototypes. Earlier ancient Near Eastern iconography and related texts alluded to the subjugation of foreign nations, but always portraying the relationship between the king and the subjects as one of antagonism. The Achaemenian art reflects the hierarchical relationship between king and subject, but instead of creating images of antagonism and oppressive subjugation, the Achaemenian imperial ideology sought to portray the relationship as one "consistently expressed as a cooperative effort of voluntary support of the king by the subject peoples."[41] Several sculptures and the accompanying inscriptions provide evidence of this form of royal propaganda.

A large sculpture of Darius I, with an accompanying inscription, was found at the monumental gate at Susa. The statue of Darius appears larger than life, reaching well over three meters tall.[42] The inscription, like many from the time of Darius, was trilingual, but strikingly included Egyptian hieroglyphics as well as cuneiform. The stone itself was apparently of Egyptian origin, suggesting that the statue was originally erected in Egypt and brought to Susa or that the statue now residing in Susa was a copy of an original statue that had remained in Egypt.[43] Because the statue had its origin in Egypt, the hieroglyphic text has the richer content. Even as Egyptian pharaohs were accorded divine status, this text appears to bestow such honors on Darius as well. He is referred to repeatedly as the "perfect god," but even more telling, Darius is referred to as the "son of Re" and as

---

41. Root, *The King and Kingship in Achaemenid Art*, 131. For representative iconographic images from Mesopotamia and Egypt, see Root, 133–44, 147–53. See also Brent Strawn, "'A World under Control': Isaiah 60 and the Apadana Reliefs from Persepolis," in *Approaching Yehud*, 85–116. Strawn's approach, similar in methodology to this study, considers the ideology present in the Apadana reliefs at Persepolis and then considers the relationship between that ideology and the one contained in Isaiah 60. Strawn's work gives evidence of "biblical writers riffing on the iconography of empire" (O'Brien, "From Exile to Empire: A Response," 212.)

42. Briant notes that the entire gate complex was some fifteen meters high and likely represents the first known example of monumental statuary in the Achaemenid dynasty (*From Cyrus to Alexander*, 216).

43. See Kuhrt, *The Persian Empire*, 479. For a translation of the cuneiform and hieroglyphic texts of DSab, see Kuhrt, *The Persian Empire*, 477–79.

the living image of Re (DSab b). Both descriptors were reserved for pharaohs and meant to validate their divine status, suggesting that those who created the statue understood well the religious and political ideologies associated with Pharaonic power and sought to blend such an ideology with the larger Achaemenid imperial ideology at work in Egypt and across the empire. In addition to Re, the text also associates Darius with Atum, Montu, Neith, and Horus, all serving to root Darius clearly within the pantheon of Egyptian deities.

The role of Darius as king is carefully articulated as well. Although the text clearly recognizes the power of Darius in his ability to conquer the "two lands" and it acknowledges that Darius "inspires fear in the heart of humanity," the text, nevertheless, offers a more sympathetic interpretation of his role as king. Drawing off the larger ancient Near Eastern notion of kingship, Darius is instead praised because "he acts in accordance with divine orders," because he is the "living image of Re." The text also explains that Atum has chosen Darius to be master of all "that the sun's disc describes" and over which he is to be the "caretaker." Further, the text records that the "lord of the two lands" has crushed the "nine bows" and those within the two lands remain united under his care.[44] The final lines of the hieroglyphic text read as though it were a charge to Darius: "I give you Upper and Lower Egypt, who adore your beautiful face, like that of Re, eternally."

As noted above, such images and inscriptions portray the king *as the king desires to be portrayed*, thus fostering a certain program of royal propaganda. Throughout the inscription Darius is lauded as a divine king, carefully selected by Re to be "lord of the earth." Although the power of Darius is acknowledged, his reign over the Egyptian regions is one that is meant to foster goodwill among its inhabitants. So generous will be the reign of Darius that all under his rule will "adore his beautiful face." Such adoration hints at the notion of a joyous participation by the subjects under Persian rule.

The joyous participation of subjects is made even more evident in the iconographic imagery that accompanies DSab. Located on the right and

---

44. The image of the nine bows played an important role in the artistic and literary expressions in Egypt. The notion of the nine bows, dating back arguably to the Predynastic period, is meant to represent regions of people who threatened the empire of the Pharaoh, consequently necessitating the defeat and subjugation of such groups. See Root, *The King and Kingship in Achaemenid Art*, 138–47.

left side of the base appear the names (written in hieroglyphics) of the empires under subjugation. The entire empire, not just the two lands of Egypt, is represented. Media, Elam, Babylon, Armenia, India, and Sardis, among others, are represented, suggesting that indeed Darius is "supreme lord of the earth (in its totality)," one to whom respect is due. Perched on top of each name is a figure kneeling in homage, with arms raised and palms turned upwards. In hieroglyphic writing such a gesture is meant to convey the idea of support.[45] As Root has observed, the entire scene is meant to suggest the support of the nations for the empire. The socle figures show support of the king as they form the base upon which the king stands, acknowledging the hierarchical relationship that exists between the king and his subjects. The artistic rendering of such figures with the palms-up gesture adds to the complexity of the iconography in that it reinforces the support of the nations for Darius.

The motif of the king being carried by the subjugated nations is found elsewhere in the iconography of the Achaemenid dynasty.[46] At Naqsh-i Rustam, the motif appears in conjunction with the tomb of Darius. The facade of the tomb is laid out in a cruciform pattern and immediately above the entrance to the tomb appears an image of Darius and his throne-bearers. Similar to the socle figures at Susa, the figures that stand beneath the royal platform at Naqsh-i Rustam represent the subjugated nations of the empire that support Darius, both literally and figuratively. Interestingly, the feet of the throne do not appear to touch the ground. Instead, the subjects appear to bear the full weight of the throne, with each standing in the atlas pose—a pose frequently found in ancient Near Eastern art.[47] The atlas pose has a lengthy history, beginning with its role in Mesopotamian art where it was reserved first for mythical beings, such as bull-men or scorpion-men, but later was employed by the Achaemenids to reinforce a particular political ideology related to the support of the empire by the subjugated nations.[48]

---

45. Ibid., 146.

46. See Gregor Ahn, *Religiöse Herrscherlegitimation im achämenidischen Iran: Die Voraussetzungen und die Struktur ihrer Argumentation* (AcIr 31; Leiden: Brill, 1992), 272–77.

47. Root, *The King and Kingship in Achaemenid Art*, 147–53.

48. Root explores the Egyptian use of the image and argues that the hieroglyphic signs for "rejoice" and "to support" both employ images of humans in the atlas pose,

This notion of imperial support is evidenced further in the actual depiction of the figures. Those that appear on the Naqsh-i Rustam carving are rendered with their palms and stiffened fingers facing the audience. The weight of the king, and hence the empire, however, appears to be supported by only the thumb and the index finger of each figure. There is a sense of effortlessness to the work of the subject nations, almost as though the platform were levitating itself. Further, the arms of the figures cross one other in a symmetrical pattern, perhaps suggesting the cooperative work of the entire empire. Root contends that the relief presents an aura of "joyous cooperation."[49]

In addition to the relief at Naqsh-i Rustam, the inscription (DNb) itself also reinforces the notion of "joyous cooperation" between the king and his subjects. Much of the text portrays Darius as a just king, one whose military might is coupled with prudence and intelligence. To these qualities of a great king, Darius adds that, "The man who cooperates, him do I reward according to his cooperation."[50] And further, Darius explains that "what a man does or performs according to his powers, satisfies me, therewith, I am satisfied; it gives me great pleasure and I give much to faithful men."[51] The image of an overzealous empire, weighing down heavily upon its subjects is altogether absent in the iconography at Nash-i Rustam and equally so, such imagery of the king and the empire in DNb has been exchanged for the image of an empire that is beneficent, one that cooperates with those who cooperate with the king.

Similar images can be found at Persepolis on the tomb of Artaxerxes as well as at the south and north doorjambs of the doorways into the massive main hall.[52] Rows of human subjects stand beneath the throne, bearing the

---

giving further evidence that the pose became associated with ideas of joyous support (*The King and Kingship in Achaemenid Art*, 149–50).

49. Ibid., 153.

50. DNb §2c (Kuhrt, *The Persian Empire*, 504–5). A similar form of the text found at Persepolis is attributed to Xerxes (XPl), again reinforcing the commitment of the dynasty to a particular imperial ideology.

51. DNb §2e.

52. Kent appears uncertain as to whether the tomb and the inscription at Persepolis should be assigned to Artaxerxes II or III (*Old Persian*, 155). Briant (*From Cyrus to Alexander*, 998) and Kuhrt (*The Persian Empire*, 484) contend that it is the former. For a brief review of the competing positions in scholarship on this issue, see Kuhrt. For the images found on the two doorjambs, see Root, *The King and Kingship in Achaemenid Art*, plates 29a and 29b.

2. THE ACHAEMENID DYNASTY AND IMPERIAL IDEOLOGY   35

full weight of the throne. And like the image at Naqsh-i Rustam, the figures appear in the atlas pose, using only the thumb and fingers to carry the throne, reflecting again the image of a joyous participation in the empire by those that stand under it. Accompanying the tomb of Artaxerxes II is an inscription that identifies each figure specifically, "This is the Persian; this is the Mede; this is the Elamite; this is the Parthian ... " with the intent of highlighting the extent of the Persian Empire.[53] More than any other inscription, however, this inscription (A?P) provides colorful descriptions of some figures, no doubt in an effort to illustrate the full range of subject nations: "this is the *hauma*-drinking Saca; this is the Pointed Hat Saca; ... this is the Scythian across the sea; ... this is the Ionian ... this is the *petasos* wearing Ionian."[54] Although the reign of Artaxerxes II (405–359 B.C.E.) began well over a century after that of Darius I, the imperial ideology associated with the Achaemenid dynasty remained intact with little change. The iconographic art continued the portrayal of humans cast in an atlas pose, while the accompanying inscriptions offered a list, albeit not an exhaustive one, of subject nations. The continuity of imagery and text no doubt reinforced the imperial ideology that sustained the dynasty and its power.

Similar to Susa and Naqsh-i Rustam, Persepolis contained images and texts that reflected the vast empire and its subjects. These lists and the others that appear on additional inscriptions are inconsistent, often failing to include known conquered people groups, or including some in one list, while omitting the same group elsewhere. Efforts have been made to explain the variation in lists, but as Briant concludes,

> It must thus be recognized that neither lists nor the representations constitute administrative catalogs yielding a realistic image of the imperial realm. It was not administrative districts that the Great Kings wanted to represent.... The inscribed lists are nothing but a selection of subject coun-

---

53. A?P (Kuhrt, *The Persian Empire*, 483).

54. The details provided suggest that the artisans for A?P were well acquainted with both the dress of the subject nations and even the cultural details that differentiate the people groups. The *hauma* was a ritual drink used in the Iranian cult (William W. Malandra, *An Introduction to Ancient Iranian Religion* [Minnesota Publications in the Humanities 2; Minneapolis: University of Minnesota Press, 1983], 20–21) and the *petasos* was a narrow-brimmed hat worn by Greeks, often for travel (Larissa Bonfante, *Etruscan Dress* [Baltimore: Johns Hopkins University Press, 1975], 67–69). The "Pointed Hat Saca" (Scythian) is also portrayed in the Behistun inscription.

tries. Darius and his successors are neither archivists nor historians. What they intend to leave to posterity is not administrative data. The inscriptions accompanying the reliefs show instead what they wished to transmit to their contemporaries was a politico-ideological message.[55]

Central to this politico-ideological message was the notion of a worldwide empire comprised of nations that could be named and identified. Further, the iconography associated with these lists intended to show that within this vast empire, all the nations participate joyfully and fully support the Achaemenid dynasty.

2.2.3. Cosmic Order and the Achaemenid Dynasty

In addition to the imperial claims of a worldwide empire comprised of cooperating nations, the Achaemenid dynasty sought to portray itself as the guarantor of cosmic order. Protests, rebellions, and insurrections were dealt with hastily because they signaled a disruption within that order, a disruption that necessitated swift action by the empire assigned by Ahuramazda to govern the world.

According to Achaemenian discourse, the chief threat to order is the *drauga*. Although the term is often translated as "lie" or "falsehoood," Kuhrt explains that *drauga* has religious and cosmological undertones, suggesting a disruption in the cosmos. Such a disruption, however, is manifested chiefly in the political realm.[56] As Herrenschmidt and Lincoln observe, the theme of cosmic disorder, and that of the "Lie" in particular, is historicized in various inscriptions and these inscriptions are rooted in the political machinations of the Achaemenid Empire.[57] Unlike other ancient Near Eastern traditions, there is no document from the Achaemenid period that waxes on the theme of cosmic disorder writ large. Rather, Old Persian evidence suggests that such disorder is encountered in the political realm and overcome by the Achaemenid dynasty, the very one established by the creative work of Ahuramazda.[58] Although a number of texts allude to this

---

55. Briant, *From Cyrus to Alexander*, 177.
56. Kuhrt, *The Persian Empire*, 152n15.
57. Clarisse Herrenschmidt and Bruce Lincoln, "Healing and Salt Waters: The Bifurcated Cosmos of Mazdean Religion," *HR* 43 (2004): 269–83.
58. In the Mazdean tradition, the god was considered good, as was the creation that reflected his nature. Consequently any disorder or break in creation could not be

2. THE ACHAEMENID DYNASTY AND IMPERIAL IDEOLOGY 37

imperial ideology, the Behistun Inscription (DB) illustrates well the role of the Achaemenid king in the maintaining of cosmic order.

The massive Behistun Inscription and the accompanying relief are inscribed on a rock face that overlooks the main road from Babylonia to Media. The inscription and relief together measure approximately fifteen meters high by twenty-five meters wide, appearing nearly one hundred meters up the rock face. The relief itself depicts Darius I standing, bow in hand, with one foot resting upon a supine figure, while nine other captives stand before Darius, hands bound, with a rope around their neck. Two court officials in Persian garb stand directly behind Darius. The captive figures are dwarfed in size by the much larger Darius and his courtiers, suggesting the power differentiation between the captured rebels and those representing the dynasty. Looking over the entire scene is the winged Ahuramazda.[59] To ensure that all who pass by understand the significance of the scene portrayed in the relief, the text of the accompanying inscription appears in Elamite, Babylonian, and Old Persian, a script that was likely commissioned under Darius (cf. DB §70).[60] As Root has reminded, "The Behistun text is not addressed to Ahuramazda, even in a token way, but rather to all the peoples of the empire."[61] Both the relief and the inscription function as imperial propaganda and stand as a reminder of Darius's claim to the throne, but even more, to the dynasty's covenant with Ahuramazda in thwarting all efforts to destabilize the ordered world created by Darius.

In the accompanying inscription Darius provides a historically dubious account of the final events surrounding the life of Cambyses and his own transition to power, but one that nevertheless advances his own imperial identity.[62] The inscription reads

---

assigned to Ahuramazda, but instead had to be attributed to a secondary principle. See Herrenschmidt and Lincoln, "Healing and Salt Waters," 269–83.

59. Root suggests that "in a symbolic way Ahuramazda is shown to deliver the concept of abstract power (embodied in the ring) as well as the concept of very concrete power (in the form of the captured rebel chieftains) into the hands of Darius. Darius fulfills his part in the covenant between king and god by affirming his righteousness and by expeditiously exterminating the followers of the Lie" (*The King and Kingship in Achaemenid Art*, 189).

60. A fourth version of the inscription, written in Aramaic, was found at Elephantine, see below, §2.3.1.

61. Root, *The King and Kingship in Achaemenid Art*, 190.

62. Briant aptly notes, "Few events in Achaemenid history raise as many ques-

> The son of Cyrus, by name Cambyses, of our family, he was king here; this Cambyses had a brother by name Bardiya; he had the same mother, the same father as Cambyses; then Cambyses killed that Bardiya; when Cambyses killed that Bardiya, the people did not know that Bardiya had been killed; then, Cambyses went to Egypt. When Cambyses had gone to Egypt, then the people became disloyal;[63] and the Lie (*drauga*) grew among the people both in Persia and Media and among the other peoples.
>
> Darius the king proclaims: Then there was a man, a magus, Gaumata by name; he rebelled in Paishiyauvada. A mountain, by name Arakadri, from there—fourteen days of the month of Viyakhna had gone (11 March 522), when he rebelled. He lied thus to the people: 'I am Bardiya, son of Cyrus, brother of Cambyses.' Then all the people became rebellious against Cambyses ... He seized the kingship ... After that, Cambyses died his own death.
>
> Darius the king proclaims: This kingship, which Gaumata the magus took away from Cambyses, this kingship belonged for a long time to our family.[64]

In the subsequent section, Darius recounts Gaumata's attempts to create his own worldwide empire, yet Darius portrays the reign of Gaumata as one marked by disorder. The people lived in fear that Guamata would kill them, especially those who may have known Bardiya previously. Further, Darius explains that under Guamata the cult centers were destroyed and that the peasants had their pastures, herds, household slaves, and even their homes taken from them. But "with the help of Ahuramazda," Darius says that he defeated Gaumata, wrested control of the empire, and "reestablished the people" (DB §14). With the rise of Darius to kingship, the text suggests, order was restored to the empire and to all those within it. The *drauga* had been overcome.

---

tions or rouse as much debate as the short period between the demise of Cambyses and the accession of Darius" (*From Cyrus to Alexander*, 98). See the evaluative comments provided by Kuhrt (*The Persian Empire*, 135–39) and Briant (*From Cyrus to Alexander*, 99–106).

63. OP *arika*, which Kuhrt explains, means "morally evil and the contravening of ties of trust and obligation" (*The Persian Empire*, 152n9). Kent simply defines the term as "evil, faithless" (*Old Persian*, 170).

64. DB §10–12 (Kuhrt, *The Persian Empire*, 143).

2. THE ACHAEMENID DYNASTY AND IMPERIAL IDEOLOGY   39

Although such a storyline makes good propaganda, it likely fails to reflect the historical record accurately.[65] In attempting to reconstruct the events, scholars have proposed that Bardiya, the brother of Cambyses, may have instigated a rebellion while Cambyses was in Egypt. Hearing of the rebellion, Cambyses set out from Egypt to put down the rebellion but died during the return trip. Darius made his way back to Persia and with the aid of a few men assassinated Bardiya. Subsequent revolts broke out across the empire as a result, but Darius managed to put down the revolts with the aid of loyal troops and secured his role as king of the empire. Grabbe surmises that "the story of the false Bardiya—the pseudo-Smerdis, the magnus Guamata—was invented to explain how an act of regicide was instead the deed of a loyal noble Persian who stepped in to combat the great Lie that had overcome so many."[66]

The latter sections of the Behistun Inscription further the claim that the text is a piece of propaganda meant to prop up Darius's assertion that he alone could secure cosmic order in the empire. Counting his alleged victory over Gaumata, Darius recounts nine uprisings that he had to quell. Herrenschmidt and Lincoln note that the first (DB §§10–14) and last of these uprisings (DB §§40–48) are associated with a mountain (*kaufah*).[67]

---

65. See the arguments proposed by Jack Martin Balcer (*Herodotus and Bisitun: Problems in Ancient Persian Historiography* [Historia Einzelschriften 49; Stuttgart: Schreiner, 1987], 150-66); Sancisi-Weerdenburg, "Darius I and the Persian Empire," 2:1035–39; and Dandamaev, *A Political History of the Achaemenid Empire*, 83–94. Some scholars, particularly those writing in the first part of the last century, argued for the veracity of the text. See for example, Albert Ten Eyck Olmstead, "Darius and his Behistun Inscription," *AJSL* 55 (1938): 392–416 and Arno Poebel, "Chronology of Darius' First Year of Reign," *AJSL* 55 (1938): 142–65, although recently the thesis has been taken up again by Mabel Lang ("Prexaspes and Usurper Smerdis," *JNES* 51 [1992]: 201–7).

66. Grabbe, *Yehud: A History of the Persian Province of Judah*, 269.

67. Herrsenschmidt and Lincoln, "Healing and Salt Waters," 276. On the rhetorical features of the Behistun inscription in general, see James Bowick, "Characters in Stone: Royal Ideology and Yehudite Identity in the Behistun Inscription and the Book of Haggai," in *Community Identity in Judean Historiography: Biblical and Comparative Perspectives* (ed. Gary N. Knoppers and Kenneth A. Ristau; Winona Lake, Ind.: Eisenbrauns, 2009), 87–117. Gernot L. Windfuhr has noted the role of the number nine in the Behistun Inscription (e.g., nine uprisings; Darius is the ninth king). As he notes, this number frequently appears in spells and may suggest something of the intended rhetorical force of the inscription ("'Saith Darius': Dialectic, Numbers, Time and Space at Behistun [DB, Old Persian Version]," in *Continuity and Change: Proceedings*

Both at Arakadri and Parga, the rebels are said to have mounted forces to challenge Darius and disrupt the ordered world established by the Achaemenid dynasty. The significance of the mountain, however, rests not in its geographical location, but in its "place within the Achaemenian *imaginaire*."[68] Although they admit the evidence is far from conclusive, Herrenschmidt and Lincoln postulate that mountains may be understood symbolically as places of "turbulence, disorder, rebellion, and violence" associated with "the Lie."[69]

In each recounting of a potential insurrection, Darius explains that "the Lie (*drauga*) made them rebellious because these (who led the rebellions) lied to the people." The connection between the Lie and a disordered world is made clear, as is the opposite: only an empire governed by an Achaemenid can thwart the political and cosmological upheaval generated by the Lie. As a warning to subsequent kings in the Achaemenid dynasty, Darius cautions, "you who shall be king hereafter, be firmly on your guard against the Lie; the man who shall be a follower of the Lie—punish him well, if you think 'May my country be secure.'"[70] The well-being and prosperity of the empire rest in the king's ability to secure order and protect it from the varied threats associated with the Lie. The implicit assumption is that so long as the empire remains under Darius, or one from the Achaemenid dynasty, the empire and those within it will enjoy the benefits of an ordered cosmos.[71]

---

of the Last Achaemenid History Workshop, April 6–8, 1990, Ann Arbor, Michigan [ed. Heleen Sancisi-Weerdenburg, Amélie Kuhrt, and Margeret C. Root; AH 8; Leiden: Nederlands Instituut voor het Nabije Oosten, 1994], 257–64).

68. Herrenschmidt and Lincoln, "Healing and Salt Waters," 276.

69. Ibid. On the role of Mount Zion in the theological rhetoric of Book 5 of the Psalter, see §5.4 in the present study.

70. DB §55 (Kuhrt, *The Persian Empire*, 148).

71. The role of the empire in guaranteeing an ordered world is apparent in several other royal inscriptions. In an inscription attributed to Darius (DSe), Darius proclaims, "Much had been done wrong that I put right; the lands were in turmoil, one smiting the other" but under Darius they were properly ordered under his reign (§4). In the same text, Darius observes that "there was much earlier building which was not in a good state" (§5), but which he restored, again bringing right order to the empire. In a text found at Persepolis, often referred to as the "Daiva Text" (XPh), Xerxes likewise states that there was turmoil in the region, particularly in one country (§4a). As king, however, he restored tranquility and order to the region. Xerxes also notes that across the empire, some countries were allegedly worshipping the *daivās* (any sort of false god), leading Xerxes to destroy the places where the *daivās* were worshipped and

2.2.4. Summary of Imperial Ideology

With Darius, the concepts and ideals of Persian kingship and imperial rule receive their definitive and lasting shape. Subsequent kings in the Achaemenid dynasty both retained and promulgated the chief tenets of this imperial ideology. The empire was envisioned as worldwide, encompassing nearly all nations, placing them under the subjugation of the Achaemenid king. Such an audacious claim was rooted in the belief that Ahuramazda had willed the world to be ordered in this way. Yet as the iconography suggests, such subjugation was recast as joyful participation in the empire. The violent and militaristic images associated with the Neo-Assyrian subjugation of nations were replaced with more tranquil images of willing subjects bearing the full weight of the empire and its demands.[72] Finally, cosmic order was predicated upon the imperial ideology generated by the Achaemenid dynasty. The imperial propaganda generated through both iconography and inscription suggests that the order of the cosmos, including the more mundane matters of life, is secured only through the able and divinely ordained Achaemenid dynasty. In short, the rhetoric of the empire is clear: those who acknowledge the worldwide empire of the dynasty and participate joyously in it will reap the benefits of an ordered world.

---

to announce that "'the *daivās* shall not be worshipped any longer.' Wherever formerly the *daivās* have been worshipped, there I worshipped Ahuramazda at the proper time and with proper ceremony" (§4b). As Briant contends, "all in all, the *daivā* inscription gives the impression of accentuating the religious justifications for the power of the Great King, the true representative on earth of Ahura-Mazda," and consequently, the only one capable of creating an ordered cosmos (*From Cyrus to Alexander*, 553).

72. This claim likely contributed to an overly generous picture of Achaemenid imperial rule in earlier scholarship and necessitated the corrective provided in more recent research literature. Kuhrt has challenged the broader notion of tolerance often attributed to the Persian Empire, suggesting instead that Persian imperial policy bears a greater semblance to Assyrian and Babylonian practices than previously considered (Amélie Kuhrt, "The Cyrus Cylinder and the Achaemenid Imperial Policy," *JSOT* 25 [1983]: 83–97). The reign of Cambyses, and in particular his subjugation of Egypt, seems indicative of the claims made by Kuhrt. See also Briant's assessment of Cambyses's campaign into Egypt (*From Cyrus to Alexander*, 50–61).

2.3. The Dissemination of Imperial Ideology

Prior to considering book 5 of the Psalter and the possible responses to the imperial ideology generated by the Achaemenid dynasty, the question of access to such an ideology must be considered. There is ample evidence that Darius, in particular, but subsequent kings as well, sought to disseminate their imperial ideology across the empire. In addition to Darius's directive, as explained below, structures inherent to the empire itself would likely have contributed to further dissemination. As noted below, the book of Ezra illustrates the types of interaction that were probably possible between the empire and those in Yehud.

2.3.1. The Behistun Inscription and Its Dissemination

Following the lengthy account of Darius's rise to power, the Behistun Inscription records that

> Darius the king proclaims: By the favor of Ahuramazda, this is the form of writing which I have made, besides in Aryan. Both on clay tablets and on parchment it has been placed.... And it was written down and read before me. Afterwards, I sent off this form of writing everywhere into the countries. The people strove (to abide by it?).[73]

The entire inscription, and this paragraph in particular, prove instructive in considering the manner in which the empire disseminated its ideology.

As mentioned in the previous section, the Behistun inscription includes the massive relief of Darius and the vanquished rebels. Surrounding the carved scene are inscribed texts written in Elamite, Babylonian, and Old Persian. These inscriptions recount the alleged events surrounding the ascendency of Darius to power. The trilingual aspect of the inscription found at Behistun is not altogether unique, however, and proves characteristic of many Achaemenid royal inscriptions found throughout the empire.[74] The multiplicity of languages on the inscriptions at Behistun and

---

73. DB §70 (Kuhrt, *The Persian Empire*, 149).

74. Besides its length, the DB does differ from other trilingual royal inscriptions in that the languages were not inscribed simultaneously; the final inscription was the result of a somewhat lengthy process, beginning with Elamite, to which was added the Babylonian text, and then finally the Old Persian text. On the historical development

elsewhere demonstrates the dynasty's awareness of the multilingual nature of the empire in its totality and likely reflects "the kings' desire to have their texts read and understood, rather than tucked away for posterity."[75] As evident in the text above, Darius indicates that he had the inscription written on clay tablets and on parchment so that he could disseminate this "everywhere into the countries." Although the narrative on the inscription related to the rise of Darius appears dubious, the point of its dissemination was not "history" but propaganda. Darius understood well the power of royal propaganda and the necessity of its dissemination in order to achieve the desired result.

Additional copies of the inscription appear elsewhere in the empire, suggesting that Darius's command for its dissemination did not go unheeded. Remnants of an Aramaic version of the inscription were found at Elephantine. The remains include two papyrus sheets and dozens of fragments likely dating from around 420 B.C.E. This date would suggest that the document was likely written under the reign of Darius II, nearly a century after Darius I. Jan Tavernier contends that Darius II may have commissioned a copy of the translation from an older document but with the primary intent of connecting his own reign with that of his great-great-grandfather.[76] If Tavernier is correct, the inscription functioned not once, but twice, as royal propaganda in the hands of those within the Achaemenid dynasty.

Two fragments of the inscription were also found in Babylon. Unlike the Aramaic inscriptions, which were found on parchment, the Babylonian texts were inscribed on basalt blocks. The first fragment was found on a block measuring 26 cm high and 40 cm long, containing lines 55–58 and 69–72 of the inscription. The second fragment, much smaller in size, appears to contain words related to lines 91–95 and 108–109 of the inscription. Although both fragments contain relatively small portions of

---

of the inscription, see Rüdiger Schmitt, "Bisotun iii: Darius's Inscriptions," *Encyclopædia Iranica*, online: http://www.iranicaonline.org/articles/bisotun-iii.

75. Cameron Howard, "Writing Yehud: Textuality and Power under Persian Rule" (PhD diss., Emory University, 2010), 40.

76. Jan Tavernier, "An Achaemenid Royal Inscription: The Text of Paragraph 13 of the Aramaic Version of the Bisitun Inscription," *JNES* 60 (2001): 161–76. For the most recent edition of the fragmentary manuscript, see Jonas C. Greenfield and Bezalel Porten, *The Bisitun Inscription of Darius the Great: Aramaic Version* (Corpus Inscriptionum Iranicarum. Part I; Inscriptions of Ancient Iran, Vol. 5; London: Humphries, 1982).

the inscription itself, they do suggest that a complete Behistun inscription was likely erected in that area in an effort to duplicate Darius's inscription, and likely, the accompanying relief.[77]

Although no Greek translation of the inscription has been discovered, the degree to which Herodotus's version corresponds to the narrative of the Behistun inscription suggests that the tradition, if not a version of the text itself, was carried to the western parts of the empire. Schmitt goes even further, suggesting that a number of statements in Herodotus's *Histories* could be read as "literal translations of the inscription."[78] The degree to which Herodotus incorporated "literal translations of the inscription" into his *Histories* may be debatable, but the correspondence of Herodotus's narrative to that of the Behistun Inscription is less so. This would again suggest that Darius's desire for the dissemination of royal propaganda had its intended result; those across the empire became well-versed in his narrative concerning the rule of the Achaemenid dynasty and its ideological foundation.

Poised on the side of a limestone rock face along a well-traveled road, the Behistun Inscription itself contributed to the dissemination of the imperial ideology associated with the Achaemenid dynasty. But Darius's command for its distribution "everywhere to the countries" extended its reach. The presence of the inscription in Babylon and Egypt, and its influence in Greek-speaking regions, implies that the inscription was widely distributed. Moreover, one may surmise that the imperial ideology associated with the text exerted a considerable influence on the regions held by the Achaemenid dynasty.[79]

---

77. See Ursula Seidl, "Ein Relief Dareios I. in Babylon," *AMI* 9 (1976): 125–30.

78. Schmitt, "Bisotun iii: Darius's Inscriptions;" Sancisi-Weerdenburg concludes that Herodotus appears simply to follow the same narrative outline of the inscription ("Darius I and the Persian Empire," 2:1036–37).

79. The Behistun Inscription no doubt influenced other royal inscriptions erected across the empire. See the Canal Stela erected by Darius I in Egypt. The Chalouf Stela, set up at Kabret, Egypt, was carved in pink granite stone with Babylonian, Elamite, and Old Persian on one side and Egyptian hieroglyphics on the observe. The stela refers to the canal commissioned by Darius, but the language is laden with imperial ideology. The artwork present on the stela incorporates both Egyptian and Persian images, employing many of the images discussed above, reflecting the dynasty's ability to embed its message within the various cultures of the empire. See Root, *The King and Kingship in Achaemenid Art*, 61–68. See also Kuhrt, "DZc," (*The Persian Empire*, 485).

2.3.2. Hypertextuality and the Persian Empire

Well-known are the biblical texts that provide ample evidence, albeit employed satirically, of the Persian Empire's obsession with royal decrees and the preservation of records (e.g., Esth 1:20; 6:1; Dan 6:8–9).[80] Despite the satirical slant of the biblical texts, they do attest to a larger depiction of the empire that is more accurate than not. In her recent study, Cameron Howard has suggested that the Persian Empire could be labeled a "hypertextual entity," arguing that the empire was "obsessed over the production of records, gripped by a bureaucratic furor, generally engaged in writing to excess."[81] The massive archives discovered at Persepolis lend credence to such a thesis. The Fortification Texts found at Persepolis span the reign of Darius, dating from 509–494 B.C.E., while the Treasury Texts can be dated from 492–458 B.C.E., a period that extends from end of the reign of Darius I, through the reign of Xerxes, and into that of Artaxerxes I. Although, the latter group of texts numbers in the hundreds, the former collection (the Fortification Texts) contains somewhere between 20,000–25,000 tablets and seals.[82] Jones and Stolper record that at least two-fifths of these and perhaps up to half of them are pieces of Elamite primary documents and that between a quarter and a third are pieces of secondary documents (Elamite journals and accounts). Another fifth are pieces of uninscribed, sealed tags.[83] Other archives, though much smaller in size have been found in Babylon at Nippur, in Egypt at Elephantine, Hermopolis, and Saqqara, along with sealed Aramaic papyri from Samaria, and bullae with seal impressions from Dascylium.[84] The texts provide insight into the complex bureaucratic and administrative system of the empire, while the seals may

---

80. David M. Valeta, *Lions and Ovens and Visions: A Satirical Reading of Daniel 1–6* (HBM 12; Sheffield: Sheffield Phoenix, 2008). Valeta has argued persuasively that, as satire, these stories respond "to the political realities of imperialism and colonialism" (5).

81. Howard, "Writing Yehud: Textuality and Power under Persian Rule," 4.

82. Concerning the precise number of fortification texts, see the analysis by Charles E. Jones and Matthew W. Stolper, "How Many Persepolis Fortification Tablets Are There?" in *L'archive des fortifications de Persépolis: état des questions et perspectives de recherches* (ed. Pierre Briant, Wouter F. M. Henkelman, and Matthew W. Stolper; Persika 12; Paris: De Boccard, 2008]), 37–44.

83. Ibid., 42.

84. See Kuhrt, *The Persian Empire*, 12–13. See also the Aramaic ostraca, likely from Idumaea, dating from the Achaemenid period; for the *editio princeps*, see Israel

have performed what has been labeled a "policing function."⁸⁵ Because these texts often record administrative minutiae (e.g., taxes, contracts, production), their importance might be viewed primarily as providing "background" for reconstructing society under the Achaemenid dynasty. While that is possible and no doubt profitable, their presence also suggests something more fundamental in the communication between center and periphery in the empire. The "spatial extent" of the tablets reflects the reach of the empire into every satrapy. Among the languages found on the Persepolis tablets was Elamite, as mentioned above, and Aramaic, but there were also Greek, Akkadian, and possibly Phrygian tablets.⁸⁶ The various languages evident in the Persepolis tablets are representative of the diversity of languages across the empire and the communication that must have existed between the center and the periphery. These documents also suggest that communication was not one-way (from center to periphery as with the Behistun Inscription), but communication also extended from the periphery to the center. The Persepolis tablets suggest that the center was well equipped for communication, but as Briant notes, so too were those in the outlying regions of the empire. In Babylonian, Egyptian, and biblical documents,

> we find exalted persons in the satrapal administration bearing the titles (sometimes multiple) *bēl ṭēmi* and *sipīru*, that is 'chancellor' and 'scribe'. It is thus very clear that all the satrapal chancelleries were organized on

---

Eph'al and Joseph Naveh, *Aramaic Ostraca of the Fourth Century B.C. from Idumaea* (Jerusalem: Magnes, 1996).

85. Michael Jursa, "Accounting in Neo-Babylonian Institutional Archives: Structure, Usage, and Implications", in *Creating Economic Order: Record-Keeping, Standardization, and the Development of Accounting in the Ancient Near East* (ed. Michael Hudson and Cornelia Wunsch; International Scholars Conference on Ancient Near Eastern Economics 4; Bethesda, Md.: CDL Press, 2004), 145–98.

86. See George G. Cameron, *Persepolis Treasury Tablets* (OIP 65; Chicago: University of Chicago Press, 1948); Richard T. Hallock, *Persepolis Fortification Tablets* (OIP 92; Chicago: University of Chicago Press, 1969). Although Aramaic would have been the lingua franca for administrative tasks throughout the empire, Elamite functioned largely as the language for the royal archives at Persepolis (see Maria Brosius, "Ancient Archives and Concepts of Record-Keeping: An Introduction," in *Ancient Archives and Archival Traditions: Concepts of Record-Keeping in the Ancient World* [ed. Maria Brosius; Oxford: Oxford University Press, 2003], 1–16).

2. THE ACHAEMENID DYNASTY AND IMPERIAL IDEOLOGY   47

the same model and that they were responsible for dispatching letters and orders and receiving and preserving letters from the royal chancellery.[87]

The hypertextual nature of the empire, as well as the structure of communication between center and periphery, readily allowed for the exchange of documents like those that appear in the various archives. Likewise, such an arrangement makes it plausible that the interaction between center and periphery in a hypertextual culture could have aided directly and indirectly in the dissemination of the Achaemenid dynasty's imperial ideology.[88]

2.3.3. LINES OF COMMUNICATION AND THE ROYAL ROAD

In addition to revealing the hypertextuality of the Achaemenid dynasty, the Persepolis Fortification archives also demonstrate the importance of the Royal Road for communication across the empire.[89] As Kuhrt has suggested, "the central authority's ability to control conquered lands, proclaim its presence, collect and monitor its profits, and maintain security, depended upon an efficient system of communication."[90] This road, and the communication it would have afforded, would have served an important role in the dissemination of imperial ideology. Herodotus (5.52–54) limits his discussion of the Royal Road to the portion that stretches from Sardis to Susa, but the system of roads was far more extensive. Roads stretched beyond Susa to Persepolis and on to the Indus River on the eastern edge of the empire. A northerly route extended from Behistun to Ecbatana and

---

87. Briant, *From Cyrus to Alexander*, 447. See also the conclusions of Lisbeth S. Fried, "The ʿam hāʾāreṣ in Ezra 4:4 and Persian Imperial Administration," in *Judah and the Judeans in the Persian Period* (ed. Oded Lipschits and Manfred Oeming; Winona Lake, Ind.: Eisenbrauns, 2006), 123–45.

88. See, for example, the use of the "Heroic Man" on the Persepolis seals and its implications (Mark B. Garrison and Margaret C. Root, with Charles E. Jones, *Seals on the Persepolis Fortification Tablets Volume I: Images of the Heroic Encounter* [OIP 117; Chicago: University of Chicago Press, 2001]).

89. The Royal Road was primarily designed for official travel and required authorization in the form of a sealed document (*miyatukkaš*) for passage (Briant, *From Cyrus to Alexander*, 364). The sheer volume of tablets uncovered at Persepolis suggests that travel between periphery and center was extensive.

90. Kuhrt, *The Persian Empire*, 730. See also Briant, *From Cyrus to Alexander*, 357–70.

Bactra in the far northeast of the empire. For the present study, however, the road from northern Syria, through Damascus and Tyre, en route to Memphis is significant. During the Achaemenid period, the main routes through Syria and Palestine were extensive, creating a Persian presence that could be visually observed in the region. Travel by royal officials and leaders within the satrapy would have been along these routes, and likely, there would have been considerable interaction between the local population and such officials.[91]

As Persian troops and the royal entourage moved across the empire, there would have been additional interaction between Persians and the local population. Each satrapy was responsible for the hostels along the Royal Road and for providing the provisions for the Persian military as it moved across the regions. Xenophon recounts the military's stay at one stop. He writes, "In these villages they remained for three days, both for the sake of the wounded and because they had abundant supplies—flour, wine, and great stores of barley which had been gathered for horses. *They had been collected by the satrap in charge of the district.*" (*Anabasis* 3.4.31, emphasis added)

In addition to the movement of troops, the travel of the Achaemenid rulers would have garnered considerable attention. Cambyses victory over Egypt in 525 B.C.E. would have involved the movement of a considerable number of Persian troops through the Syria-Palestine area. Likewise, the frequent revolts or threat of revolts in Egypt would have necessitated the movement of troops through the same region. Like Cambyses, Xerxes I and Artaxerxes III participated in military campaigns in Egypt, requiring the movement of massive numbers of people associated with the royal house.[92] In his account of Darius III's departure from Babylon to Gaugemela, Quintus Curtius Rufus describes such a scene.

> Next, at a distance of one stadium, came Sisigambis, Darius's mother, drawn in a carriage, and in another came his wife. A troop of women attended the queens on horseback. Then came the fifteen so-called *armamaxae*, in which rode the king's children, their governesses, and a herd of eunuchs ... Next came the carriages of the three hundred sixty

---

91. Jason M. Silverman, *Persepolis and Jerusalem: Iranian Influence on the Apocalyptic Hermeneutic* (LHBOTS 558; New York: T&T Clark, 2012), 89.

92. Briant suggests that with the movement of the king, thousands likely had to migrate as well (*From Cyrus to Alexander*, 187).

royal concubines, also dressed in royal finery, and behind them the six hundred mules and three hundred camels carried the king's money … At the end, closing up the rear, were the light-armed troops with their commanders. (*Historiae Alexandri Magni* 3.3.22–25)

The use of the Royal Road for the mobilization of troops, and especially the movement of the royal entourage, would have created significant opportunities for the dissemination of political ideology across the empire.

The Royal Road connected the vast Persian Empire, providing an effective form of communication while also reinforcing the rule of the Achaemenid dynasty in each region. The well-worn roads would have also provided ample opportunity for the exchange of ideas between local populations and Persian officials, as well as an official avenue to communicate the imperial ideology associated with the Achaemenid dynasty.

2.3.4. Interaction with the Empire in the Books of Ezra and Nehemiah

The likelihood of interaction between Persian officials and those in Yehud finds considerable support throughout the books of Ezra and Nehemiah. Although the books and their accounts should "be attributed to the literary genres of program and propaganda rather than ('objective') historiography," the events narrated in each prove suggestive of life under Persian imperial rule.[93] Regardless of the precise historical accuracy of the texts (see below), they do suggest that interaction of some sort existed and further that such interaction would have resulted in the dissemination of imperial ideology under Persian rule.

2.3.4.1. The Documents in Ezra

In the book of Ezra, seven documents appear throughout the book, reinforcing the notion of the Achaemenid dynasty as a hypertextual empire. As Gerstenberger contends, "More than anyone else before them in the tradition of the Hebrew writings, the authors of the book become involved in the culture of writing and the political conditions" representative of the Persian period.[94] The seven documents that appear in the book include:

---

93. Gerstenberger, *Israel in the Persian Period*, 29.
94. Ibid., 161.

Document 1: 1:2–4, The Decree of Cyrus (in Hebrew)
Document 2: 4:9–16, Letter to Artaxerxes (in Hebrew)
Document 3: 4:17–22, Reply of Artaxerxes (in Hebrew)
Document 4: 5:7–17, Letter of Tattenai (in Hebrew)
Document 5: 6:2–5, Decree of Cyrus (in Aramaic)
Document 6: 6:6–12, Reply of Darius (in Aramaic)
Document 7: 7:12–26, Decree of Artaxerxes to Ezra (in Hebrew)

These documents record letters sent to the king as well as replies sent in return, suggesting that the exchange of written material between center and periphery was extensive (see above, §2.3.2). In addition, the hypertextual nature of the empire is reinforced in Artaxerxes's reply to Rehum and Shimshai in 4:17–22 and in Darius's decree in chapter 6. Before Artaxerxes sent his reply "someone searched (the archives) and discovered that this city has risen against kings" (4:19), and then again, before Darius issued his decree, the text reads that those in the royal court "searched the archives where the documents were stored in Babylon" (6:1). Both texts suggest the connection between royal edicts and royal archives in the management of the empire, and further, both texts demonstrate the familiarity of edicts and archives by those under Achaemenid rule. The communication between center and periphery is implied in the use of documents throughout the first seven chapters. The implication in Ezra is that Persian imperial policy would have been communicated to those living in Yehud and that such communication would have had an impact on societal life.

Although the historicity of these documents has been challenged, both Grabbe and Hoglund have contended that the editor of Ezra was working with a set of documents that had likely been altered considerably to fit the narrative flow of the book itself and its larger theological purpose.[95]

---

95. Kenneth Hoglund, *Achaemenid Imperial Administration in Syria-Palestine and the Missions of Ezra and Nehemiah* (SBLDS 125; Atlanta: Scholars, Press 1992); Lester Grabbe, "The 'Persian Documents' in the Book of Ezra," in *Judah and the Judeans in the Persian Period* (ed. Oded Lipschits and Manfred Oeming; Winona Lake, Ind.: Eisenbrauns, 2006), 531–70. For a similar view, see also Hugh G. M. Williamson, *Ezra, Nehemiah* (WBC 16; Waco, Tex.: Word, 1985), xxiii–xxiv. Gerstenberger, alternatively, cautions that one should assume the narrative to be fictitious, with the embedding of such documents, and even the use of Aramaic, as an attempt at "historical authenticity" (*Israel in the Persian Period*, 159–60). Similar to Gerstenberger, David Janzen suggests that the letter to Ezra (Document 7) "may have been composed as a kind of midrash on the rest of the Ezra narrative" ("The 'Mission' of Ezra and the

The question of the historical accuracy of the *content* of the documents themselves is not at stake in the present argument. Rather, the presence of such documents in Ezra, and the apparent ease with which such documents were readily exchanged as illustrated in the book, may provide a reasonably accurate view of the exchange of documents that would have existed between the empire and the regions under its rule. Further, such an exchange would have provided a logical means for the dissemination of imperial ideology.

2.3.4.2. Nehemiah 5 and Imperial Policy

The documents in Ezra, mentioned above, reflect the type of interaction that would likely have existed between the empire and its subjects. Nehemiah 5 illustrates well the impact imperial economic policy would have had upon those living in Yehud. Williamson, followed more recently by Becking, have noted that while such events likely did not occur simultaneously with the rebuilding of the wall, they are illustrative of the economic strains experienced at a later date.[96] The people cry out to those in power for relief from the current economic and social distress brought on both by natural disasters and exacting imperial policies.

> For there were those who said, "With our sons and our daughters, we are many; we must get grain so that we may eat and stay alive." There were also those who said, "We are having to pledge our fields, our vineyards, and our houses in order to get grain during the famine." And there were those who said, "We are having to borrow money on our fields and vineyards to pay the king's tax. Now our flesh is the same as that of our kindred; our children are the same as their children and yet we are forcing our sons and daughters to be slaves, and some of our daughters have been ravished; we are powerless, and our fields and vineyards now belong to others." (Neh 5:2–5 NRSV)

Persian-Period Temple Community," *JBL* 119 [2000]: 643). For an even stronger negative assessment of the documents in Ezra, see Antonius H. J. Gunneweg, *Esra* (KAT 19/1; Gütersloh: Mohn, 1985), 85–111.

96. Williamson, *Ezra, Nehemiah*, 234–35; Bob Becking, *Ezra, Nehemiah, and the Construction of Early Jewish Identity* (FAT 1/80; Tübingen: Mohr Siebeck, 2011), 79–80.

The economic conditions under Persian rule and their impact on the colonies has been well documented.[97] Blenkinsopp has rightly cautioned that scholarship has frequently depicted the economic policies of the Achaemenid dynasty as more "benign" than its predecessors, but as he avers, "their fiscal policy was every bit as harsh and unenlightened as that of the Assyrians and the Babylonians."[98] Nehemiah 5 provides a depiction of life in Yehud that was radically shaped by imperial economic policies, a depiction that likely reflected something of reality. If imperial economic policies influenced those in Yehud to the degree suggested by Neh 5, then it is probable to reason that the imperial ideological claims of empire would have also reached the same inhabitants.

2.3.5. Summary

The above evidence suggests that the Achaemenid dynasty, beginning with Darius, sought to disseminate its imperial ideology through a variety of means, believing that such communication was essential to imperial control over a vast empire. The archives at Persepolis and elsewhere suggest that the Achaemenids were indeed a hypertextual culture, capable of continued communication between center and periphery. The Royal Road ensured the means of such communication, but also served as a constant and visible reminder of the empire's presence in the region. These same roads also served as an avenue for the manifestation of imperial ideology when military troops or royal entourages travelled upon them. Although the texts from Ezra and Nehemiah do not function as historiography in the strictest sense, they do provide a nuanced depiction of life lived under Persian imperial rule and the degree to which interaction took place between center and periphery.

2.4. Conclusion

The Achaemenid Dynasty sought to perpetuate an imperial ideology rooted in three significant claims. The empire that started under Cyrus,

---

97. Grabbe, *Yehud: A History of the Persian Province of Judah*, 189–208.

98. Joseph Blenkinsopp, *Ezra-Nehemiah: A Commentary* (OTL; Louisville: Westminster, 1988), 66–67. See also Gerstenberger, *Israel in the Persian Period*, 54–59. On the issue of the Persian Empire and a "dependent economy," see Briant, *From Cyrus to Alexander*, 388–471.

expanded under Cambyses, and organized under Darius was an empire that claimed worldwide reach, figuratively placing all nations under its dominion. This was possible only because Ahuramazda, the god of earth and heaven, had willed that the world be this way. In short, the Achaemenids possessed a divine mandate to expand, conquer, and control. The iconography of empire is quick, however, to cast such governance in terms of joyful participation by the conquered peoples. Finally, the imperial ideology generated by the Achaemenid dynasty is meant to secure cosmic order. The rhetoric of the empire is clear: those who acknowledge the worldwide empire of the dynasty and participate joyously in it will reap the benefits of an ordered world.

The rhetoric of the empire reflected what Briant referred to as "timeless attitudes" that extended beyond any one king and any one era. This rhetoric also extended beyond any one region in the empire. Beyond the Persian cities of Ecbatana, Susa, Pasagardae, and Persepolis, the rhetoric of empire, and the concomitant imperial policies, reached to Memphis, Sardis, Samaria, and Jerusalem to the west. But revolts in Egypt, Babylonia, Asia Minor (Sardis), and Cyprus, among others, suggest that the rhetoric of imperial ideology was not always fully embraced by those who were allegedly joyous participants in the empire. Although Yehud never mounted, nor could have mounted, a true revolt against an empire the size of Persia, it could mount a challenge to the *rhetoric* of imperial ideology. This challenge would be rooted in Yehud's theological and historical commitments, and manifested in its own literature.

3
Constructing and Deconstructing Power: Part 1

3.0. Introduction

Despite the longevity of Achaemenid rule, the imperial ideology associated with the dynasty remained consistent in its claims: the Persian Empire was a worldwide empire in which nations participated joyously because under Achaemenid rule the world was well-ordered. As indicated in the previous chapter, such an ideology began under Cyrus but was articulated most clearly under Darius and then adopted and transmitted by subsequent kings. This imperial rhetoric shaped and reshaped subsequent Achaemenid rulers, shaping as well those over whom they ruled.

The royal oracles in Deutero-Isaiah reflect perhaps the earliest attempt in the Hebrew Bible to blend Persian imperial ideology, or at least the chief representative of such an ideology, with that of Judean royal ideology.[1]

---

1. Over the last century, Babylon has been the likely default for the provenance of Deutero-Isaiah. Norman Whybry provides a confident assessment of the issue. According to Whybry, the prophet's "familiarity with the Babylonian scene establishes beyond a reasonable doubt that he was one of the exiles in Babylon" (R. Norman Whybry, *The Second Isaiah* [OTG; Sheffield: JSOT Press, 1983], 8). So also John Goldingay and David Payne, *A Critical and Exegetical Commentary on Isaiah 40–55: Volume 2* (ICC; New York: T&T Clark, 2006). More recently, however, a number of scholars have revisited the proposition that the provenance of Deutero-Isaiah, or portions thereof, was instead Yehud. See especially Hans M. Barstad, *The Babylonian Captivity of the Book of Exile: 'Exilic' Judah and the Provenance of Isaiah 40–55* (Institute for the Comparative Research in Human Culture, Series B, 102; Oslo: Novus, 1997), 35–75. See also, Christopher R. Seitz, *Zion's Final Destiny: The Development of the Book of Isaiah: A Reassessment of Isaiah 36–39* (Minneapolis: Fortress, 1992), 205–7; Philip R. Davies, "God of Cyrus, God of Israel: Some Religio-historical Reflections on Isaiah 40–55," in *Words Remembered, Texts Renewed. Essays in Honour of John F. A. Sawyer* (ed. Jon Davies et al.; JSOTSup 195; Sheffield: Sheffield Academic, 1995),

In Isaiah 40–48, in particular, these oracles contribute significantly to the overtly political tenor of the collection. In Isa 44:24–28 and again in 45:1–7, Cyrus is mentioned specifically by name. In addition, the prophet refers to an individual in 42:5–13, 45:11–13 and 48:12–15, likely Cyrus or a subsequent Achaemenid, as well.[2] Some have attempted to connect the rhetoric in Deutero-Isaiah to that found in the Cyrus Cylinder, suggesting a partial appropriation of the cylinder's content for the prophet's own purposes. In support of such a thesis, Joseph Blenkinsopp surmises that

> Isaiah 40–48 reads like a Jewish version of the propagandist's manifesto of Cyrus on his famous cylinder published shortly after the conquest of Babylon in 539. There is in both texts a religious polemic against the impious Nabonidus, an accusation that he had condemned his subjects to forced labor (40.2; 47.6), and a charge that he had treated their cults with contempt. In consequence of which Yhwh (not Marduk) chose Cyrus as his agent, made the vast populations of the Babylonian empire subject to him, and inspired him to exercise rule without the violence and brutality characteristic of the Babylonians.[3]

210–15; Rainer Albertz, *Israel in Exile: The History and Literature of the Sixth Century B.C.E.* (trans. David Green; Atlanta: Society of Biblical Literature, 2003), 376–433; Lena-Sofia Tiemeyer, "Geography and Textual Allusions in Interpreting Isaiah XL–LV and Lamentations as Judahite Texts," *VT* 57 (2007): 367–85; idem, *For the Comfort of Zion: The Geographical and Theological Location of Isaiah 40–55* (VTSup 139; Leiden: Brill, 2011).

2. Following recent studies on the redactional history of the collection, Albertz has suggested that the first edition of Deutero-Isaiah was written around 520 B.C.E. Consequently, he argues that the three anonymous oracles in Deutero-Isaiah should be applied to Darius. "The Deutero-Isaiah group must have been deeply impressed by the political programme proclaimed by Darius. Interpreting his political propaganda in an idealistic manner, they could not understand this coincidence other than that Yhwh himself had brought this usurper to the Persian throne" ("Darius in Place of Cyrus: The First Edition of Deutero-Isaiah [40:1–52:12] in 521 B.C.E.," *JSOT* 27 [2003], 383). Whether or not Albertz is correct in his dating of the first edition, his larger assessment concerning Deutero-Isaiah's appropriation of the Persian political program is consistent with the general argument made above: those writing Deutero-Isaiah believed it possible to blend Persian imperial ideology with traditional Judean royal ideology.

3. Joseph Blenkinsopp, "Second-Isaiah, Prophet of Universalism?" *JSOT* 41 (1988), 85. Soon after the discovery of the cylinder in 1879 at Babylon came the first attempt to study the relationship between the cylinder and that of Deutero-Isaiah. See Rudolph Kittel, "Cyrus und Deuterojesaja," *ZAW* (1898): 149–62.

Others, however, have rejected such a tight correlation. Hans Barstad has dismissed any correlation altogether, suggesting that "the cylinder is so Marduk/Babylonia oriented that it is highly unlikely that any prophet could have taken inspiration from it. Probably the prophet never knew about the cylinder at all."[4] More likely, the truth lies somewhere between the two extremes requiring a different approach to both texts.

Amélie Kuhrt has argued persuasively that the Cyrus Cylinder resembles that of a Mesopotamian building text, both in physical shape and literary genre.[5] Kuhrt compares the cylinder to the large number of building texts found in Mesopotamia and their presence over an extended period of history. The Assyrian Royal Annals, for example, appear to represent an Assyrian development of the Sumero-Babylonian genre of building texts. According to Kuhrt, these texts were often found beneath or inside the walls of buildings that were either being constructed or restored. As she notes, "This actually provides a clue to the ultimate purpose of the Cyrus Cylinder: it was composed to commemorate his restoration of Babylon like that of his predecessor Assurbanipal, to recount his accession and pious acts, and to demonstrate to subsequent generations his legitimacy as ruler of Babylon."[6] Although the text is "Marduk/Babylonia" oriented, as Barstad suggests, and likely only intended to address the plight of those in Babylon who had suffered under the reign of Nabonidus, the text did come to represent the foundational claims later asserted in the ideology associated with the Achaemenid dynasty. The portrayal of Cyrus as a "kind of saviour and model of the benign tolerance of Persian policy" suggests that while the Cyrus Cylinder may have been directed only to a Babylonian audience originally, subsequent communities familiar with Achaemenid imperial ideology appeared to appropriate its ideology in their own attempts at restoration. Whether the writer of Deutero-Isaiah made specific use of some form of the Cyrus Cylinder is difficult, if not impossible, to determine. The association of Cyrus with that of restoration, however, seems less so. Although he is identified as a foreigner, as one who does not know Yahweh (45:4, 5), Cyrus is nonetheless tasked with the restoration of both Jerusalem and the temple (44:28).

---

4. Hans M. Barstad, "On the So-Called Babylonian Literary Influence in Second Isaiah," *SJOT* 2 (1987), 94.

5. Amélie Kuhrt, "The Cyrus Cylinder and the Achaemenid Imperial Policy," *JSOT* 25 (1983), 88.

6. Ibid.

Elsewhere, the prophet signals in dramatic fashion the incorporation of Cyrus and the Persian Empire into the work of Yahweh in history.[7] The designation of Cyrus as מָשִׁיחַ יְהוָה in Isa 45:1 suggests an acceptance of the Persian ruler as a successor to the Judean dynastic monarchy.[8] Cyrus is called "my shepherd" in 44:28 and like previous Davidic kings, Yahweh pledges to subdue nations and kings (45:1) on his behalf (cf. Ps 2:8–9). It is he who will rebuild Jerusalem and lay the foundation of the temple. In short, the prophet has "delivered up to the Persian conqueror the entire theology that had defined the local king."[9]

As suggested above, the writers of Deutero-Isaiah spoke in ways that aligned somewhat with certain claims of Achaemenid imperial ideology, even assigning the Achaemenid ruler titles and claims once reserved for the Davidic dynasty alone. Such evidence suggests that the claims of Achaemenid ideology were not considered a threat to the theological tenets of Israel's faith but in fact were adapted into the theological argument put forward in Deutero-Isaiah.

In Pss 107–145 the psalmists readily acknowledge the role of political power within Israel's past but also the alleged powers that continued to threaten the small province of Yehud. Unlike the writers of Deutero-Isaiah, however, the psalmists did not adopt a more nuanced depiction of political power as expressed in the Achaemenid imperial ideology in particular, but instead the psalmists provide a thoroughly negative assessment of political power *in toto*. Rather than ignoring the political powers from the past and those in the present, the psalmists recognize such powers and seek to construct an image of power gone awry and its devastating effects upon the community. Consequently, in constructing the enemy in such a way, the psalmists deconstruct the imperial ideology promulgated most

---

7. Philip R. Davies, "God of Cyrus, God of Israel," 208.

8. Joseph Blenkinsopp, "The Cosmological and Protological Language of Deutero-Isaiah," *CBQ* 73 (2011), 498. See also Klaus Baltzer, *Deutero-Isaiah: A Commentary on Isaiah 40–55* (ed. Peter Machinist; trans. Margaret Kohl; Hermeneia; Minneapolis: Fortress, 2001).

9. Lisbeth Fried, "Cyrus the Messiah? The Historical Background to Isaiah 45:1," *HTR* 95 (2002), 392. Fried argues that local court theology was applied to Persian rulers in the initial years of Achaemenid dynasty. In Egypt, for example, Cambyses received a full Pharoanic titulary by Udjahorresnet (Miriam Lichtheim, *Ancient Egyptian Literature: Volume 3; The Late Period* [Berkeley: University of California Press, 1980], 36–41). As noted in §2 of the present study, the Egyptian titles associated with Darius can be found on a number of inscriptions at Susa and Suez.

recently by the Persian Empire. In order to identify both the construction of power and the deconstruction of such an ideology of power, this chapter and the next will consider how power is constructed in a number of psalms. In these psalms, the construction of power is complex, laden with allusions and metaphors meant to highlight the community's plight as the powerless people of God.

3.1. Psalm 107

3.1.1. The Historic Presence of Empire

Psalm 107 stands as the opening psalm of book 5, setting the tenor for the collection to follow. Although the psalm opens with the verb הוֹדוּ, "Give thanks," the psalm in its entirety might be labeled more properly a didactic meditation on Israel's deliverance out of exile.[10] The entire psalm demonstrates Yahweh's חֶסֶד in redeeming his people from hostile powers and in gathering them from the regions of the earth. The final verse in the psalm emphasizes the didactic aim of the psalm:

> Who is wise (חָכָם)? Let them give heed to these things;
>   let them understand the חֶסֶד of Yahweh.[11]

The episodes of deliverance rehearsed earlier in the psalm serve as evidence of Yahweh's חֶסֶד and should fundamentally shape those who "give

---

10. Leslie Allen proposes that a likely preexilic "summons to a service of individual thanksgiving appears to have undergone a radical reinterpretation by the addition of vv. 2–3, which transformed it into a postexilic communal thanksgiving for immigrants from the Diaspora. Verses 33–43, which take up earlier vocabulary in a new sense, represent a didactic meditation which is not necessarily inconsistent with thanksgiving" (*Psalms 101–150* [WBC 21; Waco, Tex.: Word Books, 1983], 62–3). Allen draws considerably from Walter Beyerlin's thesis, in particular the redactional function of vv. 2–3. See also Claus Westermann, *The Praise of God in the Psalms* (trans. Keith R. Crim; Richmond, Va.: John Knox, 1965), 104–5.

11. All translations are mine unless otherwise noted. Note that in v. 43b the text reads חסדי יהוה, suggesting that the acts of deliverance mentioned throughout the psalm serve as "proofs" or "acts of steadfast love" that should be considered and understood. The invitation to reflect on the "steadfast love of Yahweh" is more narrowly confined here to Yahweh's particular acts of deliverance from oppression and exile. See Klaus Seybold, *Die Psalmen* (HAT 1/15; Tübingen: Mohr Siebeck, 1996), 427–28.

heed" to them (see below). Central to the present study is the psalm's use of language that is suggestive of power and empire. Although the psalmist recognizes the cause of their plight as sin and rebellion (107:11, 17), the psalmist also understands that the חֶסֶד of Yahweh delivered them from the powers that had oppressed them.

In the opening lines, the psalmist addresses those termed the "redeemed (גְּאוּלֵי) of Yahweh." In the legal corpus, גאל frequently refers to individuals in need, and in particular, those who find themselves in slavery due to economic hardship (cf. Lev 25:48–49). Beyond the more narrowly defined familial contexts (cf. Leviticus; Ruth), the term גאל functions at the corporate level to evoke images of deliverance from imperial powers like Egypt (e.g., Ex 6:6; 15:13; Ps 74:2; 77:16; 78:35; 106:10) or Babylon (e.g., Isa 43:14; 44:23, 24; Jer 50:34). Throughout Deutero-Isaiah, the prophet couples references to the exodus from exile and deliverance from captivity with the language of redemption. Not only are the people referred to as the "redeemed" (Isa 51:10), but frequently the title "redeemer" (גֹּאֵל) is applied to Yahweh (Isa 41:14; 44:6; 47:4; 48:17; 49:7, 26; 54:5, 8). In Trito-Isaiah, the appellation for Yahweh continues (Isa 59:20; 60:16; 63:16). For the present study, however, the most striking parallel to Ps 107 appears in Trito-Isaiah. Other than Ps 107:2, the only other use of the phrase גְּאוּלֵי יהוה, "the redeemed of Yahweh," is found in Isa 62:12, a text which promises the people deliverance from the אֹיְבִים ("enemies") and the בְּנֵי־נֵכָר ("foreigners"). The political overtones are clear in Isa 62 as well as the other texts mentioned above, and no doubt such language in Ps 107 carries similar overtones.

The psalmist notes that the גְּאוּלֵי יהוה have been delivered מִיַּד־צָר. The latter word has been rendered as "trouble" in the NRSV, thereby stripping the term of the political connotations appropriately associated with it. Walter Beyerlin, however, recognized the political connotations, suggesting that the phrase "the hand of the צָר" refers to historical-political enemies.[12] Frequently צָר appears in the Hebrew Bible with clear reference to the political or military enemies of Israel or Judah.[13] In such instances, the

---

12. Walter Beyerlin, *Werden und Wesen des 107. Psalms* (BZAW 153; Berlin: de Gruyter, 1979), 13.

13. Num 10:9; 24:8; Deut 32:27; 33:7; Josh 5:13; 2 Sam 24:13 = 1 Chron 21:12; Isa 63:18; Jer 30:16; 50:7; Ezek 30:16; 39:23; Amos 3:11; Mic 5:8; Zech 8:10; Pss 44:6, 8, 11; 60:13–14 = 108:13–14; 74:10; 78:42, 61; 81:15; 105:24; 106:11; 107:2; 136:24; Lam 1:5, 7, 10, 17; 2:17; Esth 7:6; Ezra 4:1; Neh 4:5.

term צָר is best understood as coming from the root צרר II, "to be hostile," and not from צרר I, "to be in distress."[14] Further evidence for rendering צָר as a political term appears in the previous psalm.[15] In 106:10, speaking of Israel's deliverance from Egypt, the psalmist announces

> He delivered them from the hand of the foe (מִיַּד שׂוֹנֵא);
> And he redeemed (גאל) them from the hand of enemy (מִיַּד אוֹיֵב).

Later, in 106:41, the psalmist explains that Yahweh "gave them into the hand of the nations" (בְּיַד־גּוֹיִם) and they were "subdued under their hand (יָדָם)." While the term צָר has been replaced with synonymous terms, the use of the phrase "the hand of X" clearly links such language with sociopolitical realities that proved hostile to the people of God.

The nuanced language used in the opening lines of Ps 107 does more than simply connect Ps 107 to the historical reviews found in the two preceding psalms. To the contrary, such language serves to construct an image of Israel and the nations, one that highlights the role of empire within Israel's storied past. Israel's identity is bound up with the acknowledgement that the יַד־צָר has been (and continues to be) a threat to its existence, and the deliverance from such forces comes only from Yahweh. This perpetual threat of the powerful remains a constant theme throughout book 5 of the Psalter. Further, the community's self-described identity as the גְּאוּלֵי יהוה casts her as a former political prisoner "subdued under the hand" (106:41) of empires. Although the psalmist calls the community to give thanks for having been gathered from the lands (107:2–3), the suspicion of empire and power appears to linger in the poetry found in the rest of the collection.

---

14. See Ernst Jenni, "צרר," *TLOT* 2:582–83. See also Bruce Baloian, "צרר II," *NIDOTTE* 3:859.

15. Hossfeld and Zenger note that Pss 106 and 107 are semantically and conceptually bound together. See the exhaustive list of shared words and images identified in Frank Lothar Hossfeld and Erich Zenger (*Psalms 3: A Commentary on Psalms 101–150* [ed. Klaus Baltzer; trans. Linda Maloney; Hermeneia; Minneapolis: Fortress, 2011], 93–94).

3.1.2. Empire in Historical and Mythological Terms

Similar to a number of other biblical texts, the poet in Ps 107 speaks of empire in terms that are at once both historical and mythological. The opening lines of the psalm call the people to give thanks for having been gathered "from the lands, from the east and from the west, from the north and מִיָּם." Because מִיָּם apparently fails to provide a directional term, or at least not the expected term, it disrupts the parallel construction within the verse, leading a number of scholars to offer explanations for its appearance. For example, Allen has attempted to retain the term, understanding that the people were gathered from the east and the west, and from the north and from "overseas." Allen suggests that such a rendering has in full view the geopolitical powers that had held the nations in captivity.[16] Citing 2 Chr 8:17, where יָם appears to refer to the Gulf of Aqabah, Dahood retains the MT reading, understanding יָם as antithetic parallelism to צָפוֹן, thus referencing the "motif of the four cardinal points."[17] Such a reading, however, fails to capture what Hossfeld and Zenger have termed the "historical-mythical" nature of the language employed.[18] With the term צָפוֹן, the psalmist alludes to the enemies from the north (i.e., Assyria and Babylon) while also equating those locations with the more metaphorical understanding of the term as a place of disaster and chaos (cf. Ezek 38:15; 39:2). Similarly, the term יָם appears throughout the Psalter functioning often as a metaphor implying pending chaos or chaos overcome (e.g., Pss 33:7; 65:7; 74:13). To limit the interpretation of verse 3c to a geographic understanding alone fails to capture the full range of possible meanings. With the use of such robust imagery, the psalmist opens Ps 107, and arguably book 5 of the Psalter, metaphorically by associating empires and powers with places of chaos and destruction, but, nevertheless, places that are not beyond the חֶסֶד of Yahweh.

A similar blending of historical and mythical themes appears in verses 4–32. In this section, four strophes of unequal length appear, but each patterned similarly (a description of need; a cry for help; the intervention of Yahweh; the invitation to give thanks in a cultic setting). Like the

---

16. Allen, *Psalms 101–150*, 56, 58.
17. Mitchell Dahood, *Psalms III: 101–150; Introduction, Translation, and Notes with an Appendix; The Grammar of the Psalter* (AB 17A; New York: Doubleday, 1970), 81. See also John Jarick, "The Four Corners of Psalm 107," *CBQ* 59 (1997): 270–87.
18. Hossfeld and Zenger, *Psalms 3*, 104.

directional language employed in verse 3, the regions depicted carry both historical and mythical themes. The wilderness (107:4–9), imprisonment (107:10–16), sickness to the point of death (107:17–22), and shipwreck (107:23–32) all appear to portray scenes of deliverance in the face of great distress, each with a number of connections to the introductory verses. The four directional terms used in verse 3 are matched by four extended stanzas meant to rehearse deliverance from various states of despair. Repeated in each strophe is the cry

> Then they cried to the LORD in their צַר,
> and he delivered them from their distress. (107:6, 13, 19, 28)

The NRSV, as do many translations, renders the term צַר as "trouble." Unfortunately such a translation fails to capture the connection with the language used earlier.[19] The repeated refrain throughout each of the four scenes alludes back to the claim made in verse 2 that Israel was under the "hand of the foe."[20] When the term is rendered as "trouble," the connection between verse 2 and the refrain in verses 6, 13, 19, and 28 is lost, as is the thematic thread alluding to Israel's historic threat from those in power. In an effort to capture the play on imagery, Hossfeld and Zenger translate the phrase in verse 2 as "out of the hand of the oppressors (*Bedrängers*)," and in the repeated refrain, "They cried to the LORD in their oppression (*Bedrängnis*)."[21] Such a translation more nearly captures the political allusion being suggested.

The first and second stanzas, in particular, recall images associated with deliverance from the Babylonian exile and the return to Jerusalem. A number of verses allude to statements made in Deutero-Isaiah. Within the first stanza (107:4–9), the key thematic allusions include: the desert wasteland (Ps 107:4 // Isa 53:6); the plight of the thirsty and the hungry (Ps 107:5

---

19. See also Dahood, *Psalms 101–150*, 80. He laments that the "strong international note of the recurrent refrain is unfortunately lost in most modern translations."

20. Beyerlin contends that vv. 2–3 were added in the final stage of the psalm's compilation, with the primary intent to announce the triumphant warring of Yahweh with the historical-political enemies in order to bring about the final restitution of his people (*Werden und Wesen des 107. Psalms*, 13). Whether Beyerlin's reconstruction is plausible or not, his claim that vv. 2–3 significantly influence the reading of the remainder of the psalm supports the argument being constructed here.

21. See the German edition, Frank Lothar Hossfeld and Erich Zenger, *Psalmen 101–150* (HTKAT; Freiburg: Herders, 2008), 139.

// Isa 49:10); and the "straight way" (Ps 107:7 // Isa 40:3, and similarly in 42:16, and 48:17). The connections to Deutero-Isaiah and the Babylonian exile continue in the second stanza (107:10–16). They include: prisoners who remain in darkness (Ps 107:10 // Isa 49:9) and prisoners who are brought out of captivity (Ps 107:14 // Isa 42:7). The parallels between Deutero-Isaiah and Ps 107 appear as well in the third and fourth stanzas.

The most striking use of Deutero-Isaiah, however, appears in 107:16. There the psalmist announces

> For he breaks into pieces the doors of bronze,
>> and cuts in two the bars of iron.

In Isa 45:2b, the text is identical except for one fundamental difference. In Isa 45, the text is cast within a larger oracle concerning Cyrus:

> Thus says the LORD to his anointed, to Cyrus
>> whose right hand I have grasped
> to subdue nations before him—
>> and the gates shall not be closed;
> I will go before you and level the mountains,
>> I will break in pieces the doors of bronze
> and cut in two the bars of iron. (NRSV)

As suggested above, such a reference to Cyrus in Isa 45 was more than a tacit endorsement of the Persian Empire as an instrument of Yahweh. While the psalmist employs the language of Deutero-Isaiah in Ps 107, he omits any reference to Cyrus altogether. According to Isa 45, the promise to shatter the doors of bronze and cut through the bars of iron appears within the context of Cyrus' anointing, stressing God's provisions for ensuring the success of Cyrus. In Ps 107, however, Yahweh shattered doors and cut through iron in response to the cries of his people (107:13). For the psalmist, deliverance was not mediated through an empire nor predicated upon the success of a dynasty, but instead was the result of the חֶסֶד of Yahweh.[22]

A similar use of Deutero-Isaiah appears earlier in the psalm (107:7). Isaiah 45:13 reads

---

22. On the inefficacy of human power to provide deliverance, see §6.1 in the present study.

> I have aroused him (Cyrus) in righteousness,
>   and I will make all his paths straight (וְכָל־דְּרָכָיו אֲיַשֵּׁר)
> he shall build my city (עִיר)
>   and set my exiles free.

Although the language in 107:7 is not verbatim, the parallels are noticeable. Speaking of the actions of Yahweh, the psalmist recounts,

> He led them by a straight path (וַיַּדְרִיכֵם בְּדֶרֶךְ יְשָׁרָה)
>   until they arrived at a city (עִיר) in which to live.

In Isa 45, Yahweh promises to make straight the paths of Cyrus; in Ps 107:7, Yahweh makes straight the paths of the people. In Isaiah, Cyrus will rebuild the city of Jerusalem; in Ps 107, Yahweh himself ensured that the people returned to an inhabitable Jerusalem. As in the previous example, the psalmist has eradicated any mention of Cyrus or the Persian Empire, preferring instead to attribute such acts of deliverance to Yahweh and Yahweh alone.

In sum, the opening verses (107:2–3), along with the first two strophes in particular, blend mythic, traditional, and geographic themes in varying degrees, while also incorporating exodus and exilic traditions. Together, these verses imply that empires and places of power are best understood as forces of oppression, and unlike Deutero-Isaiah, there is no hint that empires can function as instruments of deliverance.

3.1.3. The Characterization of Power

The final strophe (107:33–43) stands apart both in form and tenor from the previous four.[23] The second half of the final strophe is most significant for the topic at hand. The psalmist announces,

> And they were diminished and brought low
>   through oppression (עֹצֶר), trouble, and sorrow.
> Pouring contempt upon princes
>   he made them wander in trackless wastes;

---

23. For example, Allen suggests that vv. 1–32 are a song of thanksgiving, while vv. 33–43 are hymnic with sapiential features (*Psalms 101–150*, 60). Agreeing with Beyerlin's earlier work, Seybold terms the final strophe "hymnic," but he notes the wisdom influence from Job (*Die Psalmen*, 427–28, 430).

> But he raised up the needy out of affliction
>   and made their families like flocks.
> The upright will see it and be glad
>   but all the wicked ones will shut their mouth. (107:39–42)[24]

In the final verses of Ps 107, the psalmist mentions two groups of people, the אֶבְיוֹן ("the poor") and the נְדִיבִים ("the princes"). The אֶבְיוֹן are those who have been oppressed and brought low, presumably by the יַד־צָר, the geopolitical powers mentioned in verses 2–3.[25] The second term, נְדִיבִים, however, is not synonymous with the geopolitical powers. Elsewhere in the Hebrew Bible, the term may refer to generous persons or persons of noble character (cf. Isa 32:8). In this instance, however, the usage appears to refer to persons of position and power. This particular usage appears in Job 12, a text that both Beyerlin and Seybold argue stands in the background of the final strophe.[26] In Job 12:21, the נְדִיבִים are mentioned in conjunction with "kings," "nations," and "people of the earth," thus clearly connecting the נְדִיבִים with rulers and persons of power. Yet in Ps 107, the נְדִיבִים appear to represent those in power but more specifically, those in power *within* the people of Israel as opposed to the יַד־צָר. Given the demands of the king expressed in Ps 72, the community might have expected the leading figures in society (נְדִיבִים) to deliver them from "oppression, trouble, and sorrow" (107:39). Yet the נְדִיבִים, the powerful within the people of Israel, appear to be held responsible for the disaster of the exile.[27] They were left to wander in the "wastelands without a path," bearing the brunt of the contempt of Yahweh.[28] In short, the powerful within Israel are impotent, while

---

24. The jussives in v. 42 signal a shift in the psalm. Using a typical wisdom construction, the psalmist suggests that in light of the events unfolded in Ps 107, the upright will rejoice at the demonstration of the חֶסֶד of Yahweh. The phrase וְכָל־עַוְלָה functions metonymically, referring to all who do evil and bring "oppression, trouble and sorrow" (v. 39) upon the needy (v. 41).

25. In vv. 33–38, the רְעֵבִים are mentioned, but they are not a different party; they are in fact part of the poor and pious mentioned in v. 41 (cf. v. 5).

26. Beyerlin, in referring to v. 40, suggests that it is based upon Job 12:12–25, a hymn "on the God of wisdom and power concerning the fate of humans and nations" (*Werden und Wesen des 107. Psalms*, 13).

27. Hossfeld and Zenger, *Psalms 3*, 109.

28. The second colon in the line appears to support the claim that the נְדִיבִים were in fact the aristocratic elite within the community and not foreign powers. The psalmist suggests that Yahweh "makes them wander about in a wasteland (תֹּהוּ) without a path (דֶּרֶךְ)." The implication is that while Yahweh delivered the poor, giving them a

the powerless, the אֶבְיוֹן, are "raised up out of affliction" by Yahweh. This juxtaposition between the powerful within Israel and the powerful beyond Israel is important for understanding the manner in which power is constructed in book 5. As tempting as it may be, it is not enough to suggest that only the "powers" *beyond* the borders are in view in Ps 107. In the final stanza, and verses 39–41 in particular, the psalmist also alludes to the inefficacy of the powers *within* the borders, a theme repeated within book 5. Thus the critique in book 5 appears to extend to human power writ large.

Near the end of the psalm, the psalmist reiterates the larger theme concerning deliverance from the powerful. In 107:42, the psalmist makes reference to two groups again, but rather than using the language of אֶבְיוֹן and נְדִיבִים, the psalmist shifts to declare that

> The upright will see it and be glad,
>   but all the wicked ones will shut their mouth.

אֶבְיוֹן, in essence, is paralleled with "the upright" (יְשָׁרִים) and the נְדִיבִים with "all the wicked ones" (עַוְלָה). As mentioned above, the psalmist appears to draw from portions of Job in this final strophe. In Job 21:28, נָדִיב stands parallel to the רָשָׁע, making explicit the connection between the ruling powers and wickedness. Psalm 107 makes a similar connection, opting to describe the activity of the princes as עַוְלָה rather than רָשָׁע, but nevertheless connecting the language of power with that of wickedness. Verse 42 suggests that the "upright" who are the oppressed look forward to the day when Yahweh will silence the voices of the "wicked."

If Leuenberger is correct in his assessment that Ps 107 opens book 5 thematically, then the association of terms in this opening psalm is central to reading the remainder of the book. The poor, here termed the אֶבְיוֹן, are considered the upright, thus creating an association of terms to be retained throughout the book, an association that views the poor as the righteous.[29]

---

path home (cf. v. 7), the elite were left in the wasteland as an act of judgment. Hans Joachim Kraus suggests a transposition of vv. 39 and 40 in an effort to "restore a senseless text" (*Psalms 60–150* [CC; trans. Hilton Oswald; Minneapolis: Fortress, 1993], 325n40k). Even without the transposition, however, the colon makes sense when read in light of the first strophe (vv. 4–9). Perhaps based on the usage of the term in Job, Dahood surmises that the נְדִיבִים are the Canaanite leaders driven out of Canaan by the Israelites (*Psalms 101–150*, 90). Such a reading, however, makes little sense in light of the larger psalm and should be rejected.

29. On the image of the poor in book 5, see §6 in the present study. On the use of

Similarly, then, the oppressive activity of the נְדִיבִים is characterized as "wickedness," hence suggesting that all power, both the יַד־צָר and the נְדִיבִים, will be construed, likewise, as wickedness. The only king lauded in book 5 will be the Great King introduced in book 4 (e.g., Ps 95:3).[30] The concluding verse of Ps 107, laden with wisdom language, invites the community to acknowledge such a reality. Even more, the verse encourages an "openness to new acts of divine steadfast love. It is not something to celebrate as past, but the focus of the hope for the future."[31]

3.2. Psalms 108–110: The Opening Davidic Collection

In many ways the three psalms in the first Davidic collection in book 5 extend the themes found in Ps 107.[32] Egbert Ballhorn refers to the opening collection as *"eine davidisch-politische Sammlung,"* drawing attention to the political dynamics at work in these three psalms.[33] The two framing psalms (108; 110) illustrate this most clearly in their depiction of Israel's struggle against hostile nations. In both instances, however, a divine oracle is spoken, assuring the audience that Yahweh has delivered the restored community from the political powers that threaten their existence and will continue to do so. In the opening Davidic collection, there is no approbation of these political powers, or any other empire, and no suggestion that the hope for an ordered world rests with them.

---

the multivalent term "poor" in the Psalter, see W. Dennis Tucker Jr., "A Polysemiotic Approach to the Poor in the Psalms" *PRSt* 31 (2004): 425–39.

30. With the exception of Ps 94, the psalms found in book 4 talk relatively little about challenges stemming from empires. The emphasis in that collection remains on asserting Yahweh as the Great King (Erich Zenger, "The God of Israel's Reign over the World (Psalms 90–106)" in *The God of Israel and the Nations: Studies in Isaiah and the Psalms* [ed. Norbert Lohfink and Erich Zenger; trans. Everett R. Kalin; Collegeville, Minn.: Liturgical Press, 2000], 176).

31. Howard N. Wallace, *Psalms* (Readings: A New Biblical Commentary; Sheffield: Sheffield Phoenix, 2009), 169.

32. See Martin Leuenberger, *Konzeptionen des Königtums Gottes im Psalter: Untersuchungen zu Komposition und Redaktion der theokratischen Bücher IV–V im Psalter* (ATANT 83; Zürich: Theologischer, 2004), 286–291. Leuenberger provides a detailed comparison of Ps 107 with the three subsequent psalms (291).

33. Egbert Ballhorn, *Zum Telos des Psalters: Der Textzusammenhang des Vierten und Fünften Psalmenbuches (Ps 90–150)* (BBB 138; Berlin: Philo, 2004), 147. On the role of the superscriptions in binding the collection together, see 147–49.

3. PART 1

3.2.1. PSALM 108

The first psalm in this short collection is well known for its reuse of Ps 57:7-11 (an individual song of thanksgiving) and Ps 60:5-12 (a communal lament). The rationale for the coupling of these two psalms at this point in the Psalter has generated much discussion but seemingly little consensus.[34] The anti-imperial rhetoric present in Ps 107 provides some insight as to the rationale for this new composition. In addition, the new composition makes better sense when read in light of the overall collection found in Pss 108–110.[35]

Ballhorn contends that the threat of foreign nations (*Fremdvölkerbedrohung*) is the theme that holds the two sections of Ps 108 in common.[36] In stitching Ps 57 with Ps 60, the psalmist attempts, among other things, to cast the nature of the threat in universal and, arguably, even cosmic terms. In order to accomplish this, the psalmist locates himself among the עַמִּים and אֻמִּים in verse 4. The mention of the peoples and nations actually reflects the presence of the competing powers mentioned previously in 107:40, thereby stitching Ps 108 with Ps 107.

In addition to locating himself among the עַמִּים and אֻמִּים, the psalmist alludes to the universal nature of the *Fremdvölkerbedrohung* by requesting in verse 6 that אֱלֹהִים be exalted over the heavens (שָׁמַיִם), a theme also mentioned in verse 5, and that his "glory" (כָּבוֹד) be over all the earth (אֶרֶץ). Such a petition is for the "final and universal manifestation of Yahweh's כָּבוֹד."[37] In short, only when the cosmic dimensions of Yahweh's reign are acknowledged is there hope against those in power.[38] Moreover, these

---

34. Kraus confesses, "it is … difficult, if not impossible to shed light" on reasons for this new composition (*Psalms 60–150*, 333). In an attempt to provide a historically situated context, Ernst Axel Knauf proposes that Pss 108–110 serves as a collection dated to the time of John Hyrcanus, creating what he terms a "Hyrcanus Composition" ("Psalm LX und Psalm CVIII," *VT* 50 [2000]: 62). Knauf proposes that Ps 60 represents a "promise of deliverance" and that the psalmist has incorporated that part of the psalm in an effort to portray Hyrcanus as the fulfillment (55–65).

35. Hossfeld and Zenger suggest that Ps 108 may have been created as a composite psalm specifically for the "David trilogy" (*Psalms 3*, 165).

36. Ballhorn, *Zum Telos des Psalters*, 151.

37. Craig Broyles, *The Conflict of Faith and Experience in the Psalms: A Form-Critical and Theological Study of Selected Lament Psalms* (JSOTSup 52; Sheffield: JSOT Press, 1989), 149.

38. Stephen L. Cook suggests that the exaltation of God over the earth is meant

forces appear to be so threatening to the life of the psalmist that the poet takes portions from Ps 60 and pleads, "Give victory with your right hand, and answer me, so that those whom you love may be rescued." Although the psalm opens as an individual thanksgiving psalm, the shift in verse 7 to a plural form, יְדִידֶיךָ ("your beloved ones") signals the communal nature of this plea. The shift suggests that the threatened party is not the psalmist alone, but the community that stands in need of Yahweh's deliverance.

The second half of the psalm offers a more explicit mention of the nations and peoples that appear to threaten the people of God. Frank van der Velden understands the language in verses 8–11 to be a metaphorical use of the *Feindvölkersummarium*.[39] The point of the metaphor, however, is not the identification of particular enemies, so to speak, but the construction of "a utopian concept of history."[40] Following the psalmist's plea that Yahweh deliver his "beloved ones," the psalmist interjects an oracle of God in verses 8–10.[41]

> With exultation, I will divide up Shechem
>   and portion out the Vale of Succoth.
> Gilead is mine; Manasseh is mine;
>   Ephraim is my helmet;
>   Judah my scepter.
> Moab is my washbasin;
>   upon Edom I cast my shoe;
>   over Philistia, I shout in triumph.

The oracle is pregnant with metaphorical language and imagery, particularly that of a great king dividing up his spoil following a victory with helmet in place and scepter in hand.[42] While the neighboring people groups of Moab, Edom, and Philistia may have functioned differently in Ps 60, they appear in Ps 108 as ciphers for the "nations" and the "peoples" (108:4), the

---

to be understood "in terms of a cosmic eschatological revelation of the glory (כבוד) of God in the sense of Isa 59:12; 60:2; and 66:18" ("Apocalypticism and the Psalter," *ZAW* 104 [1992]: 92). See also Jerome F. D. Creach, *The Destiny of the Righteous in the Psalms* (St. Louis: Chalice Press, 2008), 81.

39. Frank van der Velden, *Psalm 109 und die Aussagen zur Feindschädigung in den Psalmen* (Stuttgart: Katholisches Bibelwerk, 1997), 145–52.

40. Van der Felden, *Psalm 109*, 149.

41. See Rolf Jacobson, *'Many Are Saying': The Function of Direct Discourse in the Hebrew Psalter* (LHBOTS 397; New York: T&T Clark, 2004), 113–18.

42. Hossfeld and Zenger, *Psalms 3*, 120.

political powers that threaten the people of God.⁴³ As Tournay explains, "the perspectives have been universalized. Edom has become the symbol of all the enemies of God and God's people."⁴⁴ Although the geographical regions identified mark out a territory reminiscent of the Davidic Empire following the fall of Samaria, the focus of the oracle remains upon Yahweh as a warrior, the *Kreigsmann*, in overcoming the powers that threaten the people of God.⁴⁵ The oracle, then, is not primarily a map referring to the boundaries of a restored community, but instead, an affirmation that hostile forces can and will be overcome by the Divine Warrior with the goal of a new political order.⁴⁶

The final portion of the psalm shifts from the oracle of God back to the plea of the psalmist. Whereas the oracle envisions a time when enemy powers would be subdued (108:10), verses 11–14 allude to the politically charged present, suggesting that the period of restoration remains unstable. The sense of insecurity is so acute that the psalmist assumes that indeed אֱלֹהִים has forsaken (זָנַח) his people. The same verb, זָנַח, appears in the opening plea of Ps 74. In that context, the psalmist inquires, "O God, why have you forsaken us permanently?" As a communal lament, Ps 74 recounts the destruction of temple at the hands of the Babylonians, another foreign empire whose oppressive power left those in Jerusalem reeling. The claims of Zion theology leave the poet in Ps 74 no other option but to assume that such destruction can only be interpreted as godforsakenness. Likewise, the psalmist in Ps 108 surmises that the threats experienced in the present moment are, once again, evidence of forsakenness. The presence of such political threats does not signal a well-ordered world, but in fact one that necessitates the intervention of Yahweh.

---

43. See Cook, "Apocalypticism and the Psalter," 92. Cook avers, "Place names understood literally in Ps 60 are understood as symbolic aggressors in Ps 108. Because in Ps 108 we now read these geographical names in the light of vv. 3 and 5 in the first part of the psalm, they are given a more 'universal' connotation." See also Joachim Becker, *Israel deutet seine Psalmen* (SB 18; Stuttgart: Katholisches Bibelwerk, 1966), 66–67. The use of Edom, in particular, as a cipher for an empire can be found extending to the *TgPss*, where both the "wicked city of Rome" and "Constantinople" are mentioned in connection with Edom.

44. Raymond J. Tournay, *Seeing and Hearing God with the Psalms: the Prophetic Liturgy of the Second Temple in Jerusalem* (JSOTSup 118; Sheffield: JSOT Press, 1991), 181.

45. Hossfeld and Zenger, *Psalms 3*, 121–22.

46. *Contra* Hossfeld and Zenger, *Psalms 3*, 123.

The community pleads in verse 13 for Yahweh to help against "the foe" (צָר) and concludes the psalm with an affirmation that "it is he who will tread down our foes (צָר)."[47] In Ps 107:2, צָר appears to allude to geopolitical powers, as suggested above. The location of the psalmist among the עַמִּים and אֻמִּים in Ps 108:4 coupled with the plea for אֱלֹהִים to manifest himself "over all the earth" (108:6) suggests that the צָר in Ps 108, like Ps 107, must in fact be geopolitical powers, capable of continuing to threaten the people of God. In the face of such threats, there is little help to be found; even the help of humans is in vain (שָׁוְא; 108:13b).[48]

3.2.2. PSALM 109 AND AN IDENTITY OF POWERLESSNESS

The construction of power in Ps 109 deviates from the patterns seen earlier in Pss 107 and 108. In the two earlier psalms, the poet clearly and repeatedly employs vocabulary that has decidedly political connotations. In both psalms, the "foes" represent political powers from which the psalmist either sought or gained deliverance, and in both, the psalmists suggest that such powers threaten their existence. In Ps 109, however, the language concerning the "foe" remains ambiguous at best, resulting in a divergence of scholarly opinions concerning the purpose and function of the psalm.

In an attempt to understand the purpose of Ps 109, scholars have typically focused on the *Sitz im Leben* of this psalm, with the consensus being that Ps 109 would have been used within the temple complex whereby an innocent person would appear before the priestly judges in hopes of rebuffing false accusations, a position argued most notably by Hans Schmidt.[49] In an attempt to build off of Schmidt's model, while providing

---

47. Leuenberger argues that the identity of David, mentioned in all three superscriptions in the collection, is actually expanded to include the entire community. "David" functions as the "identification figure for the prayer/reader of the Psalter" (*Konzeptionen des Königtums Gottes im Psalter*, 290). See also Marko Marttila, *Collective Reinterpretation in the Psalms* (FAT 2/13; Tübingen: Mohr Siebeck, 2006) for additional examples of this hermeneutical move in the Psalter. On the role of David in book 5, see §6.2 in the present study.

48. On the inefficacy of human power, see §6.1 in the present study.

49. The classic formulation of this position is found in Hans Schmidt, *Das Gebet der Angeklagten im Alten Testament* (BZAW 49; Giessen: Töpelmann, 1928). Schmidt contends that prior to praying such a psalm, the innocent person would have been in some form of detention or imprisonment based upon the allegations levied against him (28). Gunkel labeled Schmidt's subcategory "a prayer of the accused" as dubious,

a more concrete *Sitz im Leben* for the psalm, Hosseld and Zenger more recently have argued, based on the "piety of the poor" exhibited in the psalm, that a possible setting might involve the controversy surrounding the social reforms in the fifth century B.C.E.[50] For Hossfeld and Zenger, the pray-er was a reformer being slandered in his attempt to institute justice for the poor. Consequently the psalm serves as a mirror to the conflict between the advocates and opponents of such a reform. The premise of a more general judicial setting, as suggested by Schmidt, or that of a more specific setting as outlined by Hossfeld and Zenger, remains plausible for the psalm as it may have been used *apart from the collection*. The judicial model of Schmidt, or any of the subsequent scholarly iterations, focuses on the psalm's purported use in daily life, but gives little to no attention to its function within the context of book 5 of the Psalter. The appearance of Ps 109 within the initial Davidic collection of book 5 and the collection's relationship to Ps 107, demands reconsideration of Ps 109 as it relates to its *Sitz im Buch*.[51] In that context, the pressing question concerning the construction of power in the psalm is more properly addressed.

The verbal connections between Ps 109 and the two preceding psalms underscore the relationship between the psalms. These connections also suggest that the current placement of Ps 109 was likely not coincidental and, more importantly, that the interpretation of Ps 109 is informed by its association with Ps 107 and the two other psalms in the David trilogy (108; 110).[52] Several of these verbal connections also inform the present

---

contending that the allusions identified by Schmidt are simply not explicit enough to support the claim. Gunkel surmises that any language in the psalm that appears to reflect imprisonment could equally well be understood metaphorically (cf. Ps 31:9), thus calling into question Schmidt's association of the psalm with detention (Herman Gunkel, *An Introduction to the Psalms* [MLBS; trans. James D. Nogalski; Macon, Ga.: Mercer University Press, 1998], 187–88). While more recent studies have set aside Schmidt's initial claim regarding detention and imprisonment, they have retained the emphasis on the psalm as a prayer of an unjustly accused individual. See Allen, *Psalms 101–150*, 76; Kraus, *Psalms 60–150*, 338–39; Klaus Seybold, *Introducing the Psalms* (Edinburgh: T&T Clark, 1990), 162–64.

50. Hosseld and Zenger, *Psalms 3*, 184.

51. Ballhorn argues similarly, suggesting that the collection of the psalms (Pss 108–10) actually changes the claims of the individual psalms (*Zum Telos des Psalters*, 157).

52. J. Clinton McCann Jr., "Psalms," *NIB* 4:1125. Seybold (*Die Psalmen*, 434) suggests that Pss 107–109 are linked together, creating a small cluster of enemy psalms.

investigation as it pertains to the manner in which power in constructed in the psalm. Throughout the psalm, the enemy maintains the power. In 107:42, the psalmist refers to a time when "all wicked ones will shut their mouth (פִּי)." In the opening verses of Ps 109, the psalmist prays

> Do not be silent, O God of my praise,
> for wicked and deceitful mouths are opened against me. (109:1b–2 NRSV)

Psalm 109 is about speech, both that of the enemy and the psalmist, as well as the presumed silence of God (109:2). The rhetoric is so violent that the psalmist claims the enemy "wages war" (חָלַם) against him (109:3), suggesting in fact that the mouths of the wicked ones have not been shut. Other linguistic links between the two psalms include language associated with the construction of the psalmist's self-perception. In Ps 107:41, the psalmist acknowledges that God lifts up "the poor out of affliction" (אֶבְיוֹן מֵעוֹנִי). In Ps 109:22, using nearly identical language, the psalmist self-describes, announcing "I am afflicted and poor" (עָנִי וְאֶבְיוֹן אָנֹכִי). Drawing on the larger theology of the poor in the biblical tradition, the psalmist sought to position himself as one in need, absent of power, and dependent upon Yahweh.[53] In addition, much like the godforsakenness expressed in Ps 108:10–11, the psalmist in Ps 109 anguishes over the silence of God (109:2).[54] Ultimately, these images coalesce, depicting the psalmist as powerless. For the psalmist, however, the identity of powerlessness equates with shame, consequently creating within the psalmist the

---

Further, he links Ps 109 to 110 based on the motif of Yahweh standing at the right hand (cf. 109:31; 110:5).

53. The psalmist also self-describes as a locust shaken off or a shadow quickly fading in the evening (v. 23), furthering the image of powerlessness. These images "augment and emphasize the ritual description of poverty" (David P. Wright, "Ritual Analogy in Psalm 109," *JBL* 113 [1994], 401). On the psalmists's self-description as one of the poor in book 5, see §6.2 in the present study

54. There are additional verbal connections between Psalms 107 and 109, reinforcing the claim that Psalm 107 should inform the interpretation of Ps 109. In Ps 107, for example, the psalmist celebrates deliverance from the hand of the foes (107:2) and repeatedly attributes such deliverance to the חֶסֶד of Yahweh (vv. 1, 8, 15, 21, 31, 43). In Ps 109, the חֶסֶד of Yahweh serves as the rationale for the psalmist's plea for deliverance (vv. 21, 29). Further, in 109:30, the psalmist promises to "give thanks" (יָדָה) creating a link with Ps 107 and its repeated use of the same verb (107:1, 8, 15, 21, 31).

desire for a reversal.⁵⁵ In short, the psalmist desires to see the "honor" given to the powerful for such violence be reversed so that the foes "may be wrapped in their own shame" (109:29).

The most suggestive implication of its literary placement appears in the final lines of Ps 108. In Ps 108:13–14, the psalmist concludes with both a plea for help and a confession of hope:

> Grant us help from the foe (צָר),
>   for futile is the deliverance of man.
> With God, we shall do mightily;
>   it is he who will tread down our foes (צָרֵינוּ).

The movement in Ps 108 from singular in the first portion (108:1–7) to that of plural in the latter half is instructive, as is the final image in the psalm, that of צָרֵינוּ. Psalm 108 concludes with the community under the threat of the foe and in need of deliverance, leading the community to plead with God to tread down the foes. The voice of the community and the threat of the foe that conclude Ps 108 likely informs the reading of Ps 109 and its construction of power.

Although Ps 109 is an individual rather than communal petition, Sigmund Mowinckel noted that there are a number of "I-Psalms," which are quite personal, but in reality are national (congregational) psalms.⁵⁶ He includes Ps 109 in that list.⁵⁷ Others have proposed a similar reading. Mowinckel's student, Harris Birkeland connected Ps 109 with a number of other psalms in which war appears to be a dominant theme, leading him to conclude that a collective reading of such psalms seems preferable.⁵⁸ More recent interpreters such as John Eaton and Michael Goulder

---

55. On honor and shame in the Psalter, see W. Dennis Tucker Jr., "Is Shame a Matter of Patronage in the Communal Laments?" *JSOT* 31 (2007): 465–80. See also Amy Cottrill, *Language, Power and Identity in the Lament Psalms of the Individual* (LHBOTS 493; New York: T&T Clark, 2008), 58–74.

56. Although Ps 109 might be labeled a lament, the absence of accusations leveled against God as well as the absence of genre-specific questions (e.g., "How long,?;" "Why, O LORD?") suggests that "petition" might be a more descriptive label.

57. Sigmund Mowinckel, *The Psalms in Israel's Worship* (Oxford: Blackwell, 1962), 1:219.

58. Harris Birkeland, *The Evildoer in the Book of Psalms* (Oslo: Dybwad, 1955), 31–33.

have adopted a collective or national understanding of the psalm as well.⁵⁹ While intriguing, the evidence marshaled by Mowickel, Birkeland, Eaton, and Goulder ultimately proves unconvincing. Rather than claiming the psalm was *composed* with the community in mind, Croft suggests that a collective understanding of the psalm was imposed only secondarily.⁶⁰ Although Hosseld and Zenger's proposed *Sitz im Leben* for the psalm references an individual setting, they do contend that *within the collection* (Pss 108–110), the psalm functions as a "prayer of the threatened Israel against the enemy nations."⁶¹ Such a claim is validated in Pss 108 and 110, in which the enemies are identified as international enemies. The use of "the foe" (צָר) in 108:13, 14 and "kings" (מֶלֶךְ) in 110:5 suggests that the threat is international and political in scope.

The question that remains, in part, is why such a psalm would have been appropriated within a subcollection focused on deliverance from foreign power. The answer may reside in the curses employed in verses 6–19, and in particular verses 8–13. The curses that appear in verses 6–19, in many ways, remain the *crux interpretum* for this particular psalm. The chief issue concerns whether these verses are a quote of the curses levied by the enemy, or if these are in fact curses prayed directly against the enemy.⁶² Despite the more recent arguments in favor of the latter, the view

---

59. John Eaton, *Kingship and the Psalms* (The Biblical Seminar 3; Sheffield: JSOT Press, 1980), 81; Michael D. Goulder, *The Psalms of the Return (Book V, Psalms 107-150): Studies in the Psalter, IV* (JSOTSup 258; Sheffield: Sheffield Academic Press, 1998), 133–34. Goulder interprets Ps 109 within the literary horizon of Pss 107 and 108, suggesting that "the high hopes of the returned exiles (Ps 107), threatened by the hostility of Samaria/Shechem (Ps 108), have now been frustrated, it appears permanently" (135). Psalm 109, according to Goulder, is the report of the local governor (Bishlam) to Cyrus. Clearly Goulder recognizes the political force of the text, but his attempt to constrict it more narrowly to a particular circumstance appears unwarranted. Book 5 in the Psalter appears to be making a claim about political power more generally and its oppressive forces.

60. Steven J. L. Croft, *The Identity of the Individual in the Psalms* (JSOTSup 14; Sheffield: JSOT Press, 1987), 32, 77, 134, and 180. Croft's suggestion as to a collective appropriation of the psalm differs in approach from the "collectively oriented redaction(s)" of psalms as proposed by Marttila, *Collective Reinterpretation in the Psalms*, 25–36.

61. Hossfeld and Zenger, *Psalms 3*, 184.

62. For the primary points in support of the claim that vv. 6–19 are a quote, see Kraus, *Psalms 60–150*, 338, and more recently, Hossfeld and Zenger, *Psalms 3*, 128–30. A number of scholars, however, have argued that this is not a quote, but instead the

that verses 6–19 reflect the sentiments of the enemy remains the more persuasive position for the reasons outlined by Kraus and others.

Following the presumed announcement of guilt in verse 7, a series of jussives appear in 8–13:

> May his days be few;
>   may another seize his property.
> May his children become orphans
>   and his wife a widow.
> May his children wander about;
>   may they beg and seek apart from their ruins;
> may the creditor seize all that he owns;
>   may strangers steal his property;
> may there not be anyone to show kindness to him;
>   and may there not be any to pity his orphans.
> May his posterity be cut off;
>   may their name be blotted out in the next generation.

If this psalm was indeed used in a judicial setting for an individual, the curses would have represented a crushing verdict.[63] If the psalm had a collective secondary use, as Croft and others have suggested, then the images invoked in the verdict are reminiscent of Judah's destruction at the hands of a foreign nation. In particular, the verdict echoes the communal lament voiced in Lamentations 5

> Our inheritance has been turned over to strangers,
>   our homes to aliens.
> We have become orphans, fatherless;
>   our mothers are like widows.
> We must pay for the water we drink;
>   the wood we get must be bought. …
> There is no one to deliver us from their hand. (5:2–5, 8b)

---

curses of the psalmist against the enemy. See, for example, Cottrill, *Language, Power, and Identity in the Lament Psalms of the Individual*, 138–56; Wright, "Ritual Analogy and Psalm 109," 385–404; and Gerstenberger, *Psalms, Part 2, and Lamentations* (FOTL 15; Grand Rapids: Eerdmans, 2001), 259. Gerstenberger argues that an enemy quote of this length in a psalm would be a "liturgical disaster."

63. Gerstenberger, *Psalms*, 258–59. See also Sigmund Mowinckel, *The Psalms in Israel's Worship*, 2:2–4.

To be clear, Ps 109 in its *Sitz im Leben* had nothing to do with exile, but when placed in the midst of two psalms related to foreign power, verses 8–13 might have functioned as something of a *double entendre*, alluding back to the devastation experienced at the hands of another empire. Further, such imagery reinforces the identification of the community as one who is "poor and needy" (עָנִי וְאֶבְיוֹן).

The threat of foreign destruction did not end with the exile, however, and remained a potential threat even after resettlement. Any people group that sought to challenge Persia's imperial rule met with a fate similar to that portrayed in Ps 109.[64] With the rise of Darius to power in Persia, a number of revolts broke out across the empire. The Achaemenids responded in brutal fashion. In a decisive win over the rebellious Median forces led by Fravartisch, nearly 34,000 Medes were killed and another 18,000 were taken prisoner. When Fravartisch was finally captured, Darius cut off his ears, nose, and tongue before impaling him at Ecbatana. The military associates of Fravartisch were flayed and their skins stuffed with straw and they were set alongside the fortress as a warning against revolt. In a later Babylonian revolt against Xerxes (March 481 B.C.E.), the Persian forces laid siege to Babylon, eventually destroying the city ramparts and private houses. In addition, the Persians destroyed the temples and summarily executed the cultic priests, leaving the city completely devastated. As noted above (§2), the royal propaganda portrayed the empire as generous and gracious. Accounts such as these reflect the darker side of imperial power and its capacity for oppressive action, making the claims and appeals in Ps 109 all the more plausible.

The placement of Ps 109 within the opening Davidic trilogy of book 5 recasts the scope of the psalm, in effect, transposing the language of a threatened, unjustly accused individual to that of a powerless people surrounded, both literally and literarily, by the *Feindevölkerweit*.[65] In the end, the people have no hope except to believe that Yahweh stands at the "right hand of the needy" (לִימִין אֶבְיוֹן).

---

64. See Muhammed A. Dandamaev, *A Political History of the Achaemenid Empire* (trans. Willem J. Vogelsang; Leiden: Brill, 1989), 120–21, 183–84.

65. Norbert Lohfink, "Three Ways to Talk About Poverty. Psalm 109," in *In the Shadow of Your Wings: New Readings of Great Texts from the Bible* (ed. Norbert Lohfink; Collegeville, Minn.: Liturgical Press, 2003), 134.

3.2.3. Empire and Identity in Psalm 110

In Ps 108:13–14 and Ps 109:26–29, the psalmist pleads with Yahweh for help due to the persistent presence of the enemy. Psalm 110 concludes the Davidic trilogy similarly with a plea for God to intervene from Zion and destroy the kings and nations that remain a threat. The psalm itself is an enthronement psalm that likely had its origins in the time of Israel's monarchy.[66] Its current *Sitz im Buch* within the first Davidic trilogy, however, generates a secondary use of the psalm, but nonetheless, one that reinforces the chief theme of Yahweh's rule over enemy kings and nations.

This psalm is connected most vividly with Ps 109 through the theme of the "right hand." Psalm 110:1 opens with the declaration

> Utterance of Yahweh to my lord,
>   "Sit at my right hand,
>   until I make your enemies a footstool for your feet."

The imagery need not be confused by spatial logistics, that is, who is on the right in Psalm 109:31 versus who is on the right in Psalm 110:1, rather the contextual implication is that Yahweh and the "poor" (אֶבְיוֹן) stand side by side in the midst of a hostile world.[67] Leuenberger has suggested that

---

66. Note, however, that Bernard Duhm located the psalm as late as the Maccabean period, associating it with the rise of Simon and the Hasmonean rulers (*Die Psalmen erklärt* [KHC 14; Freiburg: Mohr, 1899], 398–400). See also the work of Miriam von Nordheim, who opines that the psalm had its origins in a Jewish-Hellenistic community in Alexandria, representing the hopes of the community for a "new" David to rule (*Geboren von der Morgenröte? Psalm 110 in Tradition, Redaktion und Rezeption* [WMANT 117; Neukirchen-Vluyn: Neukirchener, 2008], 110). Although Scott R. A. Starbuck alleges that the psalm was much earlier than the Maccabean period, he does contend that the insertion of references to Melchizedek was likely a "post-Qumran development" and perhaps appropriated by the Hasmoneans in a manner similar to that proposed by Duhm (*Court Oracles in the Psalms: The So-Called Royal Psalms in Their Ancient Near Eastern Context* [SBLDS 172; Atlanta: Scholars Press, 1999], 161). On form critical matters related to Ps 110, see Thijs Booij, "Psalm 110: Rule in the midst of Your Foes," *VT* 41 (1991): 396–407; Allen, *Psalms 101–150*, 78–87.

67. McCann, "Psalms," 4:1125. On the notion of the right hand, Othmar Keel argues that being at the right hand of God implies sonship, bestowing honor upon the individual (*The Symbolism of the Biblical World: Ancient Near Eastern Iconography and the Book of Psalms* [Winona Lake, Ind.: Eisenbrauns, 1997], 255–56). On the notion of the right hand as both honor and protection, see Allen, *Psalms 101–150*, 86–87.

the figure of David appears now in "the poor collective *Volksperspective* as the identification figure for the prayer/reader of the Psalter."[68] The relationship between the psalmist and Yahweh is confirmed again in verse 5. There the psalmist announces that "Yahweh is at your right hand," clearly picking up the language that concluded Ps 109. Sitting at the right hand of Yahweh suggests a place of honor, while Yahweh sitting to the right of the psalmist implies the unceasing support of Yahweh against the enemies of the psalmist. Both images, honor and protection, suggest that Yahweh will be the guarantor of success for the psalmist. As a sign of his royal rule over the world, the enemies will serve as a footstool, a sign of utter subjection.[69]

The association between the right hand and enemies is also helpful in exploring the relationship between enemies and empire in the Psalter. The psalm opens in verse 1 with mention of "your enemies (אֹיְבֶיךָ)" and the same term appears in the following verse, as those over whom Yahweh shall rule.[70] As mentioned above, verse 1 connects the language of the right hand with the language of enemies. Later in the psalm, the psalmist announces

> Yahweh is at your right hand;
>   he will shatter kings on the day of his wrath.
> He will execute judgment among the nations (גּוֹיִם);
>   he will fill them with corpses;
> he will shatter the head over the vast earth.
> He will drink from the brook by the way;
>   therefore he will lift up his head. (110:5–7)

The identity of the enemy mentioned in verse 1 is made explicit in verses 5–6. The enemies are in fact the kings (מְלָכִים) and the nations (גּוֹיִם), those

---

68. Leuenberger, *Konzeptionen des Königtums Gottes im Psalter*, 290. Similarly, see Ballhorn, who contends "The poor from Psalm 109 are enthroned as king in Psalm 110" (*Zum Telos des Psalters*, 156). See also Wallace, *Psalms*, 171–72.

69. Although the notion of enemies being made into a footstool occurs only here in the Hebrew Bible, the image of standing on the neck of the enemy appears with regularity (cf. Josh 10:24; Isa 51:23; Ps 89:10). The image of standing on the neck of the enemy is well attested in ancient Near Eastern texts and iconography. See Keel, *The Symbolism of the Biblical World*, 297. On the Behistun inscription, Darius I stands upon the neck of Guamata, the challenger to the throne.

70. On the imagery of the scepter, see Starbuck, *Court Oracles in The Psalms*, 145–47.

in power who have threatened the people of God. These are the "head over the vast earth." Yet deliverance will be accomplished by the God who is at the right hand of the psalmist. He will fill the lands with corpses in this battle against those in power.

The meaning of the final verse and its implications for understanding the role of kings and nations in Ps 110 remains highly debated. Starbuck argues that the final line indicates an act of shaming, as Yahweh holds high the head of the defeated king. The beheading of enemies for capital punishment, only to be displayed later to the general public, was quite common in the ancient Near East and serves as the background to Starbuck's argument.[71] Read this way, verse 7 forms an *inclusio* of sorts with verse 1; the psalm opens with the mention of the kings being shamed (i.e., enemies will become footstools) and concludes with the military defeat of the "heads over the land" and a final act of shame (i.e., beheading). Von Nordheim also interprets the final verse in light of the honor-shame continuum. She contends that drinking "from a brook by the way" implies that the victors are "drinking foreign water," and that such an act would be considered a hostile and provocative act meant to indicate the superiority of one group over that of another.[72] For von Nordheim then, the "lifting up of the head" is a sign of the final triumph over the defeated foes.[73]

From beginning to end, Ps 110 suggests that the kings and nations stand over against Yahweh and his people. Without question, the psalm exhibits a thoroughly negative assessment of human empires. Consequently, the psalmist prays that the enemies and empires will be utterly routed by Yahweh and, presumably, that those who have been subject to such oppression will be raised up from their affliction (107:41). Like the preceding psalms in this small collection, kings and nations in Ps 110 function as a reminder of the persistent threat such powers present to Israel.

---

71. Ibid., 159–60.

72. Von Nordheim, *Geboren von der Morgenröte*, 110–11. Hossfeld and Zenger conclude similarly, suggesting that "the closing verse of the psalm accordingly signals the definitive and universal victory of Yhwh over the hostile kings and so the accomplishment of Yhwh's universal royal rule" (*Psalms 3*, 152).

73. Willem van der Meer understands the final line in a manner somewhat consistent with von Nordheim's suggestion that the image implies final victory, see "Psalm 110: A Psalm of Rehabilitation?" in *The Structural Analysis of Biblical and Canaanite Poetry* (ed. Willem van der Meer and Johannes C. de Moor; JSOTSup 74; Sheffield: JSOT Press, 1988), 207–34.

the earth." But clearly such spatial imagery is freighted with theological inferences.⁷⁶ Through such a portrayal, the psalmist reminds the reader that Yahweh's authority extends over all earthly political powers and all heavenly realms.⁷⁷ According to the psalmist, the throne of Yahweh sits far above all of creation, yet not so far that creation can escape the deity's gaze (113:6a). Although Persian imperial ideology extended the rule of the Achaemenid king to the ends of the earth, Psalm 113 offers a rebuttal, suggesting that even over such an expansive empire all גּוֹיִם remain within the sphere governed by Yahweh.

Like earlier psalms (107:41; 109:22), a theology of the poor emerges in connection with the nations. In Ps 113, the psalmist acknowledges that the דָּל and the אֶבְיוֹן will be lifted up from the dust and the ash heap "in order to sit with the princes (נָדִיב), the princes of his people" (113:8). For the barren woman (עֲקֶרֶת), Yahweh provides a home.⁷⁸ Unlike Ps 107, however, the psalmist in Ps 113 does not make explicit the relationship between the nations and the destitute people of Israel. Instead, the psalmist merely juxtaposes the nations (113:4a) with the poor man and barren woman (113:7–9), the powerful with the powerless. Constructed in this manner, the psalm "underscores the concern of the majestic Yhwh for the weak and poor people in Israel's history."⁷⁹ But even further, and more importantly for the present study, the psalm implies that the nations do not serve as the hope of the poor servants (113:1) of Israel nor do the princes (נָדִיב). That role belongs to Yahweh.

While the word גּוֹיִם does not appear in Ps 114, the idea of nations and empires is made explicit with the mention of מִצְרַיִם in the opening line of the psalm.

---

76. For an extended discussion on the portrayal of Yahweh as the God of heaven in book 5, see §5 in the present study.

77. John Goldingay, *Psalms 90–150* (BCOT; Grand Rapids: Baker Academic, 2008), 317.

78. On the relationship between Ps 113 and the Song of Hannah (1 Sam 2), see John T. Willis, "The Song of Hannah and Psalm 113," *CBQ* 35 (1973): 139–54; Avi Hurvitz, "Originals and Imitations in Biblical Poetry: A Comparative Examination of 1 Sam 2:1–10 and Ps 113:5–9," in *Biblical and Related Studies Presented to Samuel Iwry* (ed. Ann Kort and Scott Morchauser; Winona Lake, Ind.: Eisenbrauns, 1985), 115–21. On the larger issue of the theology of the poor in Psalm 113, see Gert T. M. Prinsloo, "Yahweh and the Poor in Psalm 113: Literary Motif and/or Theological Reality," *OTE* 9 (1996): 465–85.

79. Hossfeld and Zenger, *Psalms 3*, 184.

When Israel went forth from Egypt
>the house of Jacob from a people of a strange language,
Judah became his sanctuary,
>Israel his dominion. (114:1–2)

The mention of Egypt and the allusion to the exodus recalls a "theologically significant time when the burdens of foreign oppression were rolled away."[80] In recalling the exodus event, the psalmist parallels מִצְרָיִם with מֵעַם לֹעֵז in verse 1b, adding another interpretive layer to the psalm. The verb לֹעֵז is a *hapax legomenon* and presumed to mean "to speak unintelligibly," but it is frequently rendered "from a people of a strange language."[81] Although the term לֹעֵז does not appear elsewhere in the Hebrew Bible, biblical writers frequently mention "language that you do not know" or an "alien language" (e.g., Deut 28:49; Isa 28:11; 33:19; Ezek 3:5–6). In many of these instances the reference alludes to foreign nations within the context of an invasion or political captivity. For example, in Jer 5:15, the prophet refers to the coming invasion of Babylon when he writes

"I am going to bring upon you
>a nation from far away, O house of Israel," says the LORD.
"It is an enduring nation,
>it is an ancient nation,
A nation whose language you do not know,
>nor can you understand what they say." (NRSV)

In no case, however, does "strange language," or any of the synonymous phrases imply a beneficial aspect to foreign rule.[82]

The deliverance from a foreign nation in verse 1 is juxtaposed with deliverance from the chaotic waters in verse 3. The verbs in verse 3 (נוּס

---

80. Allen, *Psalms 101–150*, 105.

81. Allen translates v. 1b as "from a people of incoherent speech" in an attempt to remain true to the presumed meaning of the term (*Psalms 101–150*, 102). Incoherence does not seem to be the issue addressed in the psalm, however. The LXX translates the phrase as ἐκ λαοῦ βαρβάρου, "from a barbarian people," which more likely captures the original intent of the phrase.

82. Hossfeld and Zenger explain further that "the use of foreign tongues by political enemies intensifies their enmity and life-threatening character, not only because it excludes mutual understanding, but also because political enemies and especially military occupiers usually threaten and taunt in their foreign language" (*Psalms 3*, 194).

and סבב) belong to the vocabulary of war elsewhere in the Hebrew Bible. In Ps 114, the use of these terms creates an image-laden scene in which the sea and the Jordan "are terrified and in their panic, they flee away—like a hostile army that is conquered and tries to save itself from complete destruction."[83] The psalmist has taken poetic license with the language employed in Exod 14, particularly its use of נוס. In the Exodus account, the divided waters formed a wall on the right and on the left (Exod 14:22), remaining a fixed structure, collapsing only when Moses stretched out his hand over the waters (14:27). In Exod 14, the verb נוס only refers to the attempts of the Egyptians themselves in fleeing from destruction. The verb נוס in Ps 114, however, limits its reference to the water. Arguably, in Ps 114:3, there is an amalgamation of vocabulary and imagery from Exod 14; the sea replaces the Egyptian army in fleeing from the warring Yahweh. The deliverance from Egypt is cast alongside the victory over chaos, suggesting that Yahweh wages war against all powers, human and otherwise, for the sake of his people. Although the remainder of the psalm provides, in truncated form, the archetypal history of Israel and its foundation, the opening verses assert that Israel's identity is rooted in its deliverance from all power.[84]

Returning to the actual use of the word גּוֹיִם within the Hallel collection, Ps 115 contains a polemic against nations and their idols.[85] Similar to the satirical texts in Deutero-Isaiah (40:10–20; 41:6–7; 44:9–20), the psalmist derides the nations for their trust in cultic images made by human hands.[86] In Ps 115, the derision of idols is in response to the question posed by the nations in verse 2:

---

83. Hossfeld and Zenger, *Psalms 3*, 196.

84. See Elizabeth Hayes, "'Where is the Lord?' The Extended Great Chain of Being as a Source Domain for Conceptual Metaphor in the Egyptian Hallel, Psalms 113–118," in *Metaphors in the Psalms* (ed. Pierre van Hecke and Antje Labahn; BETL 231; Leuven: Peeters, 2010), esp. 63–66. On the theological force of the historical allusion, see Seybold, *Die Psalmen*, 448–49.

85. Concerning the struggle between Israel/Yahweh and the nations/gods found in Ps 115 and its thematic link across the entire Hallel collection, see Leuenberger, *Konzeptionen des Königtums Gottes im Psalter*, 293.

86. Kraus contends, however, that while dependent upon Deutero-Isaiah, Ps 115 likely came much later than Deutero-Isaiah based upon the psalm's more rational treatment of the issues posed by the idols (*Psalms 60–150*, 380). See also Allen, *Psalms 101–150*, 109.

> Why should the nations (גּוֹיִם) say,
> "Where is their god (אֱלֹהֵיהֶם)?"

This taunting question from the nations appears elsewhere in the Psalter (Pss 42:4, 11; 79:10) as well as the prophetic corpus (Mic 7:10; Joel 2:14). Although not verbatim, similar taunts by foreign nations appear in 2 Kgs 18:34–35 and Ezek 36:20 as well. In each case, the taunting nation is the superior power, challenging the efficacy of the God of Israel in light of Israel's apparent weakness in the face of foreign domination. But because this psalm does not rehearse particular needs and instead reflects upon the theological issue posed by the nations (115:2), Hossfeld and Zenger classify this psalm as "learned psalmography" or "poetic theology."[87] While the threat of the nations does not appear nearly as acute as that expressed in Psalm 79, for example, Ps 115 does suggest that Israel's subservience to the nations poses theological and existential questions that remain to be remedied (115:8–15).

The shortest psalm in the Psalter contains the third reference to the nations within Pss 113–117. The psalmist exclaims

> Praise Yahweh, all nations (גּוֹיִם)!
>   Laud him, all peoples (הָאֻמִּים)!
> For great is his steadfast love over us,
>   and the faithfulness of Yahweh endures forever. (117:1–2a)

The opening line mentions the גּוֹיִם, but adds the term הָאֻמִּים in the second half of the verse. The unusual form הָאֻמִּים has prompted a number of proposals.[88] Traditionally scholars have emended the text to read לְאֻמִּים, suggesting this term frequently stands in parallel construction to גּוֹיִם.[89] Rather than emending the text, Dahood suggests merely repointing the text to read אֵמִים, "gods," with a meaning similar to that in Ps 47:2–3.[90]

---

87. Hossfeld and Zenger, *Psalms 3*, 203, 205. See also the assessment by Walter Beyerlin, *Im Lichte der Traditionen: Psalm LXVII und CXV. Ein Entwicklungszusammenhang* (VTSup 45; Leiden: Brill, 1992), 51–137. On "learned psalmography" more generally, see Mowinckel, *The Psalms in Israel's Worship*, 2:104–25. Mowinckel includes Ps 115 within this category. Gunkel, on the other hand, suggests that the psalm more nearly follows the qualities of "prose prayers" (*An Introduction to the Psalms*, 95).

88. Note that אֻמִּים, absent the definite article, appears in 108:4.

89. Kraus, *Psalms 60–150*, 390.

90. Dahood, *Psalms 101–150*, 152.

such a rendering accords well with their interpretation of Ps 117, the proposed interpretation ultimately fails on two accounts.[102] While other texts in the Hebrew Bible assume foreigners can join themselves to Israel (e.g., Isa 56), they are never referred to as "god-fearers."[103] Second, the term "god-fearers" does in fact appear in subsequent Second Temple literature, but always as a descriptor referring to the piety of a Jewish individual, not a foreign convert.[104] Were the god-fearers a recognizable term for proselytes within the early Second Temple period, some mention of this group in the subsequent literature would be expected. The absence of such a group calls for a reassessment of the proposal by Hossfeld and Zenger. The use of the term elsewhere in the Hebrew Bible refers to trust in Yahweh (Pss 40:3; 115:11; 2 Chr 19:9) or obedience to the commands of Yahweh (Deut 10:12; 13:4; 31:12; Pss 112:1; 119:73–74), suggesting that the use of the term in Ps 118 likely refers to devout and pious Israelites (similar to its use in later Second Temple literature) and not to those converted from among the nations. The nations do remain an important part of the psalm, but the focus falls not on their conversion, but on their threat in the past and their continued threat in the present (118:25).[105]

---

102. Hossfeld and Zenger, *Psalms 3*, 226.

103. Hossfeld and Zenger connect the interpretation of this term as a proselyte with what they perceive to be a conversion of the nations in Ps 117 (*Psalms 3*, 225–26). As noted above, however, Ps 117 only asks the nations to make a confession concerning Yahweh's faithfulness to Israel; it says nothing about conversion. Psalm 103:17 uses a similar term, יְרֵאָיו, "those who fear him," but without any indication that this label represents a category of non-Jewish converts.

104. For example, see *Jub.* 11:17; *4 Macc* 15:28; 16:12; *Jos. Asen.* 4:9; 8:5–7; 20:18; 23:9, 10; 28:4; 29:3; *T. Jos.* 6:7; *T. Naph.* 1:10; *T. Ab.* 4:6; Aris. Ex. 179. The use of the term in the book of Acts and its usage there remains contested. See for example, Max Wilcox, "'The God-Fearers' in Acts: A Reconsideration," *JSNT* 13 (1981): 102–22; Thomas Kraabel, "The God-fearers Meet the Beloved Disciple," in *The Future of Early Christianity: Essays in Honor of Helmut Koester* (ed. Birger A. Pearson et. al.; Minneapolis: Fortress, 1991), 276–84. In support of the traditional interpretation of the term in Acts, see Paul R. Trebilco, *Jewish Communities in Asia Minor* (SNTSMS 69; Cambridge: Cambridge University Press, 1991), esp. 145–66.

105. Ballhorn, *Zum Telos des Psalters*, 201. Ballhorn opts for a more optimistic reading of the nations and their conversion in Ps 117, but in light of Ps 118, he is left to conclude that Ps 118 "now sees the nations again in their role as the oppressor of Israel…. This means to a certain degree that in the *Leserichtung* of the Psalter, the statements made in Ps 117 are revoked." If Ps 117 is read as proposed above, there is no

observed balance of power shifts from that of the גּוֹיִם and הָאֻמִּים to that of Yahweh, with the people of Israel as the beneficiaries.

3.3.2. Psalm 118

Of the psalms that comprise the Hallel collection, Ps 118 offers the strongest assessment of the nations and their power.[100] Similar to Ps 107, the critique of enemy power is always predicated upon the חֶסֶד of Yahweh.[101] Psalm 107 and Ps 118 begin with the same call to thanksgiving.

> O give thanks to the LORD, for he is good;
> his steadfast love (חֶסֶד) endures forever. (NRSV)

The opening declaration concerning the חֶסֶד of Yahweh in 118:1b appears subsequently as the antiphonal response in verses 2–4. The thrice-repeated colon in verses 2–4, כִּי לְעוֹלָם חַסְדּוֹ, reinforces the importance of the חֶסֶד of Yahweh in the face of the enemy nations. Each group listed is asked to make such a confession:

> Let Israel say,
> "His steadfast love endures forever."
> Let the house of Aaron say,
> "His steadfast love endures forever."
> Let those who fear Yahweh say,
> "His steadfast love endures forever." (NRSV, modified)

The first and second groups represent the people and the priesthood, respectively, but scholarly opinion concerning the third group, the יִרְאֵי יְהוָה, differs widely. Hossfeld and Zenger have proposed that the יִרְאֵי יְהוָה actually represent proselytes, or converts from foreign nations. Although

---

100. Ballhorn contends that Ps 118 may have been appended to a collection, perhaps beginning with Ps 111 and ending with Ps 117 (*Zum Telos des Psalters*, 201–2). Ballhorn, among others, has noted that the use of הַלְלוּ־יָהּ in 111:1, 112:1, and 113:1, 9 is matched by a nearly similar construction in 117:1 (הַלְלוּ), suggesting that they comprise a unique collection. Within Ps 118, however, the opening and closing lines begin with הוֹדוּ, perhaps indicating a later inclusion in the collection. Hossfeld and Zenger contend that Pss 113–18 are a discrete unit despite the different usages of הַלְלוּ־יָהּ and הוֹדוּ within the collection (Hossfeld and Zenger, *Psalm 3*, 178–79).

101. Trublet, "Approche Canonique des Psaumes du Hallel," 354–56.

Within Ps 118, the psalmist returns to another familiar source of imagery related to enemies, Exod 15, invoking both language and imagery from that poetic text.[106] Similar to the song of Moses, the psalmist makes repeated use of the divine name יָהּ (Ps 118:5, 14, 17, 18, 19). In addition, the declaration in Exod 15:2 that

> Yah will be my strength and my song;
> he has become my salvation.

appears verbatim in Ps 118:14, and the second colon of the Exodus verse likewise appears verbatim in Ps 118:21. Repeatedly in Exod 15, the "right hand of Yahweh" represents power (15:6, 11, 12, 16), and in Ps 118, the psalmist makes similar use of the metaphor (118:15b–16).[107] In referring to Israel's deliverance from the Egyptians, Exod 15:11 describes the act as a "wonder" (פֶּלֶא). The same word appears in 118:23 to describe the deliverance of the community. In the repeated use of language and imagery from Exod 15, the psalmist connects the community's most recent experience of distress at the hands of the nations (118:5, 10) to Israel's paradigmatic experience with imperial power.[108] In both accounts, however, the community confesses that nations cannot match the יְמִין of Yahweh.

Psalm 118:5–12 recounts more specifically the threats faced by the community at the hands of the nations. According to the psalmist, the nations caused מֵצַר, a term that can be translated more generally as "distress," but also can connote the idea of restriction in the sense of oppression or captivity, whether literal of figurative. The distress suffered by the psalmist and the community came at the hands of "those who hate" (שֹׂנֵא), the גּוֹיִם.[109]

---

inherent tension between the two psalms, and consequently, no need to suggest that Ps 118 requires the revocation of the claims in the previous psalm.

106. Ibid., 203.

107. On the metaphorical use of "hand," see William P. Brown, *Seeing the Psalms: A Theology of Metaphor* (Louisville: Westminster John Knox, 2002), 175–76. See also J. J. M. Roberts, "The Hand of Yahweh," *VT* 21 (1971): 244–51.

108. Ballhorn notes that "God's action at that time [the Exodus] is 'reactualized' in the present for the praying Israel" (*Zum Telos des Psalters*, 202).

109. Although the גּוֹיִם appeared as a blazing fire that threatened to ravage the landscape, in the presence of Yahweh they became little more than a blazing fire of dried thorns (118:12). They flame in intensity for a short time only to turn quickly into a smoldering heap (Goldingay, *Psalms 90–150*, 358).

In response to the threat of the enemies, the psalmist claims three times (118:10, 11, 12) that

In the name of Yahweh, indeed, I cut them off (אֲמִילַם).

The unusual use of the verb מוּל ("to circumcise") in this context has generated considerable scholarly discussion. Briggs and Briggs, who date the psalm to the Maccabean period when circumcision was prohibited, suggest that the verb may have been used in an ironic sense. "Israel would take vengeance by circumcising them; yet not with a religious significance, but as a performance of an operation extremely painful to adults."[110] Dahood suggests that the reference to circumcision implied a militaristic context similar to the one portrayed in 1 Sam 18:25–27.[111] In that context, David killed one hundred Philistines and removed their foreskins. For Dahood, the association of circumcision with a successful military campaign against the enemies fits the overall context of the psalm. Of the many neighboring enemies of Israel in the Hebrew Bible, the Philistines garnered the most attention as an "uncircumcised people," leading Israel in many ways to equate uncircumcision with a barbarous people. More recently, however, a second root for מוּל has been suggested, meaning "to fend off."[112] The second root accords well with the image of swarming bees in verse 12 and likely functions as a homonym with מוּל I, meaning "circumcision."[113] The contextual meaning of the verb in Ps 118 involves Israel having fended off the enemy, but secondarily, as a homonym, the term implies the object of Israel's actions, the "uncircumcised."

Based upon the deliverance recounted in verses 5–18, the psalmist then turns to provide a "sweeping horizon for the future."[114] The psalmist rejoices because

> The stone which the builders rejected
> has become the head of the corner. (118:22)

---

110. Briggs and Briggs, *A Critical and Exegetical Commentary on the Psalms*, 405.

111. Dahood, *Psalms 101–150*, 157.

112. מוּל, *HALOT* 1:556.

113. The metaphor of swarming bees appears also in Isa 7:18 in reference to the impending invasion of the Assyrian empire as well as in Deut 1:44 in reference to the Amorites. See Peter Riede, *Im Netz des Jägers: Studien zur Feindmetaphorik der Individualpsalmen* (WMANT 85; Neukirchen-Vluyn: Neukirchener, 2000), 254–66.

114. Hossfeld and Zenger, *Psalms 3*, 241.

The "I" of the psalm celebrates because the individual and the nation, which appeared rejected and cast aside in the eyes of the nations, now occupies a vital place within the work of God in the world.[115] Yet the psalmist acknowledges that the threats remain. Shifting to a communal plea, the psalmist and the community pray

> Save us (הוֹשִׁיעָה), we beseech you, O Yahweh;
> Cause us to prosper (הַצְלִיחָה), we beseech you, O Yahweh. (118:25)

Both lines open with the particle אָנָּא and conclude with particle of entreaty נָּא, strengthening the force of the plea. The two particles in such close proximity appear only five times in the remainder of the Hebrew Bible and strikingly only here in the Psalter (Gen 50:17; 2 Kgs 20:3; Is. 38:3; Jonah 1:14; Neh 1:11). The question remains from what are the people requesting deliverance? The very fact that Israel couples a prayer for deliverance (118:25a) with a prayer to prosper (118:25b) suggests that while the nations had been fended off previously, the present and future remain under threat, in need of intervention once more.[116]

3.4. Conclusion

As suggested in the previous chapter, the Persian Empire sought to portray itself as an empire under divine mandate to create cosmic order through the expansion of its empire. The Achaemenid dynasty portrayed itself as a beneficent power, one that would lead the citizens of the empire to participate joyfully. Following the Persian rise to power, texts such as Deutero-

---

115. Ibid., 242; Goldingay, *Psalms 90–150*, 363. Within the context of Ps 118, Briggs and Briggs suggest that the cornerstone was Zion "which the nations had done their best to reject and destroy" (*A Critical and Exegetical Commentary on the Book of Psalms*, 407). Similarly, see also Goulder (*The Psalms of the Return*, 188). Similar language appears in Isa 28:16 and Zech 4:6–10 with both texts referring to the restoration of Zion.

116. On the role of v. 25 within the larger psalm, see Gerstenberger, who suggests that this verse may have been a "scribal gloss providing existential excitement" (*Psalms*, 306). The verse need not be seen as a gloss in order to make sense of its place within the larger psalm. Mowinckel, for example, argued for its logic within the psalm, suggesting that v. 25 was a standard form prayed just before receiving the cultic blessing (v. 26). See Sigmund Mowinckel, "Psalm Criticism between 1900 and 1935," *VT* 5 (1955): 28.

Isaiah appear to have incorporated Cyrus within a Judean royal ideology, but one that resonates with the Achaemenid emphasis on order and participation. Although Deutero-Isaiah makes no concessions concerning the role of Yahweh (as opposed to Ahuramazda) in the governance of the world, the texts do appear to reflect a more positive view of empire.

Within the collections explored above from book 5, the psalms seek to construct a particular image of empire while concomitantly deconstructing its significance. Not a single psalm provides a positive assessment of empire. Although not every psalm from 107–118 deals with nations and empires, those that do, even in a tangential way, seem to deconstruct the power of such empires. In the opening psalm of book 5 and the two subsequent collections (108–110; 113–118), the psalmists continually portray the empires and nations negatively, suggesting that those in Yehud do not participate joyously with empires, both past and present. The psalmists recount the role of empire within her past; empires have scattered Israel literally and figuratively (107:2) and despite the return from exile, enemies and empires remain a threat to Yehud's existence (108:12–14; 110:2, 6). Though Yahweh has delivered Israel in the past from imperial threats (114:1; 118:10), the psalmists are emphatic that such threats have not ended (118:25).

Whatever positive associations with empire the Achaemenid dynasty sought to create, those responsible for the collection of Yehud's psalmody operated with a very different perspective in mind, a perspective that remains consistent throughout the remainder of book 5.

4
Constructing and Deconstructing Power: Part 2

4.0. Introduction

Psalms 107–118 repeatedly make reference to nations and empires, seeking to construct a particular view of empire, while also deconstructing the need for human power in a newly configured worldview in which Yahweh alone is king. The same attempt to construct and deconstruct empires appears as well in selected psalms that comprise the remainder of book 5.

4.1. The Psalms of Ascents

The issue of power takes on a more nuanced perspective in the Psalms of Ascents. The prehistory of the individual psalms, as well as the *Sitz im Leben* of the collection as a whole, remains contested. In the present study, however, the *Sitz im Leben* of the psalms remains secondary to the question of the *Sitz im Buch*. Loren Crow identified two themes that appear to dominate the psalms in this collection as they now stand. Some texts appear to reflect the agrarian concerns of everyday life for the small landowner or farmer, while other texts appear driven by a strong Zion theology. Crow contends that a secondary redaction involving Pss 121–122 and 132–134, in particular, creates a political horizon. He opines, "The most important new direction provided by the redactor was a tendency to nationalize the songs" and "to see Jerusalem as an *omphalus mundi*, a center from which God's blessing flows forth."[1] The confession of Zion as the center of world,

---

1. Loren Crow, *Songs of Ascents (Psalms 120–134): Their Place in Israelite History and Religion* (SBLDS 148; Atlanta: Scholars Press, 1996), 13. On the role of Zion as dispenser of the gifts from Yahweh, see §5.4 in the present study.

however, remains in tension with a vision of the world in the Psalms of Ascents that is shaped by "social and political antagonism."[2]

As noted below, the opening psalm in the collection highlights the social and political tension which underlies much of the collection. While a number of psalms allude more generally to a threatened existence, Pss 120, 124, 125, and 129, in particular, allude to the threat of foreign power over the people of God. Together, these four psalms function as the opening and closing psalms in the first two subgroups of the larger collection.[3] In effect, these four psalms, which create an *inclusio* in each of the first two subgroups within the Psalms of Ascents, reveal the "social and political antagonism" generated by foreign powers. These psalms may also further support Crow's thesis that the Psalms of Ascents, regardless of their prehistory, may have been nationalized in an effort to address political threats faced by those who prayed the psalms.[4]

4.1.1. Psalm 120

Although Ps 120 has occasionally been classified as a song of thanksgiving, the psalm is better understood as a song of lament, albeit one that is *sui generis* because of the reversal of the lament elements (lament, petition, affirmation of confidence). Such an unusual construction of a lament psalm has lead Hossfeld and Zenger to propose that the psalm itself was a literary composition created as an introduction for the entire collection (Pss 120–134).[5] As attractive as such a proposal may be, it remains speculative at best. Whether there is evidence to support Hossfeld and Zenger's claim that this psalm, or any psalm, was composed specifically for its literary setting, Hossfeld and Zenger are surely correct in their assessment that the psalm, as it now stands, does function as an introduction to the Psalms of Ascents. The themes present in this psalm not only resonate with the

---

2. Frank Lothar Hossfeld and Erich Zenger, *Psalms 3: A Commentary on Psalms 101–150* (ed. Klaus Baltzer; trans. Linda Maloney; Hermeneia; Minneapolis: Fortress, 2011), 298.

3. The Psalms of Ascents may be divided into three subgroups (120–124; 125–129; and 130–134) following Hossfeld and Zenger (*Psalms 3*, 296).

4. See also Marko Marttila's treatment concerning the "collectivizing" (or nationalizing) elements present within Psalms 120–134 (*Collective Reinterpretation in the Psalms: A Study of the Redaction History of the Psalter* [FAT 2/13; Tübingen: Mohr Siebeck, 2006], 167–76).

5. Hossfeld and Zenger, *Psalms 3*, 305.

themes of unchecked power found elsewhere in book 5, the themes in Ps 120 both inform and shape the ideologies present within Pss 120–134.

In the opening line of the psalm, the psalmist alludes to a previous situation of distress in which he cried to Yahweh. The language of distress, צָרָה, in Ps 120 invokes the language employed in Ps 107 where foe (צָר) and oppression (צָרָה) appear in tandem. As in Ps 107, the situation of distress in Ps 120 appears connected to the oppressive power of another. The previous experience with distress mentioned in verse 1 is meant to buttress the faith of the psalmist in a world where such oppressive activities have not ceased.

The nature of the distress currently experienced by the psalmist appears initially in verse 2 ("lying lips" and "a deceitful tongue"), yet the remainder of the psalm suggests that this contestation between the psalmist and the hostile other is more than simply a battle of words. Göran Eidevall has tracked in the book of Isaiah numerous occurrences in which the prophet associates the use of arrogant and deceitful language with the behavior of empires.[6] Arguably, a similar usage appears in Ps 120. As the psalm progresses, the militaristic overtones in the text increase in intensity, culminating in the final claim of the psalmist: "They are for war" (120:7b). As Amy Cottrill has suggested, the metaphor of battle posits "a one-dimensional hostile other, ruthless and volatile, with no motive other than to harm the supplicant" and constructs a "perilous, violent social world in which the psalmist is endangered."[7] The mention of arrows in verse 4 parallels usage elsewhere in the Psalter where the term functions as a metaphor for speech or verbal attack (e.g., 64:4). Yet such a meaning is not omnipresent in the Psalter. In Ps 11, for example, the arrows (11:2) allude to the violence (11:5) being done to the psalmist. In Ps 120:4, the psalmist implores Yahweh to return to the hostile other what has been doled out to him. The language associated with speech in verse 2 would suggest that the abuse in question is primarily that of speech, yet the comments to follow in verses 6–7 would infer that such language is only the precursor to potential violence at the hands of those more powerful than

---

6. Göran Eidevall, *Prophecy and Propaganda: Images of Enemies in the Book of Isaiah* (ConBOT 46; Winona Lake, Ind.: Eisenbrauns, 2009), 23–131.

7. Amy Cottrill, *Language, Power, and Identity in the Lament Psalms of the Individual* (LHBOTS 493; New York: T&T Clark, 2008), 88.

the psalmist. Or put more simply, "violent action, signaled in the warrior's arrows, is here seen as an inevitable result of malicious speech."[8]

Similar to the move made in Ps 108, the apparent historical references in Ps 120 have been loosened from their historical moorings in an effort to heighten the drama of the text, and in particular, to reinforce the notion of threat that comes from foreign power.[9] In Ps 120, the psalmist laments,

> Woe is me, that I sojourn in Meschech
>   that I dwell among the tents of Kedar.
> Too long have I had my dwelling
>   among those who hate peace.
> I am for peace,
>   but when I speak,
>   they are for war. (120:5–7)

Interpreters have frequently sought to identify Meschech and Kedar geographically.[10] Both place names appear to allude to warring people groups. Those from the tribes of Kedar are first mentioned in Gen 25 and recognized elsewhere for their skills in battle, especially with the bow (Isa 21:13–17). Geographically, Kedar would have been associated with the tribes in the Arabian Desert to the south. Although more difficult to locate, Meschech has generally been associated with a region in the far north where a warlike people group lived south of the Black Sea.[11] David Mitchell is no doubt correct, however, in his assessment that these place names are now functioning metaphorically for hostile peoples.[12] The metaphorical use

---

8. Ibid., 98n116.

9. Michael Goulder rejects a symbolic reading of Meschech and Kedar and instead, attempts to connect the activity of Sanballet with Meschech and Geshem with Kedar. Such a move is consistent with his larger project of reading the Psalms of Ascents in light of the fourteen testimonies of Nehemiah, an approach that has yet to win significant support (*The Return of the Psalms [Book V, Psalms 107–150]: Studies in the Psalter, IV* [JSOTSup 258; Sheffield: Sheffield Academic Press, 1998], 37–39). Crow does acknowledge that Geshem could be associated with the reference to Keder, but lists this as only one of several options (*The Songs of Ascents*, 36–37). Goulder, much more than Crow, seeks a historical period, along with historical personages, in which to locate the psalm.

10. See, e.g., Cuthbert C. Keet, *A Study of the Psalms of Ascents: A Critical and Exegetical Commentary upon Psalms CXX to CXXXIV* (London: Mitre, 1969), 22–24.

11. Hossfeld and Zenger, *Psalms 3*, 309.

12. David C. Mitchell, *The Message of the Psalter: An Eschatological Programme*

of geographical regions appears elsewhere in the Hebrew Bible, with the most relevant text for the present study appearing in Ezek 38 and 39. There Gog, the apocalyptic marauder, is said to be the chief prince of Meschech and Tubal, the one who comes from the north with bow and arrow in hand to meet final destruction at the hands of Yahweh.

> [Yahweh] will bring you up from the remotest parts of the north and lead you against the mountains of Israel. I will strike the bow from your left hand and will make your arrows drop out of your right hand. You shall fall upon the mountains of Israel, you and all your troops and the peoples that are with you. (Ezek 39:2b–4a; NRSV)

The book of Ezekiel associates the people groups in the region of Meschech with war and devastation, a theme replicated in Ps 120.

As noted above, Kedar appears in the far south while Meschech in the far north, yet both function metaphorically in Ps 120. The two locations portray a world from south to north, filled with regional and political powers that threaten the life of the psalmist. The psalmist announces

> I am for peace,
>   but when I speak,
>   they are for war. (120:7 NRSV)

In short, the entire psalm laments the presence of enemies that are portrayed as slanderous foreign powers opposed to peace.[13] Such a claim, however, extends beyond Ps 120, and resonates with the assertions made in the opening psalm of book 5 (Ps 107) and the fourth Davidic psalter (Pss 108–110). Within the context of book 5, the community that seeks a restored life finds itself continually "among those that hate peace" (120:6).

---

in the Book of Psalms (JSOTSup 252; Sheffield: Sheffield Academic Press, 1997), 118. Hossfeld and Zenger refer to the geographical terms as "theological topography" (*Psalms 3*, 309). See also, Erhard Gerstenberger, *Psalms, Part 2, and Lamentations* (FOTL 15; Grand Rapids: Eerdmans, 2001), 319.

13. Crow, *The Songs of Ascents*, 34. Susanne Gillmayer-Bucher suggests that while Zion stands as the central space within the Psalms of Ascents as a whole, the opening psalm, Ps 120, is meant to "introduce a lyrical speaker at the margins of the world," under foreign threat ("Images of Space in the Psalms of Ascents," in *The Composition of the Book of Psalms* [ed. Erich Zenger; BETL 238; Leuven: Peeters, 2010], 498).

4.1.2. Psalm 124

Through the use of mythopoeic imagery, the psalmist both rehearses and recasts the language of threat for the community. The attempt to locate a specific historical circumstance, however, for either the threat or the deliverance mentioned in this psalm is challenging at best.[14] Instead, following the suggestion of Philip Satterthwaite, the psalm is meant to "recount the perennial hostility endured by Israel."[15] The particularities of the original threat fade into the background as the psalmist implores the community in verse 1b, "Let Israel now say," in essence calling upon Israel "to make this expression its own."[16] The remainder of the psalm explores the threat to the people, suggesting that Israel's identity is shaped in part by its encounter with the foes that threaten them.

In verses 1b and 2a, the psalmist formulates two unreal conditional statements with the term לוּלֵי, posing the question of what *would have been* had not Yahweh been on the side of his people. The chief threat named in verse 2b is אָדָם. Rather than "man" or "human being," the term may be better understood either as "every man" who comes against Israel, in the sense that the term signifies the hostile world that surrounds them, or even further, that the term signifies a collective plural, referring to the enemies of the nation.[17] Gert Prinsloo suggests that the term was intentionally employed as a value judgment, inferring that the enemies of Israel were merely אָדָם.[18] The labeling of the enemy as אָדָם, however, in no way diminishes the perceived threat. Egbert Ballhorn notes that although the traditional enemy language is absent, the opposition presented in Ps 124 is

---

14. Nevertheless, for an attempt at historical location, see Goulder, *The Psalms of the Return*, 53–55, as well as Alexander F. Kirkpatrick, *The Book of Psalms 3* (The Cambridge Bible for Schools and Colleges 16; Cambridge: Cambridge University Press, 1903), 744. Both attempt to situate Ps 124 within the Nehemiah narratives, especially Neh 4.

15. Philip E. Satterthwaite, "Zion in the Songs of Ascents," in *Zion, City of our God* (ed. Richard S. Hess and Gordon J. Wenham; Grand Rapids: Eerdmans, 1999), 120.

16. Frank Crüsemann, *Studien zur Formgeschichte von Hymnus und Danklied in Israel* (WMANT 32; Neukirchen-Vluyn: Neukirchener 1969), 167.

17. Gerstenberger, *Psalms, Part 2, and Lamentations*, 335.

18. Gert T. M. Prinsloo, "Historical Reality and Mythological Metaphor in Psalm 124," in *Psalms and Mythology* (ed. Dirk J. Human; LHBOTS 462; New York: T&T Clark, 2007), 184.

depicted as an anonymous *Übermacht*.[19] His claim appears substantiated by the metaphorical language that follows in the three apodoses.

> Then they would have swallowed us up alive,
>   when their anger was kindled against us;
> then the flood would have swept us away,
>   the torrent would have gone over us;
> then over us would have gone the raging waters. (124:3–5 NRSV)

Three times the psalmist employs water imagery (מַיִם; נַחְלָה) to depict the threat that would have resulted had not Yahweh been on Israel's side. Such language is often employed in the Psalter to signal the threat of chaos (e.g., 42:2; 46:3; 69:2–3; 144:7), but as William Brown suggests, its usage within Ps 124 follows other occurrences where the term has an explicit "political target domain."[20] In Jer 47:2, both terms appear, operating within a similar "political target domain." In referring to the judgment coming upon the Philistines, the text reads

> Thus says the LORD: See, waters (מַיִם) are rising out of the north
>   and shall become an overflowing torrent (נַחַל);
> They shall overflow the land and all that fills it,
>   The city and those who live in it. (NRSV)

The metaphorical language is rich, associating waters and torrents with the freighted image of the enemy from the north (צָפוֹן) in an effort to reinforce the political threat that was to come.[21]

Elsewhere in the Hebrew Bible, מַיִם functions as a metaphor for invading nations (Isa 8:7–8; Dan 11:10). Typically נַחְלָה has a positive connotation, suggesting something that is a source of life, but in Ps 124, its meaning shifts due to its pairing with מַיִם. Three times the psalmist employs "water" imagery in verses 4–5 and in each occurrence the presumption is that such an event would result in nothing short of death.[22]

---

19. Egbert Ballhorn, *Zum Telos des Psalters: der Textzusammenhang das Vierten und Fünften Psalmenbuches (Psalmen 90–150)* (BBB 138; Berlin: Philo, 2004), 230.

20. William P. Brown, *Seeing the Psalms: A Theology of Metaphor* (Louisville: Westminster John Knox, 2002), 114.

21. Brevard S. Childs, "The Enemy from the North and the Chaos Tradition," *JBL* 78 (1959): 187–98.

22. Brown explains, "The image of inundating waters is deployed to heighten the

The menacing watery abyss mentioned in verses 4–5 is understood in light of verse 2b. Or perhaps better stated, the אָדָם mentioned in verse 2b, and the threat implied by their presence, is better understood in light of the metaphors that follow. That the אָדָם would rise up against Israel (124:2b) provides only limited information; that the אָדָם is described as a watery abyss that "swallows up" those in its path suggests that the enemy possesses a power that cannot be thwarted by Israel. The fate of one caught in such an abyss mirrors the fate of what *might have* happened had Yahweh not been on the side of his people.

Similar to the metaphor of threatening waters in verses 3–5, the two images present in the second half of the psalm contain a "political target domain" as well. In 124:6, the psalmist invokes the people to bless Yahweh, the one who "did not give (נָתַן) us over as prey to their teeth." As Hossfeld and Zenger have noted, the verb נָתַן "plays on the well-known formula according to which Yhwh 'gives' Israel or Jerusalem 'into the hands' of the enemies."[23] For example, in Ps 106:41, the psalmist recalls that following Israel's disobedience in the land,

> He gave them into the hand of the nations (וַיִּתְּנֵם בְּיַד־גּוֹיִם).

In Ps 124, however, the psalmist has opted to replace the metaphor "hand" with that of "teeth," another frequently occurring metaphor in the Hebrew Bible, and as apparent in Ps 35, one that can signify a threat imposed by foreigners (35:15b–16).[24] More specifically, in Ezek 22, the Babylonians are said to be "like roaring lions tearing the prey; they have devoured human lives" (22:25). The image constructed in verse 6, like that constructed in

---

mortal danger posed by Israel's national enemies" (*Seeing the Psalms*, 115). The final image, הַמַּיִם הַזֵּידוֹנִים, is often translated as "raging waters," yet the term הַזֵּידוֹנִים also carries political overtones, referring to "insolent or rebellious ones." A political usage of the term can be found in Exod 18:11 and Jer 50:29, while its adjectival form is used elsewhere in the Psalter to speak of the oppression of another (Pss 19:14; 86:14; 119:21, 51, 69, 78, 85, and 122).

23. Hossfeld and Zenger, *Psalms 3*, 357. See 2 Kgs 18:30; 19:10; Jer 20:4–5; 34:20–21.

24. Following the *BHS* note, read נָכְרִים ("foreigners") in place of נכים ("smiters"). The image of being caught in the teeth of a wild animal appears with great regularity in the Hebrew Bible (and the larger ancient Near Eastern context). See Peter Riede, *Im Netz des Jägers: Studien zur Feindmetaphorik der Individualpsalmen* (WMANT 85; Neukirchen-Vluyn: Neukirchener, 2000), 150–94; Brown, *Seeing the Psalms*, 139.

verses 3–5, is meant to convey a sense of certain death, had not Yahweh been on their side.

Arguably, the most politically overt metaphor in Ps 124, however, appears in verse 7:

We have escaped as a bird from the snare of the fowlers.

In some ancient Near Eastern texts, the image of a bird caught in a snare serves as a metaphor for death more generally.[25] In a similar vein, the sage writes,

For no one can anticipate the time of disaster. Like fish taken in a cruel net, and like birds caught in a snare, so mortals are snared at a time of calamity, when it suddenly falls upon them. (Qoh 9:12 NRSV)

When the metaphor of a bird trapped in a cage or a snare appears to have a collective sense, as apparent in Ps 124, the image seems to be a stock metaphor in the ancient Near East for a city under siege.[26] In the Annals of Sennacherib, the siege of Jerusalem is recounted, making use of this ornithological metaphor.

As for Hezekiah, the Judean, I besieged forty-six of his fortified walled cities and surrounding towns.… He himself, I locked up within Jerusalem, his royal city, like a bird in a cage.[27]

The celebration of having escaped such a snare as mentioned in Ps 124:7 presumably refers to the lifting of a siege—deliverance from a foreign occupier.[28] Although all three images, water, teeth, and a snare, suggest

---

25. See Prinsloo, "Historical Reality and Mythological Metaphor in Psalm 124," 200–201. Prinsloo notes that in Ishtar's Descent into the Netherworld (lines 1–10) and in the Epic of Gilgamesh (7.182–92), those who have journeyed to the netherworld are apparently clothed in garments that resemble birds.

26. Such a statement appears in the El Armana letters as well as in Hittite literature. See the comments by Crow, *The Songs of Ascents*, 53n39. The metaphor does not appear to relate to the return from exile, *contra* Satterthwaite, "Zion in the Psalms of Ascents," 120.

27. "Sennacherib's Seige of Jerusalem," trans. Mordechai Cogan, COS 2.119B: 302–3.

28. On the frequency of the "hunt" metaphor in the Hebrew Bible, see Riede, *Im Netz des Jägers*, 339–76. In his comments on Ps 127:7, Riede explains, "Israel saw itself

the presence of a force so menacing that it could snuff out the lives of the inhabitants of the city, the psalmist recounts the deliverance experienced by Israel. As Brown has observed, other psalms that speak of deliverance frequently allude to the fate of the oppressor.[29] Strikingly, however, in Ps 124 the psalmist remains silent about the fate of the enemy. Clearly, Yahweh has enabled Israel to escape the net of the fowler, but there is no indication that the net, much less the fowler, has been destroyed. Perhaps the silence of the psalmist in this regard suggests that Israel will always need the help of the one "who made heaven and earth" because the enemy, אָדָם, remains a perpetual threat in the history of Israel. The psalm also reinforces particular ideas associated with foreign powers. The political imagery present in the psalm supports the notion that empires and foreign powers do little to create order. To the contrary, their actions threaten to "sweep away" Israel like raging waters (124:3–5), resulting in death and destruction (124:6).

4.1.3. Psalm 125

The threat of foreign power stands, literally, at the center of this communally oriented psalm, holding in tension the community of Israel and the foreign power that seeks to undo that community.[30] The language throughout the psalm reinforces the communal orientation of the text. In addition to the opening participial phrase (הַבֹּטְחִים בַּיהוָה), the substantival use of the adjective throughout appears consistently in the plural (טוֹבִים; יְשָׁרִים; הַצַּדִּיקִים).[31] Moreover, the psalmist refers to Israel as "his people" (עַמּוֹ), no doubt reinforcing the collective emphasis in the psalm.[32] Although the final phrase in the psalm, שָׁלוֹם עַל־יִשְׂרָאֵל, is likely a later gloss, its appearance nonetheless stresses the collective perspective of the psalm in its *Sitz im Buch*. Although the psalm repeatedly focuses on the

---

caught in a trap like a bird. Deliverance from the threat of death was only possible if the trap was destroyed.... The psalm praises the act of deliverance by Yahweh who sees the threat and danger to his people" (351).

29. Brown, *Seeing the Psalms*, 146.

30. Martilla, *Collective Reinterpretation in the Psalms*, 168–69.

31. Gerstenberger suggests that the initial participial phrase is similar to a beatitude (cf. Ps 1:1) in both form and meaning (*Psalms, Part 2, and Lamentations*, 337).

32. Ballhorn suggests, "God surrounds the whole nation (v. 2) and the whole nation is to be counted among the righteous (v. 3)" (*Zum Telos des Psalters*, 231).

community as a whole, the psalm also implies that the community appears to have little if any power in the face of opposition. The strength of the community, instead, is predicated upon the work of Yahweh (125:2, 5b). Similar to the affirmation made in Ps 124:1b and 2a ("If Yahweh had not been for us… "), Ps 125 appears to suggest that Israel's fate rests in the faithfulness of Yahweh and Yahweh alone.

The communal state of bliss mentioned in verses 1–2 is interrupted abruptly with the introduction of a foe.[33] The "scepter of wickedness" (שֵׁבֶט הָרֶשַׁע) mentioned in verse 3 invokes language of an oppressive rule at the hands of a foreign power.[34] Hossfeld and Zenger suggest that the synecdoche implies both "a political and social system" as well as "practices of injustice in the exercise of its power."[35] Although not precisely identical in language, similar phrases appear in the Hebrew Bible alluding to political systems known for their oppression of Israel. In Isa 9:3, the phrase שֵׁבֶט הַנֹּגֵשׂ, "the rod of the oppressor," is used in reference to the rule of Assyria. Similarly, in Isa 14:5, the writer places שֵׁבֶט מֹשְׁלִים "the scepter of the ruling ones," in apposition to מַטֵּה רְשָׁעִים, "the staff of the wicked ones," in reference to the king of Babylon. Further, the שֵׁבֶט הָרֶשַׁע stands as a symbol of oppressive foreign rule, understood in contrast to the שֵׁבֶט מִישֹׁר, "the scepter of equity" (Ps 45:7), a phrase meant to symbolize the just rule of Israelite kings. Although the psalmist fails to mention the particularities regarding an unjust rule in the land, 125:3b alludes to an

---

33. Gerstenberger, *Psalms, Part 2, and Lamentations*, 337. Gerstenberger contends that the lack of reference to Yahweh in v. 3, despite its repeated use in vv. 1–2 and 4–5 leads him to "believe in the original autonomy" of this verse (337). Hossfeld and Zenger suggest, however, that while there is no overt reference to Yahweh in v. 3, the mention of the land allocated to the righteous no doubt refers to Yahweh implicitly (*Psalms 3*, 366).

34. In 125:3, the psalmist states that the "scepter of wickedness shall not remain (נוּחַ) upon the land allotted to the righteous." The verb נוּחַ can mean "to rest," which would suggest in this context that the scepter of wickedness has yet to "rest" upon the land. While possible, the preferred meaning, however, seems to be "to remain" (Allen, *Psalms 101–150*, 166). Verse 5 implies that those within the community who turn aside to the wicked ways will be led away with the "evildoers." As Allen avers, the psalmist makes "a plea for Yahweh to deal with renegades who have broken the covenant and forfeited their share in the land, by expelling them and their foreign patrons" (166). By implication the "evildoers" are already in the land, suggesting that the "scepter of wickedness" has already exerted its influence. See also John Goldingay, *Psalms 90–150* (BCOT; Grand Rapids: Baker Academic, 2008), 485–86.

35. Hossfeld and Zenger, *Psalms 3*, 366.

influence so pervasive that it threatens the covenantal faithfulness of the righteous ones.

Among the ramifications of foreign oppression is the negative influence of such political power upon the identity of the community (125:3b).[36] The psalmist contends that the presence of the "scepter of wickedness" in the land may cause the righteous to "stretch out their hands in iniquity (עַוְלָה)" (125:3b). Allen notes the word play in verses 1b and 5a, which creates an *inclusio*.[37] This *inclusio* highlights the potential shift in the character of the righteous when faced with the pressures that come from foreign occupation. In verse 1b, the righteous are those "who cannot be moved (יִמּוֹט)," much like Zion itself (Ps 46:6a). Later in the psalm, due to the influence of the "scepter of wickedness," some individuals will "bend (הַמַּטִּים) their crooked ways" (125:5a). Their fate will match that of the occupiers; they will be led away with the פֹּעֲלֵי הָאָוֶן, "the evildoers." As evident in other psalms, the view of foreign rule remains persistently negative, with dire consequences for those within the community who choose to align themselves with the ways of the foreign power.

4.1.4. Psalm 129

Psalm 129 concludes the second collection in the Psalms of Ascents by announcing that Israel has been oppressed throughout her history. As the psalmist avers, affliction at the hands of the enemy is nothing new; it is part of Israel's identity. In 129:1a and 2a, the psalmist remembers "Often they have oppressed (צָרַר) me from my youth." The use of צָרַר in the opening of the psalm recalls Ps 107 and the mention of the יַד־צָר in 107:2. The corporate response of the people in 129:1b, "Let Israel now say," reinforces the claim that Israel, *as a community*, remembers those

---

36. Following the larger thesis of his work, Goulder proffers a context in which political collusion leads to "godless cruelty," suggesting the psalm is referencing the crisis outlined in Neh 5 (*The Psalms of the Return*, 58–59). Hossfeld and Zenger, however, center their argument on the appearance of the term גּוֹרָל, "lot," and suggest that the inference is to "the practice of officially bestowing confiscated land on new owners ... This practice of unjust distribution of land was probably given public protection by the Persian or Ptolemaic powers" (*Psalms 3*, 366). Further, the psalmist may have been referring to the righteous participating in the confiscating of land in v. 3b, thereby, "stretching forth their hand in wickedness" (עַוְלָה).

37. Allen, *Psalms 101–150*, 168.

who have oppressed them.³⁸ Throughout Ps 129, however, the language is replete with images and metaphors alluding to the exploitation of God's people by foreign powers.

The use of חֹרְשִׁים ("plowers") in verse 3a underscores the theme of foreign oppression.³⁹ The psalmist cries out

> Upon my back, the plowers have plowed;
> they made long furrows.

Metaphorically, the language suggests heavy oppression at the hands of the enemy.⁴⁰ The term חֹרְשִׁים invokes the image of a work animal whipped while laboring, an image the poet believes accords well with Israel's servitude to another group.⁴¹ Crüsemann offers an alternative reading of the metaphor suggesting that the imagery of plowing upon the back may reflect the practice of cutting one's back as a sign of grief and mourning in light of the arduous reality faced by the community.⁴² Yet in verse 3, the injury is not self-inflicted, but carried out by the חֹרְשִׁים. The image of plowing functions as a metaphor for total destruction in Mic 3:12 and Jer 26:18, suggesting further a political rendering of the image in verse 3. Elsewhere in the Hebrew Bible, similar agricultural imagery appears in reference to oppression at the hands of foreign powers. In Isa 9:3 (Eng. 4), the prophet writes,

---

38. Allen notes that the opening of the psalm is in the singular, but suggests that perhaps there is a personification of Zion at work, with Zion speaking this psalm on behalf of all her inhabitants, notably in vv. 2–4 (*Psalms 101–150*, 189). The close association between the inhabitants of Zion and Zion herself may explain the first-person language in vv. 2–4.

39. The LXX reads οἱ ἁμαρτωλοί, obviously reading רְשָׁעִים for חֹרְשִׁים. In 11QPsa, רשעים appears as well, thus leading Crow to contend that in the Hebrew *Vorlage* רְשָׁעִים was the original term (*The Songs of Ascents*, 77). The MT should be retained. Hossfeld and Zenger attempt to explain the altered reading in the LXX. "While in the MT, the metaphors for plowing, sowing, and harvesting, drawn from the world of farm life, shape the whole psalm—as images for exploitation by foreign powers—the LXX changes the image world in the first section of the psalm (vv. 1–4), probably because in its urban cultural context that imagery was foreign and perhaps incomprehensible (*Psalms 3*, 418).

40. Satterthwaite, "Zion in the Songs of Ascents," 123n74.

41. Allen, *Psalms 101–150*, 187.

42. Crüsemann, *Studien zur Formgeschichte von Hymnus und Danklied in Israel*, 170–71.

> For the yoke of their burden
>> and the bar across their shoulders,
> The rod of their oppression,
>> you have broken as on the day of Midian. (NRSV)

Although the word "yoke" is absent in Ps 129, the image of plowing infers the larger metaphorical field that suggests forced labor. In a relief from a tomb at Edfu (ca. 1500 B.C.E.), the scene depicts a plow being pulled by human slaves, a scene similar to the one envisioned in 129:3.[43] In short, the imagery of pulling a plow in verse 3 no doubt functioned metaphorically, but its meaning was likely one not too far removed from reality itself.[44]

The חֹרְשִׁים, the "plowers," mentioned in verse 3 are labeled רְשָׁעִים, "the wicked," in verse 4. In Ps 125, the first psalm in this subcollection within the Psalms of Ascents, the psalmist alludes to foreign powers metonymically, שֵׁבֶט הָרֶשַׁע, "the scepter of the wicked," associating the "wicked" and "wickedness" with foreign powers who oppress the people of God. Continuing the agricultural metaphor, the psalmist announces that Yahweh "has cut (קִצֵּץ) the cords of the wicked," implying that at some point in the past, Israel was freed from those who had oppressed her. As suggested above, the cord would have tethered literally and figuratively the animal or human to the plower, the oppressed to the oppressor. As a remedy, however, Yahweh "cut" the cords. The term קִצֵּץ appears elsewhere in the Hebrew Bible, describing graphically the cutting off of hands (2 Sam 4:12), cutting off thumbs and toes (Judg 1:6–7), and the destruction of weapons of war (Ps 46:10). Its usage in Ps 129 suggests "the disempowerment of the wicked/enemies."[45] The affirmation that Yahweh has cut the cords of the wicked in times past provides the necessary foundation for the imprecations that follow.

The curses that follow in 129:5–8 suggest that a persistent threat remains, a threat that must be redressed by Yahweh. The psalmist dramatically shifts metaphors and language in verse 5, picking up militaristic images and momentarily suspending the agricultural theme.[46]

---

43. Hossfeld and Zenger, *Psalms 3*, 415

44. The whole process, including the yoke and plowing, function as a "metaphor for compulsion and foreign rule, for oppression, exploitation, forced labor, and slavery" (ibid., 415).

45. Ibid., 407.

46. The use of the verb קִצֵּץ in v. 4 already portends this shift, but beginning in

> May all those who hate Zion
> be put to shame and turned back.

Admittedly, the military themes in verse 5 are not as overt as the agricultural metaphors that appear earlier in the psalm, yet as with the agricultural image, the militaristic language reinforces the oppressive threat of foreign powers. The psalmist refers to the enemies as "all who hate Zion," thus pitting all of Israel (129:2) against "all who hate Zion" (129:5). The desire of the psalmist is that the enemies of Zion be shamed (בּוֹשׁ) and turned back (סוֹג).[47] Both verbs, which appear to function as a hendiadys in this context, can allude to militaristic and political upheaval.[48] Frequently בּוֹשׁ appears in texts related to warfare, signaling the shame endured by those routed or yet to be routed in battle (cf. Isa 20:5; Jer 2:26, 36; 51:51; Zech 10:5). When used in the *niphal* elsewhere, סוֹג suggests the repelling of an attacking force (cf. Ps 35:4; 40:15; 70:3). Just as the community had experienced deliverance from the oppressing foes (129:1a, 2a) in the past, the psalmist implores Yahweh to mount up and rout the forces that threaten the community.

In the verses that remain, the psalmist returns to agricultural imagery, but one that undermines the perceived power and strength of the enemy. The psalmist prays

> Let them be like grass on the housetops
> that withers before it can be pulled out.

The "grass" that withers is here understood as the grass that grows on the rooftop, a harmful weed that threatens the integrity of the roof. Because there is no fertile soil on the roof, such weeds can only develop shallow roots, and hence under an oppressive sun, are prone to wither. The agricultural metaphor in verse 6, however, alludes to the more militaristic

---

v. 5, the agricultural imagery is suspended altogether. Klaus Seybold suggests that v. 5 was secondarily inserted based upon its thematic differences with the remainder of the psalm (*Die Wallfahrtspsalmen: Studien zur Entstehungsgeschichte von Psalm 120–34* [Biblisch-theologische Studien 3; Neukirchen-Vluyn: Neukirchener, 1978], 28–29). The mixing of metaphors, however, is a common occurrence in Hebrew poetry, thereby making such a conjecture unnecessary.

47. On the role of shame in the Psalter, see W. Dennis Tucker Jr., "Is Shame a Matter of Patronage in the Communal Laments?" *JSOT* 31 (2007): 465–80.

48. Goldingay, *Psalms 90–150*, 518.

imagery in verse 5. Although the *BHS* note suggests the deletion of יֵבֹ֑שׁוּ, Dahood is no doubt correct in his observation concerning the paronomasia at work in these verses with the presence of יֵבֹ֑שׁוּ ("be put to shame") at the beginning of verse 5 and the presence of יָבֵֽשׁ ("will wither") at the end of verse 6.[49] "All those who hate Zion" will be a people put to shame, withering under the might of Yahweh, the Righteous One (129:4).

In 129:6b, the poet apparently opts for another term, שָׁלַף, that while appearing to have an agricultural meaning in the present context, carries with it military connotations. In texts related to battle and military struggle, שָׁלַף refers to the act of pulling out a sword in battle (cf. Num 22:23, 31; Josh 5:13; Judg 3:22; 8:10, 20; 9:54; 20:2, 15, 17, 35, 46; 1 Sam 17:51; 31:4; 2 Sam 24:9; 2 Kgs 3:26; Job 20:25). Within the present context, the term no doubt refers to the uprooting of a plant. Read this way, the psalmist requests that the enemy wither up before there is even time for it to be uprooted. If the term functions as a *double entendre*, the psalmist may be requesting that the enemies wither up before they have the opportunity to pull out the sword again in military conquest.

Once again, the imperial ideology of a well-ordered world is thwarted by the militaristic allusions in Ps 129. From Israel's "youth," she has experienced affliction at the hands of foreign powers (129:1a, 2a), and while Yahweh "cut the cords" of wickedness in past times of affliction, the psalmist and all of Israel remain in need of similar deliverance (129:5–7).

4.1.5. PSALMS 135 AND 136

Similar to the final two psalms in book 4 (Pss 105–106), Pss 135–136 provide a cursory recital of Israel's history.[50] Although each psalm does

---

49. The association of shame with a withering plant is found as well in 2 Kgs 19:26 and Isa 37:27.

50. Hermann Gunkel classifies Pss 105 and 106 (along with Ps 78) as "legends," a genre he suggests belongs "to a very late period of psalmody" (*Introduction to the Psalms* [trans. James D. Nogalski; MLBS; Macon, Ga.: Mercer University Press, 1998], 247). For Gunkel, legends are a subgenre of other classifications, including the hymn, the communal complaint, and the instructional poem. Psalms 135–136, however, are more broadly classified as "hymns" (22). Kraus follows similarly, although he does note the similarities of Ps 136 with Pss 105–106 (*Psalms 60–150*, 316–17). Gunkel understands the difference between legends and hymns to be one of intent, with the legends having a "didactic tendency" as a final goal. The present study suggests, however, that Psalms 135–136, *even as hymns*, do in fact have a didactic function in the

in fact address specific elements of Israel's history, a significant difference remains between the concluding psalms in book 4 and the historical psalms in book 5, a difference germane to the thesis of this book. Psalm 105 concludes with the admonition that the people "should keep his statutes and observe his laws" (105:45). Psalm 106 recounts Israel's history from Egypt until the entry into the land of Canaan. Yet the psalmist does more than recount the גְּבוּרֹת יְהוָה, "the mighty works of Yahweh." Psalm 106 repeatedly rehearses the guilt of Israel throughout her history. In 106:6, the psalmist confesses

> Both we and our ancestors have sinned;
> we have committed iniquity; we have acted wickedly.

The overriding assumption through the remainder of Ps 106 is that the desperate plights faced by the people of Israel throughout their history are the consequence of disobedience. The psalmist explains

> He gave them into the hand of the nations,
> so that those who hated them ruled over them. (106:41 NRSV)

As the psalm concludes, the psalmist pleads for Yahweh to deliver his people by gathering them from the nations. Unquestionably, the psalmist associates the scattering of the people with their disobedience. The historical recital in Psalms 105 and 106, drawing from the tenets of retribution theology, offer justification for the punishment experienced by the people of God.[51]

Psalter. In reciting significant moments in Israel's canonical history, both psalms testify to the power of Yahweh over kings and empires in Israel's past with the implied assertion that current threats present no challenge to the God of Israel.

51. Kraus explains "The entire history of Israel is viewed as a single vast judgment of the wrath of Yahweh, which again and again was interrupted by the helpful intervention of God, by an answer to the cry of distress and by a merciful 'remembrance of his covenant'" (*Psalms 60–150*, 321). Gerstenberger, however, suggests that the primary message of Ps 106 can be found in vv. 43–46 and 47: "Yahweh's untiring care for his people does overcome sufferings and captivity under foreign powers" (*Psalms, Part 2, and Lamentations*, 243–44). Judith Gärtner arrives at a conclusion similar to that of Gerstenberger, suggesting that "the text is not concerned with the deliverance from specific enemies, but generally with Jhwh saving his people from enemies" ("The Torah in Psalm 106," in *The Composition of the Book of Psalms* [ed. Erich Zenger;

In Pss 135–136, however, there is no reference to retribution theology. Strikingly, however, both psalms focus on the נַחֲלָה, the "heritage" of the land, and the apparent threats in the form of foes (135:10; 136:24). In both psalms, the audience is depicted as "helpless playthings of the enemy powers."[52] As will be suggested below, the נִפְלָאוֹת גְּדֹלוֹת, "the great wonders," in Israel's history function as theological confessions of hope in the face of those that stand against the people of God.

The intertextual references throughout Ps 135 are numerous, leading Allen to suggest that the reader finds himself or herself "assailed by a conglomeration of snatches" from other texts in the Hebrew Bible.[53] Although a number of the allusions or direct quotes come from texts elsewhere that deal specifically with oppression at the hands of political enemies, three examples are particularly illustrative. First, in 135:4, the psalmist acknowledges that "Yahweh has chosen Jacob for himself" and that Israel is "his own possession." While not a direct quote, the psalmist appears to allude to Deut 7:6, "For you are a holy people to the LORD your God; the LORD your God has chosen you out of all the peoples on the earth to be his people, his treasured possession" (NRSV).[54] Earlier in the chapter, Deut 7 opens with instructions for entering the land, noting that Yahweh will

---

BETL 238; Leuven: Peeters, 2010], 481). She contends that Ps 106 highlights *both* the deliverance of God's people as well as the destruction of the enemies. Despite Gerstenberger's and Gärtner's suggestion, Ballhorn's more moderating analysis appears most logical. According to Ballhorn, Ps 106 serves as *Lernparadigma*, indicating that the "greatest danger may be in the apostasy (*Abfall*) of Israel from its God," a threat brought on by nations around them (*Zum Telos des Psalters*, 133).

52. Ruth Scoralick, "Hallelujah für einen gewalttätigen Gott? Zur Theologie von Psalm 135 und 136," *BZ* 46 (2002), 267.

53. Allen, *Psalms 101–150*, 224. See also Leuenberger, *Konzeptionen des Königtums Gottes im Psalter*, 314–15. The intertextual connections between Pss 135 and 136 have led to a considerable diversity of opinion regarding which psalm, if either, has priority. Hossfeld and Zenger conclude that Ps 135 was written well after Ps 136, drawing heavily from it (*Psalms 3*, 496). Both Allen (*Psalms 101–150*, 224) and Seybold (*Die Psalmen*, 503–4) argue likewise. Goulder suggests that the same individual wrote both psalms, with Ps 136 expanding the themes in Ps 135 (*The Psalms of the Return*, 221). Dirk Human contends that neither psalm drew from the other, but instead, both drew from a common source of tradition ("Psalm 136: A Liturgy with Reference to Creation and History," in *Psalms and Liturgy* [ed. Dirk J. Human and Cas J. A. Vos; LHBOTS 410; New York: T&T Clark, 2004], 72–73).

54. See also Deut 14:2; 26:18.

"clear away many nations before you … seven nations mightier and more numerous than you" (7:1).

A more explicit "snatch" appears in Ps 135:5.

> For I know that the LORD is great,
>   and that our Lord is above all gods. (NRSV)

Drawn from Exod 18:11, where Jethro addresses Moses, the line is nearly verbatim, with a little poetic license. This theological confession by Jethro, however, follows the account given by Moses concerning Israel's deliverance from the hardships exacted upon them by the Egyptians.[55]

A third example appears in 135:14.

> The LORD will vindicate his people
>   and have compassion on his servants. (NRSV)

The verse adapts the language of Deut 32:36 to serve as "past proof of the patronage" of Yahweh.[56] Strikingly, the larger context of Deut 32 refers to the enemies that oppress God's people. In Deut 32:40–42, God announces,

> For I lift up my hand to heaven,
>   and swear: As I live forever,
> when I whet my flashing sword,
>   and my hand takes hold on judgment;
> I will take vengeance on my foes (צָרָי),
>   and will repay those who hate me.
> I will make my arrows drunk with blood,
>   and my sword shall devour flesh—
> with the blood of the slain and the captives,
>   from the long-haired enemy. (NRSV)

To this, the people reply,

---

55. Similar to Ps 107:2, Exod 18:9–10 employs the formula "from the hand of X" to refer to political enemies. In Exod 18, the narrator uses both מִיַּד־מִצְרַיִם and מִיַּד־פַּרְעֹה interchangeably to allude to oppressive political power.

56. Allen, *Psalms 101–150*, 227. On the notion of patronage in the Psalter, see Tucker, "Is Shame a Matter of Patronage in the Communal Laments," 469–74. See also Cottrill, *Language, Power, and Identity in the Lament Psalms of the Individual*, 100–137.

> Praise, O heavens, his people,
> > worship him, all you gods!
> For he will avenge the blood of his children,
> > and take vengeance on his foes (צָרָיו);
> he will repay those who hate him,
> > and cleanse the land for his people. (Deut 32:43 NRSV)

All three examples illustrate the politically charged contexts associated with many of the allusions and quotes employed in Ps 135, heightening the political nature of Ps 135 itself.

As seen elsewhere in book 5, the psalmist employs both mythological and historical themes in the psalm. In 135:5–7, the psalmist recounts the universal reign of Yahweh over all creation, stressing that

> Everything that Yahweh desires he does,
> > in heaven and on earth,
> > in the seas and all the deeps.

As Gerstenberger has suggested, the emphasis on Yahweh's supreme authority over creation functions as "theologoumena" for subsequent reflections regarding Yahweh's capacity to deliver his people from oppressive forces. The psalmist refers to the seas (יַמִּים) and the deeps (תְּהוֹמוֹת) in verse 6, no doubt alluding to the chaos imagery present throughout the Old Testament.[57] Rebecca Watson has suggested that "the imagery [of chaos] appears as a paradigm for endangered national stability or even for fear of the collective annihilation by the relentless onslaught of imperial expansion."[58] The proximity of יַמִּים and תְּהוֹמוֹת in verse 6 with the political powers in verses 8–12 appear to substantiate such a claim. Consequently, the psalm seeks to connect the chaotic forces in creation with the chaotic forces that threaten life politically.

In the subsequent section (135:8–12), the psalmist recounts the oppressive enemies that threatened Israel in the past. In each instance, it is the action of Yahweh, "the one who does what he desires" (135:6), that proves decisive in the annihilation of the empires that threatened

---

57. Kraus, *Psalms 60–150*, 493.

58. Rebecca Watson, *Chaos Uncreated: A Reassessment of the Theme of 'Chaos' in the Hebrew Bible* (BZAW 341; Berlin: de Gruyter, 2005), 4. Watson's attempt throughout the monograph to remove any notion of combat from the biblical notion of chaos, however, seems overdrawn.

the people of God. The list of vanquished foes is impressive: Pharaoh and all his servants; mighty kings;[59] Sihon, king of the Amorites; Og, king of Bashan; and all of the kingdoms of Canaan. In recounting these victories, the psalmist employs the verb נָכָה, "to strike," in verses 8a and 10a, a verb found frequently in texts referring to a battle between political powers.[60] The psalmist is clear, however, that it is Yahweh, the "Lord over all gods," who remains responsible for the overturning of empires.[61] The psalmist's use of the Sihon and Og traditions, in particular, substantiate this claim. In the Pentateuch and Joshua, Israel and Moses are traditionally given credit for the slaying of Sihon and Og (Num 21:24, 35; Deut 1:4; 3:2; 4:46; 29:6; Josh 2:10; 21:1).[62] In nearly every account, the narrator credits either Israel or Moses for having struck down (נָכָה) the two kings. In the two accounts where נָכָה is absent (Deut 3:2; Josh 2:10), the verb employed is עָשָׂה. Arguably, the psalmist has reworked the tradition, crediting the work of Israel and Moses to Yahweh, "the one who does (עָשָׂה) what he desires" (135:6), the one capable of striking down (נָכָה) all human threats.

The victory of Yahweh over kings and nations in the past provides a rationale for the claim made in verse 14.

> For Yahweh will judge his people;
>   and over his servants he will have compassion.

The actions of the past serve as guarantees for present deliverance. While Pharaoh, Sihon, Og, and the "mighty kings" have been put down, the community apparently stands in need of deliverance once more by Yahweh. The apparent "hymnic interlude" in verses 13–14 does more than separate the second major strophe from the third.[63] Instead, verse 14 articulates

---

59. The connection of עָצוּם with the noun מֶלֶךְ occurs only here and in Dan 8:24 and 11:24.

60. For example, see Gen 14:7, 15, 17; 36:35; Num 14:45; Deut 29:6; Josh 11:10-12. See also the repeated use of the verb throughout Exod 2–15.

61. Scoralick explains that such usage is meant to show "the superior power of God over against the potency of other nations and their rulers" ("Hallelujah für einen gewalttätigen Gott," 257).

62. The only two exceptions are Deut 31:4 and Josh 9:10. In those instances, Yahweh is given credit for the victory.

63. Kraus, *Psalms 60–150*, 493. Kraus offers scant treatment of vv. 8–12 and devotes only one sentence to vv. 13–14.

the community's expectation that Yahweh will serve as judge and king in defense of Israel "against the dominant groups."[64]

Psalm 136, traditionally labeled the Great Hallel (b. Pesahim 118a), provides a similar recital of significant moments in Israel's history with the added refrain of כִּי חַסְדּוֹ לְעוֹלָם following each line. The rich language and allusions employed in Ps 136 suggests the psalmist's familiarity with pentateuchal traditions.[65] Like Ps 135, Ps 136 rehearses the great wonders (נִפְלָאוֹת גְּדֹלוֹת) of Yahweh, with particular focus on his work in creation (136:5–9) and his victory over the forces that have historically threatened his people (136:10–20). Although the repeated refrain in Ps 136 may be its most unique feature, the extensive attention given to the defeat of kings and nations should not be overlooked. The language and imagery in Ps 136 does little to minimize the legitimate threats posed by Pharaoh and his army or those posed by the many kings encountered en route to settlement in the land. To the contrary, the legitimation of such threats in Israel's past *and* the legitimation of Yahweh's power over them provide the necessary theological underpinnings for the claims made in verses 23–24.

In verses 10–20, the psalmist recounts Israel's deliverance from threatening nations. The opening verse (136:10) in this section of the psalm employs the verb נָכָה, clearly invoking the political and militaristic overtones suggested above. In verse 10, the object of such action is Pharaoh. When the verb appears again in verse 17, the object is the "great kings," suggesting that no political power, be it the ruler of an empire or that of a regional king or chieftain, can unseat the God of Israel. In verse 11, the psalmist states that Yahweh "brought Israel out from among them" (מִתּוֹכָם), alluding to Egypt.[66]

---

64. Gerstenberger, *Psalms, Part 2, and Lamentations*, 381.
65. Human, "Psalm 136," 76–82. Among the comparisons listed by Human are the following: Ps 136:7–9 with Gen 1:14–16; Ps 136:11 with Exod 7:5; 18:1; 20:1; Ps 136:12 with Exod 6:1, 6; Ps 136:13 with Exod 14:16–17, 21; Ps 136:14 with Exod 14:22; Ps 136:15 with Exod 14:27; Ps 136:17–22 with Num 21:21–24, 33–35; Ps 136:2 with Deut 10:27; Ps 136:11 with Deut 1:27; 4:20; 5:15; Ps 136:12 with Deut 4:34; 5:15; 7:19; 9:29; 11:2; 26:8; Ps 136:16 with Deut 8:15; 32:10; Ps 136:19 with Deut 2:33; Ps 136:22 with Deut 32:36.
66. Hossfeld and Zenger, *Psalms 3*, 507. Hossfeld and Zenger, however, have proposed that a subtle word play is at work in the final word of the line. If מִתּוֹכָם, "from among them," is vocalized differently, then the phrase could be read "from their oppression," taken from the noun תֹּךְ, "oppression, violence," highlighting further the oppressive nature of enemy rule (cf. Ps 72:14). Although there is no textual witness

The psalmist alludes to the threat of foreign powers even further by employing mythic imagery in recounting the deliverance of Israel at the יַם־סוּף. Yahweh is praised as לְגֹזֵר יַם־סוּף לִגְזָרִים, "the one who cut the *Yam Suf* into pieces." The use of גָּזַר in 136:13 recalls the battle waged against the "dragon" in Ugaritic literature as well as the splitting of Tiamat into pieces as recorded in the *Enuma Eli*sh tale.[67] As Scoralick has contended, this language of cutting into pieces "carries mythological overtones of the warring enforcement of Yahweh against the sea, suggesting the powerful enforcement of Yahweh not only against the nations, but against all powers."[68] In the hands of Yahweh, the vanquished forces of cosmic chaos (136:13) become an instrument of death to those that represent political chaos to the people of Israel (136:15).

As in Ps 135, Yahweh's victory over kings extends beyond the deliverance experienced in Egypt to that associated with the settlement in the land. The psalmist acknowledges Yahweh's achievements:

> To him who struck down (נָכָה) great kings (מְלָכִים),
>   for his steadfast love endures forever;[69]
> and slew noble kings (מְלָכִים),
>   for his steadfast love endures forever;
> Sihon, king (מֶלֶךְ) of the Amorites,
>   for his steadfast love endures forever;
> and Og, king (מֶלֶךְ) of Bashan,
>   for his steadfast love endures forever. (136:17–20)

Although Josh 12:24b records that altogether thirty-one kings were killed in the settlement of the land, the four-fold mention of kings in Ps 136 deserves consideration. Obviously the list in Ps 136 is not meant to be

---

for such a reading, the phrase מְתוֹכָם may have functioned as a *double entendre* (cf. Amos 7:7–8).

67. See Kraus, *Psalms 60–150*, 499; Human, "Psalm 136," 81. See also, René Dussaud, *Les Découvertes de Ras Shamra (Ugarit) et l'Ancien Testament* (Paris: Geuthner, 1941), 84. On depictions of chaos more generally in the ancient Near East, see Othmar Keel, *The Symbolism of the Biblical World: Ancient Near Eastern Iconography and the Book of Psalms* (Winona Lake, Ind.: Eisenbrauns,1997), 47–56, and Brown, *Seeing the Psalms*, 143–44.

68. Scoralick, "Hallelujah für einen gewalttätigen Gott," 262.

69. Gerstenberger translates כִּי חַסְדּוֹ לְעוֹלָם as "yes, his solidarity forever," capturing well the political nature of the relationship between Yahweh and his people, a point not lost upon the psalmist (*Psalms, Part 2, and Lamentations*, 388).

comprehensive, as verses 18–19 suggest, but those on the list serve as "exemplary prototypes of enemies in Israel's history."[70] Moreover, the fourfold mention of kings in the psalm reinforces the anti-imperial bent in book 5. Kings and kingdoms have provided nothing of benefit to Israel in her past, only serving as an obstacle to Israel enjoying the נַחֲלָה that is theirs (136:21).

In the final section of Ps 136, the psalmist alludes to political enemies once more. The psalmist praises Yahweh as one

> who remembered us in our low estate,
>   for his steadfast love endures forever;
> and rescued us from our foes (מִצָּרֵינוּ),
>   for his steadfast love endures forever. (136:23–24)

In the previous two sections (136:4–9, 10–22), the psalmist opted to rehearse the events in the third person. In verses 23–24, however, the psalmist breaks with the previous strophes, introducing first-person plural language (שִׁפְלֵנוּ; מִצָּרֵינוּ). The subtle shift in person and number suggests the hermeneutical move being made by the psalmist. The story of a people plagued by kings and political powers becomes, for the present community, the operative lens through which to view its own history; the story is "not merely of a generation dead and gone, but of 'us.'"[71] The connection between past and present, however, extends beyond simply the use of first person language. The psalmist refers to the community's most recent threat as מִצָּרֵינוּ, "our foes," a term that appears repeatedly in book 5, beginning with Psalm 107, and one that typically refers to political and military enemies. The term מִצָּרֵינוּ (136:24) is no doubt a partial homophone with מִצְרַיִם, the initial empire mentioned in verse 10. With the use of מִצָּרֵינוּ, the psalmist connects the most recent oppressive threat with the empire of old.[72] But unlike the particularities reported in the previous strophe

---

70. Human, "Psalm 136," 82. In Ps 108, the list of nations there performs a similar function (see §3.2.1 in the present study).

71. Christian Macholz suggests that "the community speaking here emphasizes its own historical experiences as the acts of God in line with the acts of God of the earlier *Heilsgeschichte*" ("Psalm 136: Exegetische Beobachtungen mit methodologischen Seitenblicken," in *Mincha. Festgabe für Rolf Rendtorff zum 75. Geburtstag* [ed. Erhard Blum; Neukirchen-Vluyn: Neukirchener, 2000], 186).

72. J. F. J. van Rensburg, "History as Poetry: A Study of Psalm 136," in *Exodus 1–15, Text and Context: Proceedings of the 29th Annual Congress of the Old Testament*

(136:10–22), the community reports of its deliverance without providing specific details.⁷³ In making such a connection, the psalmist suggests that any oppression, be it מְצָרֵינוּ or מִצְרַיִם, will be met by the חֶסֶד of Yahweh.

Psalms 135 and 136 do more than recount the significant moments in the history of Israel. Rather these historical moments provide the psalmists with a rich resource for theological construction and confession.⁷⁴ As these psalms note, opposition from empires and nations dots the history of the people of God. In neither psalm does the psalmist offer a positive assessment of these powers. Rather, in both psalms, such opponents are vividly connected with the powers of chaos, but even more striking, such opponents appear as the chief obstacle to Israel enjoying its נַחֲלָה.⁷⁵ Such opposition is not, however, an event reserved for Israel's past. To the contrary, in the additional "confession" found in 136:23–24, the community interprets its own present deliverance as an act of God, one that stands in line with the previous events recounted.⁷⁶ In so doing, the community affirms the legitimate threat of the present foes, while also acknowledging that their continued hope is in the God "who remembered us in our low estate."

4.2. Psalm 137: Recalling the Power of Empire

The reference to enemies and empires continues in Ps 137, but in a manner considerably different from the two preceding psalms. In Pss 135 and 136, the psalmist mentioned kings and empires as part of a confession rooted in Israel's historical tradition. In Ps 137, however, the psalmist has narrowed the focus considerably. The psalmist vividly recalls a scene from

---

Society of South Africa (OTSSA) (ed. J. J. Burden; Pretoria: OTSWA/OTTSA, 1987), 87. Human surmises that the wordplay "suggests that the current danger is similar to the suffering of the slavery in Egypt and the submission to the Pharaoh" ("Psalms 136," 83).

73. Seybold, *Die Psalmen*, 508.

74. Macholz recognizes the political and militaristic dimensions of the text, contending that the community understood "holy history" (*heilige Geschichte*) in terms of "the militant (*kämpferischen*) acts of the power of Yahweh" ("Psalm 136," 186).

75. As Scoralick has summarized, "The smiting (*schlagen*) and slaying (*erschlagen*) God of both psalms evokes the idea of the warring king who defeats the enemy that embodies the powers of chaos" ("Hallelujah für einen gewalttätigen Gott," 265).

76. Macholz, "Psalm 136," 185.

exile, one which reflects the oppression those from Jerusalem experienced at the hands of Babylonian officials.

The oppressive power of the Babylonian empire, as remembered by the psalmist, becomes evident in the language employed in the opening strophe (137:1–3). In verse 3, the psalmist refers to the Babylonians as שׁוֹבֵינוּ ("our captors") and תוֹלָלֵינוּ ("our tormentors"). The verb שבה means "to take captive" and carries with it heavy political and militaristic overtones elsewhere in the Hebrew Bible (e.g., 1 Kgs 5:2; Jer 41:10, 14; 1 Chr 5:21; 2 Chr 6:36). The oppressive connotations continue with the use of תוֹלָלֵינוּ. Although, the term itself is a *hapax legomenon*, the most likely root is יָלַל, meaning "to wail or howl."[77] Bob Becking contends that תוֹלָלֵינוּ "indicates the mocking and dehumanizing behavior" of the Babylonian officials, thus suggesting a "sense of harshness" regarding the fate of those carried away to Babylon.[78] The two terms together contribute to a larger understanding of life under an empire such as Babylon. As Becking explains

> In labeling these Babylonians שׁוֹבֵינוּ and תוֹלָלֵינוּ, the Yehudite community offered a view of the cause of the Exile. To them the Exile was not a neutral event in history, nor a punishment by YHWH in view of their sins, but a brute act of a cruel enemy.[79]

---

77. Hossfeld and Zenger, *Psalms 3*, 512. Alfred Guillaume explains תוֹלָל in 137:3 as based upon the Arabic word, *talla*. In Arabic, the term refers to the driving of animals. Guillaume alludes to the Assyrian and even Achaemenid iconography, which frequently depicts humans bound by the neck as they are driven into captivity. Guillaume concludes, "Thus it is clear beyond all doubt that the תוֹלָל were the harsh, pitiless slave-drivers who drove the prisoners they had plundered hundreds of miles eastward to distant Babylon" ("The Meaning of *twll* in Psalm 137:3," *JBL* 75 [1956], 144). Alternatively, the word could derive from a secondary meaning of הלל, "to mock." This may explain the rendering of Ps 137:3 in σ´ (καὶ οἱ καταλαζονευόμενοι ἡμῶν). Although numerous emendations have been proposed, Allen rejects all of them, preferring instead the MT. Allen's preference for the MT stems largely from what he perceives to be a word play between תָּלִינוּ ("we hung") in v. 2 and תוֹלָלֵינוּ in v. 3 (Allen, *Psalms 101–150*, 236).

78. Bob Becking, "Does Exile Equal Suffering: A Fresh Look at Psalm 137," in *Exile and Suffering: A Selection of Papers Read at the 50th Anniversary Meeting of the Old Testament Society of South Africa OTWSA/OTSSA, Pretoria August 2007* (ed. Bob Becking and Dirk Human; OTS 50; Leiden: Brill, 2009), 197.

79. Ibid., 198.

The object of scrutiny in Ps 137 is not Israel nor her history, but empires and their malevolence.

Traditionally, the scene and events depicted in verses 1–3 have led some to suggest that Babylon may have been not only the locus of the action, but in fact the provenance of the psalm itself.[80] More recently, however, a growing number of interpreters have argued that the psalm was likely written as a retrospective, reflecting upon an event in exile, yet done so at some distance, both chronologically and physically, from the original event.[81] Among the evidence marshaled to support such a claim, three points dominate most discussions related to the issue.

The use of שָׁם in verses 1 and 3 suggests that the psalmist is no longer in Babylon, preferring instead to speak of it as "there."

> By the waters of Babylon,
>   there (שָׁם) we sat and we wept
>   when we remembered Zion.
> Upon the poplars in her midst,
>   we hung up our lyres.
> For there (שָׁם), our captors

---

80. Seybold, *Die Psalmen*, 509–10. Seybold considers the psalm likely to be "early exilic," perhaps as early as the initial deportation in 598 B.C.E., and absolutely no later than 539 B.C.E. Rainer Albertz suggests a date more likely subsequent to the rise of Cyrus (*Israel in Exile: The History and Literature of the Sixth Century* B.C.E. [trans. David Green; Atlanta: Society of Biblical Literature, 2003], 159). Kraus states matter-of-factly that "Psalm 137 is the only psalm in the Psalter that can be dated reliably" (*Psalms 60–150*, 501). Based upon his translation of v. 8a, Kraus suggests that Babylon was still in power when the psalm was written. Briggs and Briggs opted for a Babylonian setting, claiming that the psalm could not have been written very long after the destruction of Jerusalem (*A Critical and Exegetical Commentary on the Psalms*, 2:485). For a more recent defense of an exilic provenance, see John J. Ahn, *Exile as Forced Migrations: A Sociological, Literary, and Theological Approach of the Displacement and Resettlement of the Southern Kingdom of Judah* (BZAW 417; Berlin: de Gruyter, 2011), 73–80. Based on his analysis of the three displacements (597, 587, 582 B.C.E.), Ahn argues for a date somewhere between the second and third displacement, but with the origin of the psalm in Babylon.

81. Hossfeld and Zenger, *Psalms 3*, 513–14; Goldingay, *Psalms 90–150*, 600–601; Goulder, *Psalms of the Return*, 224–25; Dahood, *Psalms 101–150*, 269. See also Birgit Hartberger's assessment of the various proposals related to dating (*"An den Wassern von Babylon ... ": Psalm 137 auf dem Hintergrund von Jeremia 51, der biblischen Edomtraditionen, und babylonischer Originalquellen* [BBB 63; Frankfurt am Main: Hanstein, 1986], 4–7).

> asked us for words of a song,
> and our tormentors, in joy,
> "Sing to us one of the Songs of Zion." (137:1–3)

The repeated use of the adverb (שָׁם) coupled with the *qatal* verb forms in the opening strophe reinforces the claim that the poet spoke of an event presumably from another time.

Second, Goulder and Gerstenberger argue that the three-fold use of the shortened form of the relative pronoun (-שׁ) may also indicate a late date.[82] While such usage does occur in some earlier texts affiliated with the North, this form of the relative pronoun appears with great regularity after the exile (e.g., two hundred times in the Song; sixty-eight times in Qoh). In the Psalter itself, this form of the relative pronoun appears ten times in the Psalms of Ascents and nine times in various psalms from 135–150. Strikingly, however, the term is altogether absent from earlier portions of the Psalter, including Pss 107–119.

A third point to support a Jerusalem provenance is possible, contingent upon the translation of הַשְּׁדוּדָה in verse 8. The verse opens with an address to "daughter Babylon" (בַּת־בָּבֶל), followed by הַשְּׁדוּדָה in apposition. Although the word is pointed as a passive participle in the MT, Kraus, Allen, and Seybold, among others, follow σ´ by rendering the term as an active participle, "the devastator."[83] Other scholars, however, have recognized the MT as the *lectio difficilior* and opted instead to retain the passive construction.[84] The passive construction could be rendered, "the one devastated," implying that Babylon has already fallen, or it could be rendered passively but implying a future devastation of Babylon, "O Daughter Babylon, you who are condemned to devastation." The subsequent "beatitudes" in verses 8a–9 suggest that the psalmist longs for future action that will utterly and finally devastate the city of Babylon making retribution complete. Although the Achaemenid dynasty under Cyrus had defeated the

---

82. Goulder, *The Psalms of the Return*, 229; Gerstenberger, *Psalms, Part 2, and Lamentations*, 395.

83. Kraus, *Psalms 60–150*, 501n8e; Allen, *Psalms 101–150*, 251n8b; Seybold, *Die Psalmen*, 509n8a; Becking, "Does Exile Equal Suffering," 193.

84. David N. Freedman, "The Structure of Psalm 137," in *Near Eastern Studies in Honor of W. F. Albright* (ed. Hans Goedicke; Baltimore: Johns Hopkins University Press, 1971), 202–3; Ulrich Kellerman, "Psalm 137," *ZAW* 90 (1978), 45–46; Norbert Rabe, "'Tochter Babel, die verwüstete!' (Psalm 137,8)—textkritisch betrachtet," *BN* 78 (1995), 84; Goldingay, *Psalms 90–150*, 608–9.

Babylonians, the city of Babylon itself apparently suffered little under the hands of the new empire.[85] Based upon *lex talionis*, the psalmist desired to see the city of Babylon devastated even as Jerusalem had been (137:8). Even further, the psalmist wanted any possibility of its restoration to power through one of its own eradicated (137:9). By declaring Babylon to be the one condemned to devastation, the psalmist asserts that empires, even empires like Babylon, cannot escape the judgment that is to be theirs.

If the psalm is postexilic, as suggested, then the psalm was likely written from Jerusalem, with Yehud under the thumb of another empire internationally, and more locally, in tension with her political neighbors.[86] As suggested in Pss 108 and 136 above, the mention of nations, or Babylon in this case, functions on two levels. The mention of Babylon recalls a specific empire within Israel's past, but as a postexilic text, Babylon comes to represent the threats currently experienced.[87] As Goldingay has noted, "the imperial authority that controls and oppresses [Yehud] after the exile could be thought of as Babylon," and indeed was in other postexilic texts (e.g., Ezra 5:13; Neh 13:6).[88]

The power of an imperial empire comes to the fore in Ps 137, reinforcing the image thus far in book 5 that empires fail to create an ordered world where its people joyously participate. Instead, the psalmist claims

---

85. According to the Nabonidus Chronicle (15–16, 18–19), "On the sixteenth day of Ug, Gubaru, governor of Gutium, and the army of Cyrus without battle entered Babylon ... Cyrus entered Babylon. They filled the *haru*-vessels in his presence. Peace was imposed on the city" (Amélie Kuhrt, *The Persian Empire: A Corpus of Sources from the Achaemenid Period* [London: Routledge, 2007], 51)

86. Kellermann posits a date some time between 520 and 445 B.C.E. for the psalm, suggesting similarities with Haggai, Zechariah, and Trito-Isaiah. Further, he terms this period in Yehud as a *Zeit der Resignation*—a time that would have led to laments, curses, and prayers of vengeance ("Psalm 137," 51–52).

87. Leuenberger suggests that Ps 137 functions as an "orphan psalm," connecting Ps 136 with the final collection (Pss 138–145). The emphasis on the "international setting" in Ps 137 provides a link to one of the major themes in the last David Psalter, the *Feind-Frevler-Bedrohungsklage*. The mention of Babylon and Edom shifts the collection in part to the "national and largely historical opposition between Israel and the nations" (*Konzeptionen des Königtums Gottes im Psalter*, 341–42).

88. Goldingay, *Psalms 90–150*, 601. Howard Wallace argues similarly, suggesting that the psalm "anticipates the question of continued foreign domination after return from exile" (*Psalms* [Readings: A New Biblical Commentary; Sheffield: Sheffield Phoenix, 2009], 187). See also Hossfeld and Zenger, *Psalms 3*, 519.

that under such an empire, the people are left to sit down and weep (137:1) while longing for the active intervention of Yahweh into their history.[89]

4.3. Psalms within the Final Davidic Collection

Psalm 138 opens the fifth Davidic collection in the Psalter (138–145) and the final collection in book 5, and likely serves as a response to the crisis articulated in Ps 137.[90] The fifth Davidic collection, as a whole, portrays the psalmist in considerable need. In Ps 139, the psalmist bemoans the threat of the wicked (רָשָׁע) and seeks deliverance from the "men of blood" (139:19). Similarly, the psalmist pleads three times in Ps 140 for deliverance from the "violent men."[91] In Ps 141, the psalmist struggles to survive against the "evildoers" (פֹּעֲלֵי אָוֶן) and the wicked (רְשָׁעִים). The psalmist seeks deliverance from his persecutors (רֹדְפַי) and yearns to be brought out of prison in Ps 142. Throughout Ps 143, the enemy (אוֹיֵב) threatens the psalmist, leading the psalmist to pray

> And in your חֶסֶד, cut off my enemies,
>> and destroy all the foes (צֹרְרֵי) of my life,
> for I am your servant. (143:12)

In short, nearly all of the psalms in this collection reflect "prayers for deliverance from distress."[92] In Pss 138 and 144, however, the psalmists refer

---

89. See Kellerman's suggestion regarding the possible features of a noncultic lament in vv. 1–4 ("Psalm 137," 53–57). Similar scenes of sitting and weeping appear in Isa 47:1, Ezek 26:16, and Job 2:8.

90. Ballhorn, *Zum Telos des Psalters*, 267; Christoph Buysch, *Der letzte Davidpsalter: Interpretation, Komposition und Funktion der Psalmengruppe Ps 138–145* (SBB 63; Stuttgart: Katholisches Bibelwerk, 2009), 70–71.

91. In Ps 140:2a, the poet refers to "evil men," אָדָם רָע, which stand in parallel relationship with "violent men," אִישׁ חָמָס, in 140:2b. The latter phrase appears subsequently in the psalm (140:5, 12).

92. Gerald Wilson, *The Editing of the Hebrew Psalter* [SBLDS 76; Chico, Calif.: Scholars Press, 1985], 222. For proposals on the place and function of the fifth Davidic collection in the Psalter, see especially Buysch, *Der letzte Davidpsalter*, 15–19, 324–27. See also Harm van Grol, "David and his *Chasidim*: Place and Function of Psalms 138–145," in *The Composition of the Book of Psalms* (ed. Erich Zenger; BETL 238; Leuven: Peeters, 2010), 309–37. Van Grol challenges the approaches to the collection espoused by both Ballhorn (*Zum Telos des Psalters*, 264–98) and Leuenberger (*Konzeptionen des Königtums Gottes im Psalter*, 320–67).

explicitly to foreign powers. Both psalms, in decidedly different ways, reconfigure the role of imperial power within the world, dismantling the image constructed by the dominant imperial ideology.

4.3.1. Psalm 138

The image of empire in Ps 137 deconstructed many of the claims associated with a Persian imperial ideology, as suggested above. Ps 138 proves illuminating in that it further unseats the claims of such an ideology. In Ps 137, the empire, via its representatives, calls for the people of God to sing songs. But as noted above, the capacity for joyous participation is altogether absent. Such songs cannot be sung in a foreign land. In Ps 138, however, the psalmist musters the capacity to sing praises to God, confessing his faith "with all of [his] heart" (138:1a) despite the presence of gods (138:1b) and kings (138:4a). The reference to kings praising Yahweh in 138:4 might suggest that the image of kings and empires has been rehabilitated by the psalmist, but closer investigation suggests otherwise. Similar to the mention of nations in Ps 117, the mention of kings and their activity in Ps 138 actually continues to undermine the dominant imperial ideology.

Some have categorized Ps 138 as a thanksgiving psalm, but as Buysch suggests, the classical form of a thanksgiving psalm is only partially fulfilled here. "Neither a hint of a thanksgiving offering … nor a separate report of need, crying out, and deliverance is found in the psalm."[93] He contends that while the thrice-repeated verb יָדָה in Ps 138 can mean "to give thanks," the notion of acknowledgement or confession is fundamental to its meaning.[94] Consequently, for Buysch, the recognition and confession of God appears to stand in the foreground of the psalm.[95]

The claim in verse 1b illustrates the psalmist's desire to confess something about Yahweh. In that colon, the psalmist vows to sing praises (זמר) to Yahweh "before the gods." Similar to Pss 86:8 and 96:4, the referent for

---

[93]. Buysch, *Der letzte Davidpsalter*, 24. Goldingay opts to label the psalm a "psalm of testimony" (*Psalms 90–150*, 616).

[94]. Ibid., 25. See also Claus Westermann, "יָדָה," *TLOT* 1:674–82. Westermann notes that "the concept that binds the two meanings could be rendered 'to acknowledge' or 'to confess'; we could speak of a 'confession of praise.'" See also, Leslie C. Allen, "יָדָה," in *NIDOTTE*, 2:405–8.

[95]. Buysch, *Der letzte Davidpsalter*, 25.

אֱלֹהִים in Ps 138 is clearly the gods of the nations.[96] Hossfeld and Zenger argue that such a statement likely reflects "the reality of a Diaspora situation" of the psalmist.[97] They envision a context in which the psalmist is surrounded figuratively by the gods of other nations. The subsequent clause in verse 2a, "I will bow towards your holy temple," lends credence to Hossfeld and Zenger's claim that the provenance of the psalm may have been on foreign soil. Similar acts of bowing towards the temple appear elsewhere in the Hebrew Bible (1 Kgs 8:48; Dan 6:11; Tob 3:11–12; Jonah 2:5, 8). Regardless of whether the psalmist was in a Diaspora situation or in Yehud, but under the rule of a foreign empire, the mention of "gods" in verse 1b and the need to bow down "towards the temple" in verse 2a suggests that the psalmist perceived himself to be in a position that engendered a sense of distress (צָרָה).

The reference to the אֱלֹהִים in Ps 138 appears at first glance to differ markedly in tone from the rhetoric found in Deutero-Isaiah. In that collection, the idols are mocked relentlessly as vacuous creations of human hands (e.g., Isa 41:29; 44:9–20; 46:1–7). In Ps 138, however, the psalmist speaks not of idols, but of אֱלֹהִים, "gods." While Deutero-Isaiah mocked the idols, the psalmist, with the use of the phrase נֶגֶד אֱלֹהִים, promises to sing the praises of Yahweh "in defiance [of the gods.]"[98] Rather than mocking the ineffectiveness of idols or gods, the psalmist opts to testify about Yahweh's חֶסֶד and אֱמֶת before them, in effect establishing Yahweh's supremacy over any other presumed deity. In making such a claim, the psalmist also posits a political claim. Because gods and nations were so closely associated in the ancient Near East, the psalmist's defiant claim of Yahweh's faithfulness "in the face" of the gods also implies a certain rejection of the claims of supremacy by the nations associated with such gods.[99]

---

96. As Goulder suggests, the use of אֱלֹהִים in Ps 82:1 does not resemble its usage in this context. In Ps 82, the אֱלֹהִים are clearly inferior figures while in Ps 138, the defiant tone of the psalmist suggests that the אֱלֹהִים represent some form of challenge (*The Psalms of the Return*, 231).

97. Hossfeld and Zenger, *Psalms 3*, 528. Kraus interprets the phrase in v. 2a altogether differently, suggesting instead that the psalmist was in the temple precinct and bowing towards the temple (*Psalms 60–150*, 507).

98. Goulder, *The Psalms of the Return*, 231. Similarly, J. Clinton McCann Jr. suggests that the phrase creates a polemical tone ("Psalms," *NIB* 4:1232).

99. McCann, "Psalms," 4:1232.

The political imagery of Ps 138 becomes more overt in verse 4. There the psalmist announces

> All the kings of the earth shall testify about you, O Yahweh,
>   when they have heard the words of your mouth.
> They shall sing of the ways of Yahweh,
>   for great is the glory of Yahweh.

In verse 4, the kings of the earth confess (יָדָה) Yahweh and sing (שִׁיר) of his ways. The kings of the earth will join the people of God in their praise, participating joyously in the ways of God. Royal imperial ideology, as suggested above (§2), posited the claim that the Persian Empire was a worldwide empire in which nations participated joyously because under Achaemenid rule the world was well-ordered. The vision set forth in Ps 138 however reverses such imagery. According to the psalmist, the empires of the world will participate joyously in the praise and confession of Yahweh and shall celebrate the intended order of the world as outlined in the "ways of the Yahweh." The kings of the earth will apparently know of the ways of Yahweh when they "have heard the words of your mouth (אִמְרֵי־פִיךָ)."[100] Buysch has noted that פִּי occurs seven times in the Psalter. Of these seven occurrences, the term makes reference to God in three of those texts (119:13, 72, 88). In each of the three instances from Ps 119, פִּי stands in a construct relationship with terms such as תּוֹרָה, מִשְׁפָּט, and

---

100. Because the verb in v. 4b (שָׁמְעוּ) is perfect, Goulder assumes that the kings have in fact *already* heard the "words" of Yahweh. He explains that "the change from imperfect to perfect suggests that some cognizance of Yahweh has been taken by the Persian kings" (*The Return of the Psalter*, 233). He attempts to ground this claim in history by suggesting that the Persian kings would not have allowed Ezra and the others to "go up" to Jerusalem without some "cognizance" of Yahweh. Further, he opines, "Artaxerxes and his predecessors *have heard the words of thy mouth*, they have taken seriously the petitions based on the exilic prophecies; and in time it may be expected that, as in Isa 52 and 60, they will shut their mouths and come with tribute" to Zion (emphasis original). Goulder's claim, however, ultimately proves unconvincing. A far simpler rationale for the use of the perfect in 138:4b seems preferable. The second half of v. 4 provides the precondition for what is announced in the first half. The kings will not confess Yahweh *until* they have heard first the אִמְרֵי־פִיךָ. Allen captures the meaning well in his translation, "Let all the kings in the world give you thanks *in reaction to* hearing of the promises of your mouth" (*Psalms 101–150*, 243; emphasis added). Hossfeld and Zenger follow similarly (*Psalms 3*, 526).

עֵדָה, all three *termini technici* for the Torah.[101] Cosmic order, then, is not predicated upon the rule of Achaemenids, nor any other imperial ruler, but upon the אִמְרֵי־פִיךָ.

Psalm 138 both challenges and reconfigures imperial ideology. The psalmist not only challenges the gods of other nations through his testimony (138:1b), but he also reconfigures the role held by the kings of the world. Rather than creating an empire in which all nations will joyously participate, the kings of the world will joyously participate in the worship of the God of Israel. As Ballhorn explains, "Israel gives the sound and the kings of the nations bring freely the tribute of praise to God (138:4)."[102] The kings of the world no longer maintain a dominant grasp upon the world, but instead testify to the God of Israel.

4.3.2. Psalm 144

Throughout the final collection in book 5 (Pss 138–145) the themes of persecution, violence, and destruction appear repeatedly with Ps 144 highlighting the dire circumstances of the psalmist. As Ballhorn has observed, the first part of the psalm strikes a "warring tone," and the language in verse 1 appears confirmed in verse 14 with its implication that there is crying in the streets due to the present threat.[103] The psalmist explains that the threat is מִיַּד בְּנֵי־נֵכָר literally, "from the hand of the sons of the foreigner." The word נֵכָר occurs with great regularity in the Hebrew Bible, most often functioning adjectivally with אֱלֹהִים ("foreign gods"). The phrase that appears in Ps 144:7 and 11 (בְּנֵי־נֵכָר) occurs only eighteen times in the Hebrew Bible, with the highest concentration appearing in Isa 56–66, frequently with overt political connotations.[104] For example, in Isa 60:10, the text reads

> Foreigners (בְּנֵי־נֵכָר) shall build up your walls,
>   and their kings (מַלְכֵיהֶם) shall minister to you.

---

101. Buysch, *Der letzte Davidpsalter*, 32. Hossfeld and Zenger suggest that the image of the kings singing of the "ways" of Yahweh "presumes in the petitioner a conviction about the universal quality of the Torah" (*Psalms 3*, 530).

102. Ballhorn, *Zum Telos des Psalters*, 267.

103. Ibid., 280.

104. See also Gen 17:12; 17:27; Ex 12:43; Lev 22:25; 2 Sam 22:45, 46; Isa 56:3, 6; 60:10; 61:5; 62:8; Ezek 44:7, 9; Ps 18:45, 46; Neh 9:2.

The pairing of בְּנֵי־נֵכָר with מַלְכֵיהֶם reinforces the political overtones present in the Isaiah text and are suggestive for understanding the meaning of בְּנֵי־נֵכָר within Ps 144.[105]

The phrase מִיַּד בְּנֵי־נֵכָר also recalls the opening psalm of book 5. In 107:2, the psalmist praises Yahweh for having redeemed the people מִיַּד־צָר. As suggested above (§3), the phrase "the hand of צָר" typically refers to historical-political enemies, a meaning which appears consistent within the context of Ps 107. In Ps 144, מִיַּד בְּנֵי־נֵכָר appears twice, and like the similar phrase in Ps 107, implies a hostile, political threat.

The parallel construction in verse 7 further defines the nature of the threat. The phrase מִיַּד בְּנֵי־נֵכָר stands parallel to the phrase מִמַּיִם רַבִּים, "from the many waters," with מִמַּיִם רַבִּים appearing first in the parallelism. The direct allusion to foreign powers, then, is filtered through the first image of the "many waters." Similar to the imagery in Ps 124, the psalmist employs the metaphor of "many waters" in an effort to recast the present threat in cosmological terms. As J. J. M. Roberts has suggested, such cosmological themes are fundamental to Israel's construction of the identity of Yahweh. These cosmological themes articulate Yahweh's imperial rule over the world, while concomitantly, generating an anti-imperial theology with reference to the power of the nations that populate the world. Roberts writes, "It is these primeval, cosmogonic victories of Yahweh that the psalmist cites, not the exodus or the conquest of Canaan, as a motivation to stir Yahweh to act against the historical enemies that now threaten the people of God."[106] The cosmological language employed in reference to the בְּנֵי־נֵכָר only confirms the more specific language of threat articulated in verses 7 and 11. It is this threat, the threat of foreign powers, that must be thwarted.

In an effort to fashion a challenge to the foreign powers, the psalmist adapts the language of Ps 18 and 2 Sam 22. Virtually all commen-

---

105. Further evidence of the political connotations of בְּנֵי־נֵכָר can be found in Isa 61:5

Strangers (זָרִים) shall stand and feed your flock,

foreigners (בְּנֵי־נֵכָר) shall till your land and dress your vines (NRSV).

The Hebrew word זָרִים (parallel to בְּנֵי־נֵכָר) is translated as "strangers" in 61:5a, but in the use of the term elsewhere, the meaning is more explicit, suggesting foreigners who are also enemies.

106. J. J. M. Roberts, "God's Imperial Reign According to the Psalter," *HBT* 23 (2001), 217.

tators have noted the anthological style found in Ps 144, but as Ballhorn has suggested, the use of Ps 18 is an "act of receptive contextuality (*Kontextualität*)."[107] The question, however, that remains is how does Ps 144 appear as an act of "receptive contextuality" and perhaps more significantly, to what end?

The use of Ps 18 in Ps 144, however, differs markedly from the manner in which the psalmist in Ps 108 made use of Pss 57 and 60. Psalm 108 results from the wholesale reuse of major portions of the two earlier psalms, with virtually no adaptation or variation. In Ps 144, however, the use of the earlier psalm is much more subtle with considerable variation and adaptation. The citations of the earlier psalm appear throughout Ps 144. For example, 144:1a, "Blessed be Yahweh, my rock," is drawn from 18:3 and also 18:47. The phrase "who trains my hands for war" in Ps 144:1b is drawn from 18:35 and much of the language in 144:2 compares to that found in 18:3. The theophanic language found in Ps 144:5–6 is found in 18:10a and 18:15. The imagery of being drawn up from the "many waters" found in Ps 144:7 finds its parallel in 18:17 and perhaps 18:18a. Even the phrase בְּנֵי־נֵכָר, mentioned in Ps 144:7 and 11 appears near the end of Ps 18 in verses 45–46. And as will be discussed below, the mention of kings and David in Ps 144:10 appears in 18:51.

While the parallels in language prove instructive regarding the sources of Ps 144, it is the variations that prove most illuminating. Michael Goulder has noted variations that relate directly to the thesis at hand.[108] He observes, as do most commentators, that the indicative statements found in Ps 18 have become imperatives in Ps 144. In Ps 18, the king gives thanks for having been "delivered from the strong enemy" (18:18), yet in Ps 144, the psalmist pleads for Yahweh to "rescue me and deliver me" (144:7, 11). In Ps 18:10, the psalmist recounts how Yahweh "bowed the heavens and came down," but in 144:5, cries out, "Bow the heavens, O Yahweh, and come down." Yahweh is praised for having stretched forth his hand to deliver the psalmist from the many waters in Ps 18:17 while the psalmist craves for such action in 144:7. The song of thanksgiving has been transformed. In Ps 18, the threat has been resolved; in Ps 144, the threat lingers.

---

107. Ballhorn, *Zum Telos des Psalters*, 279.
108. Goulder, *The Psalms of the Return*, 274–75.

Secondly, the highest concentration of parallels between the two psalms is drawn from 18:1–18, with additional parallels found in 18:45–46 (בְּנֵי־נֵכָר) and 18:51 (the mention of David and the king). Noticeably absent in Ps 144, however, is any reference to the militaristic tone found in Ps 18:33–49. The only exception can be found in Ps 18:35, "he trains my hands for war." Following this phrase in Ps 18, the psalmist exclaims,

> I pursued my enemies and overtook them;
>   and did not turn back until they were consumed.
> I struck them down, so that they were not able to rise;
>   they fell under my feet.
> For you girded me with strength for the battle;
>   you made my assailants sink under me.
> You made my enemies turn their backs to me,
>   and those who hated me I destroyed....
> I beat them fine, like dust before the wind;
>   I cast them out like the mire of the streets. (18:37–40, 42 NRSV)

Given the psalmist's appropriation of Ps 18 and the psalmist's penchant in Ps 144 to shift verbs from the indicative to the imperative, one might expect the psalmist to plead for Yahweh to cause him to strike down the בְּנֵי־נֵכָר so that they are not able to rise again, to cause them to fall under the feet of the psalmist, or better yet, the psalmist might plead for Yahweh to "beat them fine, like dust in the wind." But such language from Ps 18 is lacking in Ps 144. Although the psalmist prays in Ps 144:1 that his hands be trained for battle, there is no mention of the psalmist potentially engaging in battle. Deliverance from the foreign power comes from the outstretched hand of Yahweh (144:7), a theme that appears repeatedly in book 5.

The identity of the kings in Ps 144:10 is significant for the present study. The verse nearly repeats that found in Ps 18:51. The psalmist concludes Ps 18 stating,

> Great victories he gives to his king (מַלְכּוֹ)
>   and shows steadfast love to his anointed (לִמְשִׁיחוֹ)
>   to David and his offspring forever.

In Psalm 144:10, the psalmist declares of God,

> the one who gives victory to kings (מְלָכִים),
>   the one who rescues David his servant (עַבְדּוֹ).

Hossfeld and Zenger, as well as Buysch, argue that with the use מְלָכִים in Ps 144:10a, the psalmist claims that Yahweh provides victory to all the kings of the world.[109] According to Hossfeld and Zenger, the psalmist refers to the kings of the nations in verse 10a while verse 10b refers to David and the Davidic dynasty. In support of such a claim, scholars have suggested that the plural form of מֶלֶךְ appears frequently in the Psalter (e.g., 2:10; 72:10; 102:23; 138:4) and in such contexts, the word refers to the kings of earth, necessitating a similar rendering in Ps 144.[110] Those following this line of reasoning also point to Ps 138:4 ("all kings of the earth will praise you") and contend that just as the kings turned to Yahweh in Ps 138, so also is Yahweh turning to the kings of the earth in Ps 144, guaranteeing victory to them. The context of Ps 144 itself and its intertextual relationship with Ps 18, however, suggests a different, albeit, more straightforward interpretation. As noted above, Ps 144:10 draws from Ps 18:51. In Ps 18, the psalmist places David in parallel with "his [Yahweh's] king." The poet makes a similar move in Ps 144. The psalmist maintains the same parallelism found in Ps 18 despite a slight change in verbiage. According to Kraus, the psalmist declares that Yahweh "bestows on the 'kings'—and that means the kings of David's lineage—תְּשׁוּעָה."[111] Although Hossfeld and Zenger and Buysch are correct that מְלָכִים in Ps 138:4 does in fact refer to the kings of the nations, the use of that term in Ps 138 and its meaning there provides little justification for the decoupling of the parallelism evident in Ps 144, a parallelism initially established in Ps 18. In addition, Ps 144 depicts a crisis at the hands of the בְּנֵי־נֵכָר, a crisis that necessitates the "bending of the heavens" and the direct intervention of Yahweh. The two figures used in Ps 144:10, David and the kings of David's lineage, serve as a reminder of Yahweh's faithful intervention on behalf of his people in the past. Yahweh's faithfulness in the past provides the rationale for the psalmist that a שִׁיר חָדָשׁ, "a new song," can be sung in the face of the בְּנֵי־נֵכָר.

The precise function of verses 12–15 within Ps 144, including whether it was an original part of the psalm, has received considerable attention.

---

109. Hossfeld and Zenger, *Psalms 3*, 586; Buysch, *Der letzte Davidspsalter*, 291–92.

110. See Christoph Rösel, *Die messianische Redaktion des Psalters: Studien zu Entstehung und Theologie der Sammlung Psalm 2–89* (Calwer theologische Monographien Bibelwissenschaft 19; Stuttgart: Calwer, 1999), 188–89.

111. Kraus, *Psalm 60–150*, 543; see also Leuenberger, *Konzeptionen des Königtums Gottes im Psalter*, 331; Allen, *Psalms 101–150*, 289–90.

As suggested above, the traditions from Ps 18 were in fact employed, but in a way that appears to emphasize the threat of foreign power while also reinforcing the communities utter reliance upon Yahweh for deliverance from such foes. Although appropriation of previous traditions does not occur with the same regularity in verses 12–15, the function of the final verses nevertheless appears consistent with verses 1–11, that of challenging foreign kings.

Jon Berquist, in his work on imperialization, has suggested that central to the formation, administration, and continuation of an empire is its ability to extract resources. He argues,

> Functionalist sociological discourse defines an empire as a large-scale social unit that extracts resources (including labor) from other social units, the colonies.… An empire is not a static social unit or a category that a social unit attains once it reaches a certain size and power as compared to its neighbors, or once its military defeats another empire. In this sense, it is more correct (or at least more advantageous) to discuss the process of imperialization than the social unit of the empire, since the empire exists only insofar as it continues to extract resources.[112]

Berquist suggests there are "multiple modes of extraction," but included among such resources would be food, products, and human capital. In addition, empires may extract resources through taxation, "leading to a decreasing colonial ability to survive."[113]

The scarcity of resources and the threat of survival due to mistreatment at the hands of the בְּנֵי־נֵכָר likely stands behind the imagery present in verses 12–14. Markus Saur has suggested the final section in Ps 144 "was designed from the beginning as a wish … for material welfare."[114] The psalmist longs for sons and daughters to grow to full stature, like full-grown plants and beautiful corner pillars on a palace. Likewise, the psalmist wishes that the storehouses, now empty, would provide for the people food "from all kinds," and that the sheep and cattle would be prolific in their reproduction. And finally, in verse 14c, that there would be "no cry of distress in our streets." The word צְוָחָה, "cry of distress," occurs elsewhere

---

112. Jon L. Berquist, "Postcolonialism and Imperial Motives for Canonization," *Semeia* 75 (1996), 16–17.

113. Ibid., 17.

114. Markus Saur, *Die Königspsalmen. Studien zur Entstehung und Theologie* (BZAW 340; Berlin: de Gruyter, 2004), 254

only in Isa 24:11, Jer 14:2, and 46:12. In all three instances the meaning is connected to community destruction and situations of depravity.[115]

Kraus, Weiser, Eaton, and more recently, Shalom Holtz have suggested that these final verses are those articulated by a king, given the king's responsibility to provide for the nation, as seen most clearly in Ps 72.[116] In Ps 72, however, nearly half of the psalm focuses on the establishment of the human king's reign over the nations and the obeisance due him from all peoples and nations. The political dimensions so clearly observed in Ps 72 are altogether absent in the final verses of Ps 144, and are instead replaced with a focus on what Ballhorn terms *häusliches Glück*, "domestic bliss."[117] However much these verses may resemble a royal ideology, as has been argued, the emphasis is not on the execution of royal power or even royal prerogative, but instead appears to be upon the reversal of oppression at the hands of foreigners. The descriptively pictorial language in these verses situates the psalmist and his community within the throes of imperial might, recognizing full well the disastrous results of power apparently unchecked. Yet the anticipation of such a reality reversed suggests that in the ideology of the psalmist, political power does in fact remain in check by the one who rescued David from the evil sword.

In summary, the psalmist in Ps 144 appears to have appropriated royal language and imagery from earlier psalmic material in an effort to address the politics of power. Although the language associated with kingship and power in ancient Israel has been employed against the power of the בְּנֵי־נֵכָר, the psalmist is fully cognizant that he and his community cannot challenge empires in the manner rehearsed in Ps 18. Instead, the psalmist must call upon the power of the one who will bow the heavens, deliver the community from the cruel sword, and in the end, overturn the work of imperial power gone awry. The Persian image of a beneficent empire in which the nations joyously participate, and together, enjoy cosmic harmony is foreign to the psalmist in Ps 144. Instead, the בְּנֵי־נֵכָר produce

---

115. Ballhorn, *Zum Telos des Psalters*, 283; Christoph Buysch, *Der letzte Davidpsalter*, 295–96.

116. Shalom E. Holtz, "The Thematic Unity of Psalm cxliv in Light of Mesopotamian Royal Ideology," VT 58 (2008): 367–80.

117. Ballhorn, *Zum Telos des Psalters*, 283. Gerstenberger refers to the five categories mentioned as important to the family life in the ancient Near East (*Psalms, Part 2, and Lamentations*, 430–31).

lamentation in the streets (144:14) and breaches in the wall, leaving the community to yearn for a day of reversal brought about by Yahweh.

4.4. Conclusion

Similar to the psalms explored earlier (§3), these psalms repeatedly undermine the dominant imperial ideology with their consistently negative portrayal of empires and foreign powers. These psalms appears to reflect a world shaped by "social and political antagonism," resulting in at least three images of empire that dominate these psalms.[118]

First, various psalms depict empires and foreign powers as tormentors and captors who threatened Israel's existence. In reference to nations that rose up against Israel in the past, the psalmist resorts to mythopoeic language in an effort to capture the nature of the threat. The psalmist writes that had not Yahweh been on their side

> then they would have swallowed us alive,
>   when their anger raged against us;
> then the waters would have overpowered us;
>   the torrent would have passed over us;
> then the raging waters would have passed over us. (124:3–5)

The depiction of the nations as chaotic waters threatening to swallow Israel alive shifts the account from mere historical recital. The enemy nations assume a cosmological quality, intensifying the threat posed by them.

A more graphic depiction of the threat levied by foreign powers appears in Ps 129. In that psalm, the foreign powers are said to be like "plowers," plowing long furrows upon the backs of their captors (129:3). As suggested above, the agricultural image invokes claims associated with political captivity, forced labor, and slavery. Such images lead Israel to confess as a nation, "they have afflicted me from my youth," implying an enduring image of empire, one rooted in Israel's repeated attempts to thwart the advances of powerful empires (129:1, 2). The taunting of the Babylonian captives in Ps 137, while less vivid in depiction, reinforces the image of affliction that can be levied by empires.

Second, several psalms depict empires and kings in general as obstacles which prevent Israel from enjoying the land as her נַחֲלָה. In Pss 135:12

---

118. Hossfeld and Zenger, *Psalms 3*, 298.

and 136:21–22, the psalmists explain that the land was given to Israel as a נַחֲלָה ("heritage"). Yet, in both psalms, the psalmist is clear: empires and foreign kings had to be overcome if Israel was to enjoy her נַחֲלָה. But even within the land, the threat of a "scepter of wickedness" resting upon the land (125:3) suggests that the continued threat associated with empires may inhibit Israel's capacity to enjoy her נַחֲלָה.

A third image, closely relate to the second, is the depiction of empires as foreign powers that "stunt" Israel's capacity to flourish. In Ps 144, the psalmist prays

> May our sons in their youth
>   be like plants full grown,
> our daughters like corner pillars
>   cut for the structure of a palace.
> May our garners be full,
>   providing food of all kinds ...
> May there be no cry of distress in our streets. (144:12–13a, 14c)

The need for such a prayer stems from the presence of the בְּנֵי־נֵכָר who threaten Israel. Whether Israel perceives itself as a "bird in a cage" (124:6–7), a people tempted to do iniquity (עַוְלָה) by the influence of the "scepter of wickedness" (125:3), or a nation filled with "cries of distress" (144:14c), Israel understands that the presence of empires and foreign powers inhibits her capacity to flourish as the people of God.

The Persian imperial ideology provided a consistent message regarding the beneficial qualities of empire: all nations should participate joyfully in the Achaemenid empire because under that empire, the cosmos will enjoy order and the nations will prosper. As suggested above (§2), the Persian imperial ideology remained essentially static throughout the Achaemenid period with little change in its ideological claims. Over the course of two centuries the propagation of such a strong and consistent message likely would have seeped into the vast reaches of the empire, perhaps even shaping the subject nations's view of empire. The language and images crafted in the Psalter, however, provide a subtle, yet important, challenge to the imperial claims associated with Persia. For the psalmist, there is no joyous participation in empire by Israel, both in her past, and presumably, in her present. Rather, the psalmist asserts that empires continually wreak havoc upon Israel, stripping her of the prosperity she is meant to enjoy.

By portraying empires in such a negative light, the psalmists effectively discount allegiance to empire as a means of securing identity moving forward. Israel's identity instead is conceived in ways that are altogether different, as will be suggested in the subsequent chapters.

5
Reconstructing Power:
Images of Yahweh in Book 5

5.0. Introduction

As suggested in the previous two chapters, the psalms in book 5 consistently and repeatedly cast the nations in a less than favorable light and certainly portray them in a way that is inconsistent with the imperial ideology promulgated by the Persians. Yet deconstructing and challenging the image of the nations and their presumed power is not the chief end for these psalms. In addition to discounting the power of the nations and their capacity to secure cosmic order and joyous participation by all people, the psalmists sought to reconstruct the identity of those in Yehud. Central to constructing their own identity was a reaffirmation of Yahweh and Yahweh's capacity to deliver his people. Although Persian ideology venerated Ahuramazda as the supreme deity responsible for all of creation, including the present Achaemenid dynasty, the psalmists countered by reasserting their belief in Yahweh as the divine King capable of delivering his people. Despite the unchecked reign of the Persians, the psalmists refused to give up their claim on the absolute power of Yahweh. The social, historical, and political dynamics, however, necessitated subtle shifts in their theological confession concerning God's presence in the world and the role of Zion.

Prior to evaluating the theological claims made about Yahweh in book 5, a cursory review of the chief tenets of Zion theology, and particularly those relevant for the present study, is necessary. These ideas and their subsequent iterations in book 5 prove formative in understanding Israel's claim concerning the power of Yahweh.

5.1. The Chief Tenets of Zion Theology and the Notion of Power

In his unpublished Heidelberg doctoral dissertation under the supervision of Gerhard von Rad, Edzard Rohland identified and explicated the general contours of the Zion tradition in the Hebrew Bible.[1] Focusing chiefly upon Psalms 46, 48, and 76, Rohland identified four motifs foundational to this tradition: (1) Zion as the peak of Zaphon, the highest mountain; (2) the presence of the paradisiacal river within the precinct of Zion; (3) Yahweh's routing of the chaos waters there; and (4) Yahweh's ultimate victory over the nations and their kings.[2] While subsequent scholarship has retained the primacy of these four motifs, scholars have, nevertheless, supplemented and expanded these motifs with additional themes identifiable in various biblical texts. Corinna Körting's assessment of Zion as a "magnet of theological concepts" is at once both true and understated.[3]

Beyond the four motifs identified by Rohland, J. J. M. Roberts, among others, has noted the explicit association of Zion with the kingdom of Yahweh, and relatedly, the choice of Zion as the dwelling place of the Divine King.[4] According to Roberts, because Zion was the dwelling place of the Most High, there are additional attributes of Zion that can be identified. Among those, two attributes relate directly to the argument at hand. The first is the inviolability of Zion amid the political machinations of the

---

1. Edzard Rohland, "Die Bedeutung der Erwählungstraditionen Israels für die Eschatologie der alttestamentliche Propheten" (DTheol diss., University of Heidelberg, 1956).

2. More recently, see the exhaustive study on Zion by Corinna Körting (*Zion in den Psalmen* [FAT 1/48; Tübingen: Mohr Siebeck, 2006]). On the influence of Rohland, see also Ben C. Ollenburger, *Zion the City of the Great King: A Theological Symbol of the Jerusalem Cult* (JSOTSup 41; Sheffield: JSOT Press, 1987), 13–22; Ronald E. Clements, *Isaiah and the Deliverance of Jerusalem: A Study in the Interpretation of Prophecy in the Old Testament* (JSOTSup 13; Sheffield: JSOT Press, 1980), 72–89. See also Odil Hannes Steck, *Friedensvorstellung im alten Jerusalem: Psalmen, Jesaja, Deuterojesaja* (Theologischen Studien 111; Zürich: Theologischer, 1972).

3. Körting, *Zion in den Psalmen*, 225–26.

4. J. J. M. Roberts, "Zion in the Theology of the Davidic-Solomonic Empire," in *Studies in the Period of David and Solomon and Other Essays: Papers Read at the International Symposium for Biblical Studies, Tokyo, 5–7 December, 1979* (ed. Tomoo Ishida; Winona Lake, Ind.: Eisenbrauns, 1982), 93–108. Körting contends that the two aspects identified by Roberts are crucial to understanding the Zion tradition and its varied nuances (*Zion in den Psalmen*, 227–28).

time (Ps 46:6–7; 48:5–7).[5] If Zion was indeed the dwelling place of the Most High God, then it seemed to follow logically that such a location was immune to the militaristic threats of neighboring peoples. Second, Zion represented the nearness of God. Because Zion was the high mountain that symbolically reached to the heavens, the psalmists could also claim the nearness of Yahweh in Zion while concomitantly referring to Yahweh's presence in the heavens.

The elasticity of the Zion tradition allowed psalmists to speak of Yahweh as intimately connected with Zion, even enthroned within the city, while also allowing psalmists to locate Yahweh in the heavens. In selected texts and at selected times, one spatial location frequently received greater attention than the other. Yet as Konrad Schmid has cautioned, one cannot assume a strictly linear development, as though Israel shifted the presence of Yahweh exclusively from Zion to heaven over the course of time.[6]

With the exile and the destruction of the temple, the fundamental claim of God's presence, or more precisely, God's nearness, was radically challenged, and the claim to the inviolability of Zion was eviscerated. These challenges produced a flurry of theological reflection. The responses offered necessitated an evaluation of previous traditions, consequently resulting in a renewed, albeit differentiated appropriation of those same traditions.[7]

---

5. On the inviolability of Zion, see Hans Joachim Kraus, *Theology of the Psalms* (Translated by Keith Crim; CC; Minneapolis: Fortress Press, 1992), 81–82. Kraus contends that the traditions of holy war and the rebuking of the chaotic waters form the backdrop to the motif of the "unconquerable city of God" (82). See also Roberts, "Zion in the Theology of the Davidic-Solomonic Empire," 102–4. Clements, however, has maintained that the inviolability of Zion is actually an outgrowth of the conflict motif present in the Davidic royal ideology, and only later became associated with the sacred mountain (*Isaiah and the Deliverance of Jerusalem*, 80–89).

6. See further Konrad Schmid, "Himmelsgott, Weltgott, und Schöpfer: 'Gott' und der 'Himmel' in der Literatur der Zeit des Zweiten Tempels," in *Der Himmel* (ed. Martin Ebner and Irmtraud Fischer; JBT 20; Neukirchen-Vluyn: Neukirchener, 2005), 111–48.

7. On the transformation and amplification of themes associated with the older temple and Zion theology in the exilic and postexilic period, see Bernd Janowski, "Die heilige Wohnung des Höchsten: Kosmologische Implikationen der Jerusalemer Tempeltheologie," in *Gottesstadt und Gottesgarten: Zu Geschichte und Theologie des Jerusalemer Tempels* (ed. Othmar Keel and Erich Zenger; QD 191; Freiburg: Herder, 2002), esp. 58–59.

In countering the claims of absolute power articulated by the Persian imperial ideology, the psalms in book 5 of the Psalter have clearly adopted and expanded the notion of Yahweh as the "God of heaven." In so doing, however, they have also reassigned the previous theological claim concerning inviolability, suggesting that inviolability no longer characterizes Zion, per se, but instead, is associated with the rule of the God of heaven. Yet, for these psalmists, the declaration of Yahweh as the God of heaven in no way vitiates the claim concerning the nearness of God to his people. Through the use of metaphorical imagery, and in particular that of the hand, the psalmists reassert Yahweh's accessibility to his people. This theological move also appears to reconfigure somewhat the role of Zion within the life of God's people, as will be suggested below. Together, these subtle shifts prove significant in constructing the notion of power in book 5 of the Psalter.

5.2. Yahweh as the God of Heaven

The loss of the first temple, the subsequent exile, and the difficulties associated with the return all likely proved to be contributing factors to the frequent references to the God of heaven in the exilic and postexilic literature. Schmid opines that the loss of the first temple, in particular, likely "triggered" a greater emphasis on this theological perspective. Accordingly, he contends that "the temple ceased as the exemplary place of the earthly presence of God ... which almost necessarily forced the development of the idea that from now on God resides in the heavens."[8] In analyzing a number of exilic and postexilic texts, Schmid observes that the biblical writers opted for one of several constructs in attempting to speak of Yahweh as the God of the heavens. Each construct, in varying ways, employs spatial metaphors and images in an effort to place Yahweh over or beyond the events transpiring in the human sphere.[9]

---

8. Schmid, "Himmelsgott, Weltgott, und Schöpfer," 6–7. See also Beate Ego, "'Der Herr blickt herab von der Höhe seines Heiligtums': Zur Vorstellung von Gottes himmlischen Thronen in exilisch-nachexilischer Zeit," ZAW 110 (1998): 556–69. For an extensive treatment of the theme of Yahweh as the God of heaven, see Cornelius Houtman, *Der Himmel im Alten Testament: Israel's Weltbild und Weltanschauung* (OtSt 30; Leiden: Brill, 1993), 319–68.

9. In some ways, Schmid's work has an affinity with the recent developments in critical spatial theory and biblical interpretation. Scholars working with critical space

5.2.1. The Heavenly (*uranisierend*) Concept

The first construct, which he labels as the "heavenly (*uranisierend*) concept," locates the actual dwelling place of God in the heavens, or even the "heaven of heavens."[10] This imagery appears frequently in book 5. In Ps 113, for example, the psalmist writes

> Who is like Yahweh our God
> who is seated on high,
> who looks far down
> upon the heavens and the earth? (113:5–6)

Whereas some psalms that appear earlier in the Psalter (books 1–3) employ the same image (i.e., the enthroned Yahweh looking down from the heavens), the imagery in these psalms has a more foreboding sense, implying that this divine glance is reserved primarily for the testing of the people of God (11:4; 14:2; 17:2–3). In Ps 113, however, the motive appears altogether different. In this instance, the divine glance from the heavens ensures the powerless (דָּל) and the needy (אֶבְיוֹן) of Yahweh's commitment to deliver them.[11] As Ps 113 suggests, the location of Yahweh in the heavens in no way precludes the possibility of deliverance by Yahweh, nor exempts Yahweh from the responsibility of delivering his people. To the contrary, the presence of Yahweh in the heavens reinforces the hope for deliverance amid hostile foes.

---

theory trace this methodological development back to Henri Lefebvre and his groundbreaking work *The Production of Space* (trans. Donald Nicholson-Smith; Oxford: Blackwell, 1996) and to a subsequent iteration of the theory by Edward W. Soja (*Thirdspace: Journeys to Los Angeles and other Real-and-Imagined Places* (Cambridge, Mass.: Blackwell, 1996) and his earlier work *Postmodern Geographies: The Reassertion of Space in Critical Space Theory* (London: Verso, 1989). For examples of its use in biblical scholarship, see Jon L. Berquist and Claudia V. Camp, eds., *Constructions of Space I: Theory, Geography, and Narrative* (LHBOTS 481; New York: T&T Clark, 2007); idem, eds., *Constructions of Space II: The Biblical City and Other Imagined Spaces* (LHBOTS 490; New York: T&T Clark, 2008). Note in particular the recent work on spatial theory and the psalms by Till Magnus Steiner ("Perceived and Narrated Space in Psalm 48," *OTE* 25 [2012]: 685–704) and that of Christl M. Maier in her study of Zion (*Daughter Zion, Mother Zion: Gender, Space, and the Sacred in Ancient Israel* [Minneapolis: Fortress Press, 2008]).

10. Schmid, "Himmelsgott, Weltgott, und Schöpfer," 7.
11. Ego, "'Der Herr blickt herab von der Höhe seines Heiligtums,'" 563.

Other psalms within book 5 make a similar move in locating Yahweh amid the heavens. In Ps 123:1, the psalmist acknowledges that Yahweh is the one "enthroned in the heavens" and in so doing, the psalmist asserts that this God has the capacity to bend down and bring to an end the distress experienced by the despised and poor.[12] Similarly, in response to the taunting by the nations, the psalmist in Ps 115 confesses that "Our God is in the heavens" (115:3) but rather than being a distant deity, this God is Israel's help and shield (115:11). Further, the Great Hallel, Ps 136, concludes

> O give thanks to the God of heaven
>   for his steadfast love endures forever. (136:26)

The entire psalm rehearses Yahweh's חֶסֶד as the God of heaven who ordered the world (136:4–9) and put down the mighty political powers throughout Israel's history that sought to create disorder out of order for Israel (136:10–22). Yet in the final lines of the poem, the community acknowledges

> It is he who remembers us in our humiliated state (שָׁפָל)
>   for his steadfast love endures forever
> and delivered us from our foes (צָר)
>   for his steadfast love endures forever.

The most explicit example in book 5 appears in Psalm 144, a psalm that appropriates the language and imagery of Psalm 18.[13] In light of an apparent, but unnamed, foreign threat (מִיַּד בְּנֵי־נֵכָר), the psalmist pleads with the God of heaven

> O Yahweh, bend your heavens and come down;

---

12. Frank Lothar Hossfeld and Erich Zenger, *Psalms 3: A Commentary on Psalms 101–150* (ed. Klaus Baltzer; trans. Linda Maloney; Hermeneia; Minneapolis: Fortress Press, 2011), 347.

13. As Hans-Peter Mathys has suggested, "Psalm 144:1–11 builds a systematic exegesis of Psalm 18" but one that shifts the genre of thanksgiving found in Psalm 18 to that of lament (*Dichter und Beter: Theologen aus spätalttestamentlicher Zeit* [OBO 132; Göttingen: Vandenhoeck & Ruprecht, 1994], 263–65). See also Michael Goulder, *The Psalms of the Return (Book V, Psalms 107–150): Studies in the Psalter, IV* (JSOTSup 258; Sheffield: Sheffield Academic Press, 1998), 271–76.

> touch the mountains so that they may smoke.
> Cast lightning and scatter them;
> > send out your arrows and rout them.
> Stretch forth your hand from on high;
> > free me and deliver me
> > > from the mighty waters,
> > > > from the hand of the foreigner. (144:5–7)[14]

Although Yahweh is clearly located within the heavens or perhaps even above the heavens, the psalmist nonetheless acknowledges the readily felt presence of this God, calling him "my shield" and the one "in whom I take refuge" in verse 2.

In each psalm mentioned above, the location of Yahweh in the heavens is juxtaposed with the plight of the praying community, yet in each instance, the distance between the two is overcome by Yahweh's capacity to "bend down" to his suffering people.

5.2.2. The "Cosmos-Theistic" Concept

Schmid labels the second construct the *Kosmotheistische* conception. By this, he suggests that through other metaphors and spatial imagery, the biblical writers attempted to extend the idea of the heavenly throne of Yahweh, yet instead of enthroning Yahweh *above the heavens*, the writer prefers to speak of the cosmos itself as the temple of Yahweh which allows him to be "experienceable and present [in the world] in fundamental ways."[15] Similar to the "heavenly conception" mentioned above, the cosmos-theistic conception is not limited to book 5 of the Psalter. The clearest example of this construction actually appears in book 4. There the psalmist says of Yahweh

> You are clothed with honor and majesty,
> > The one wrapped in light as with a garment.
> The one who stretches out the heavens like a tent,
> > the one who has set the beams of your chambers on the waters.

---

14. The notion of Yahweh as being "on high" (מָרוֹם) appears at the beginning of the final Davidic collection (Pss 138–145) as well (138:6). On the contribution of מָרוֹם to the larger idea of the God of heaven, see Houtman, *Der Himmel im Alten Testament*, 342–46.

15. Schmid, "Himmelsgott, Weltgott, und Schöpfer," 15.

> The one who makes the clouds your chariot,
> > the one who rides on the wings of the wind,
> the one who makes the wind his messengers,
> > the one who makes the blazing fire his ministers. (Ps 104:1a–4)

In Ps 104, the entire cosmos functions as the throne room of Yahweh. The images construct a throne room, and by implication an empire, that extends far beyond Jerusalem or even Yehud. Yet such an interpretation of the world not only stresses the sovereignty of Yahweh over the world, but equally stresses his "sacral presence in the cosmos" itself.[16]

Within book 5, Ps 139 provides the clearest, albeit somewhat truncated, notion of the cosmos-theistic construction. In this familiar text, the psalmist claims that there is no place within the created order where one can escape Yahweh's presence. Using both vertical and horizontal spatial images, the psalmist constructs a cosmos fully saturated with the presence of the Divine King. Both in heaven and Sheol (139:8), Yahweh is present, fully cognizant of those realms of his empire. In alluding to the "wings of the morning dawn," the psalmist poetically alludes to the borders of the east.[17] The horizontal dimension is completed with the reference to farthest edges of the sea (139:9) in the west.

Similar to the heavenly construct in the preceding psalm (138:6) that portrays Yahweh as lofty (רָם), the psalmist in Ps 139 repositions Yahweh beyond the domain of Zion. In both constructs, the "heavenly" and the "cosmos-theistic" conceptions, the psalmists connect this confession of Yahweh with a desire for deliverance from the "enemies" (138:7) and the "men of blood" (139:19). Despite the differing spatial images employed in these constructs, the underlying assumption remains the same. Yahweh's location beyond Zion reinforces the belief that Yahweh remains readily available to deliver his people regardless of location or circumstance (cf. 138:7; 139:19–22).

---

16. Ibid., 17.

17. Hossfeld and Zenger, *Psalms 3*, 541. On the cosmological dimensions depicted in these verses, see Othmar Keel, *The Symbolism of the Biblical World: Ancient Near Eastern Iconography and the Book of Psalms* (Winona Lake, Ind.: Eisenbrauns, 1997), 23–24.

5.2.3. Yahweh as "Maker of Heaven and Earth"

Similar to the constructs proposed by Schmid, the use of the participial phrase עֹשֵׂה שָׁמַיִם וָאָרֶץ by the psalmists has a similar effect.[18] The phrase appears four times in book 5 (115:15; 121:2; 124:8; 134:3) and once in the final Hallel (146:6) but strikingly, nowhere else in the Psalter.[19] The use of the participle עֹשֵׂה creates a link with Deutero-Isaiah and the extensive usage of the term in that collection (41:4, 20; 43:7, 19; 45:7, 9; 46:4, 10, 11; 48:3, 5, 11). Although the full phrase עֹשֵׂה שָׁמַיִם וָאָרֶץ does not appear in Deutero-Isaiah, the verb itself in its participial form does "accent the idea of *creatio continuata*," suggesting that Yahweh remains attentive to the world he made and seeks to keep it and protect it.[20] In Deutero-Isaiah, the prophet seeks to emphasize that Yahweh is doing a new thing (Is 48:6–8) and by employing the participle עֹשֵׂה, the prophet attributes the "new thing" to the creative power that is Yahweh's.

In the book of Psalms, however, the use of the phrase עֹשֵׂה שָׁמַיִם וָאָרֶץ appears to take on a more nuanced usage. In each of its five appearances, the phrase functions appositionally, modifying Yahweh, while also functioning more nearly in a titular sense, "Yahweh, the maker of heaven and earth." While the participial phrase no doubt implies the idea of *creatio continuata*, the emphasis resides in the claim that it is Yahweh who has the power, "the one who makes heaven and earth." As the "maker," Yahweh stands over his creation as a king does over an empire, prepared to address

---

18. On the word-pair שָׁמַיִם and אֶרֶץ, see Houtman, *Der Himmel im Alten Testament*, 26–49.

19. The closest parallel in the Psalter is 135:5–6. The relative lateness of this psalm may be suggestive of the theological importance of עֹשֵׂה שָׁמַיִם וָאָרֶץ in late postexilic thought. On the late dating of Ps 135 and its *relecture* of earlier psalms, see Mathys, *Dichter und Beter*, 259–62. Outside of the Psalter, the closest form appears in 2 Chron 2:11 but in a more expanded version, employing the relative pronoun אֲשֶׁר along with the definite direct object marker. The lack of both items in the texts from the Psalter can easily be explained by the classical features associated with Hebrew poetry. On the phrase more generally, see Jonathan Magonet, "Convention and Creativity: The Phrase 'Maker of Heaven and Earth' in the Psalms," in *"Open thou mine eyes ...": Essays on Aggadah and Judaica Presented to Rabbi William G. Braude on his Eightieth Birthday and Dedicated to his Memory* (ed. H. Blumberg, Benjamin Braude, and Bernard Mehlman; Hoboken, NJ: Ktav, 1992), 139–53. See also Norman Habel, "Yahweh Maker of Heaven and Earth: A Study of Tradition Criticism," *JBL* 91 (1972): 321–37.

20. Hossfeld and Zenger, *Psalms 3*, 323.

those who challenge his rule or threaten his people. To this point, Houtman explains that from the phrase עֹשֵׂה שָׁמַיִם וָאָרֶץ "one gets the impression that Yahweh's 'Schöpfer-sein' and his 'Herr-sein' are inseparable aspects of Yahweh's work of redemption which is revealed in the creation of the cosmos and since then, manifested in various forms within the cosmos."[21]

In Pss 121 and 124, the psalmists allude to an unnamed political threat, but confess that their help (עֵזֶר) comes from Yahweh, עֹשֵׂה שָׁמַיִם וָאָרֶץ. In Ps 146, the correlation between עֵזֶר and the participial phrase also appears, and similar to the two other usages, the psalmist alludes to the dire circumstances that threaten the people (146:5–9). Notably in the final verse (146:10), the psalmist confesses that Yahweh will reign forever, making explicit the connection between Yahweh as "maker" and Yahweh as the king who stands ready and able to deliver his people.[22]

The use of the phrase in Ps 115:15 and Ps 134:3 appears to diverge from its use in the other three psalms, yet the fundamental claim suggested by Houtman remains the same. In Pss 115 and 134, Yahweh, the one who makes the heavens and the earth, appears as the one who will bless (בְּרָךְ) his people.[23] In Pss 121, 124, and 146, the threat of the nations is apparent and demands a response. In Ps 134 and to a lesser degree, Ps 115, the enemies do not dominate the psalm. Rather both psalms depict Yahweh as the God who is the עֹשֵׂה שָׁמַיִם וָאָרֶץ and consequently the one who has the power to stand over all of creation and pour forth his blessing.

---

21. Houtman, *Der Himmel im Alten Testament*, 96. "The psalmist wants in a sense to show that as creator, he is even now Lord over creation."

22. Hossfeld and Zenger suggest that "Yahweh's creative power is thus praised as the precondition for his saving action for Israel" (*Psalms 3*, 323). See also Martin Klingbeil, *Yahweh Fighting from Heaven: God as Warrior and as God of Heaven in the Hebrew Psalter and Ancient Near Eastern Iconography* (OBO 169; Göttingen: Vandenhoeck & Ruprecht, 1999), esp. 38–157. See the extended discussion of Ps 146 in §7 of the present study.

23. Magonet incorrectly claims that Psalm 134 "is meant to invoke the totality of creation that is to be the beneficiary of the blessing that comes from Zion" ("Convention and Creativity," 152). Magonet appears to blur the identity of the one receiving the blessing with the identity of the one who issues the blessing. The psalm invokes the "servants" to bless Yahweh (vv. 1–2) which is followed in turn by the psalmist's wish that Yahweh would bless the servants themselves (v. 3). Like the other psalms, the participial phrase, עֹשֵׂה שָׁמַיִם וָאָרֶץ, functions appositionally and is meant as a statement about Yahweh, and does not imply that all of creation is in view and meant to receive blessings from Yahweh.

Similar to the "heavenly" conceptualizing of Yahweh that Schmid noted, this phrase functions to assert Yahweh's creative and kingly power over all *and* above all of creation. Yet even in positioning Yahweh conceptually in this manner, the psalmist does not rule out the nearness of Yahweh both to deliver and bless.

While the reference to Yahweh as עֹשֵׂה שָׁמַיִם וָאָרֶץ suggests that such language and imagery was drawn from the Priestly creation tradition, the phrase also runs counter to the imperial claims of the Persians and world governance.[24] As Darius and subsequent kings sought to create an entrenched ideology of empire, the notion of its worldwide reach was a central component. The Achaemenid dynasty, particularly beginning with Darius, attempted to root the political ideology of a worldwide empire in the creation narrative involving Ahuramazda. As already discussed above (§2), the inscription at Naqsh-i Rustam reads, "A great god is Ahuramazda, who created this earth, who created yonder heaven, who created man, who created happiness for man, who made Darius king, one king of many, one lord of many."[25] Whether an explicit or implicit challenge, the affirmation of Yahweh as "the maker of heaven and earth" stands in tension with the official ideology of the empire. The confession of Yahweh as the "maker of heaven and earth" not only unseats any claims associated with Ahuramazda as the supreme deity, it also buttresses further Israel's claim that it is Yahweh alone who can deliver Israel from the hands of oppressive powers.

5.3. The Hand of Yahweh and the Nearness of God

Among the bodily images employed across the Psalter that of the hand (יָד; יָמִין) occurs with considerable regularity, but with a wide range of meaning.[26] In book 1 of the Psalter, for example, the image of the hand of God

---

24. Klaus Seybold suggests that the phrase is the "quintessential statement of creation theology" (*Die Psalmen* [HAT 1/15; Tübingen: Mohr Siebeck, 1996], 452).

25. DNa §1 (Amélie Kuhrt, *The Persian Empire: A Corpus of Sources from the Achaemenid Period* [London: Routledge, 2007], 502). The Achaemenid inscriptions sought repeatedly to link the rule of the Achaemenian king with the rule of Ahuramazda, the maker of heaven and earth. For similar conclusions, see also Bruce Lincoln, *Religion, Empire, and Torture: The Case of Achaemenian Persia with a Postscript on Abu Ghraib* (Chicago: University of Chicago Press, 2007), esp. 51–65.

26. In the Psalms, יָד occurs ninety-four times and יָמִין forty-two times. Only לֵב, נֶפֶשׁ, and פָּנִים occur with greater regularity (144 times, 132 times, and 107 times,

is often associated with the judgment of God upon the psalmist. Having failed to confess his sins, the psalmist explains that God's hand "was heavy upon me" (32:4). In Ps 38:2, God's "hand has come down" upon the psalmist, like arrows that have sunk deep into the body (cf. Ps 39:10). In texts that deal with the enemy, however the image of the hand functions differently. Susan Gillmayr-Bucher explains the role of bodily depiction in various psalms, noting that "the depiction of the body presented is a fictitious model. This fiction offers a new perception of the enemies, God and the lyrical subject."[27] More specific to the present study, she also notes that with the help of body language not only is nearness expressed, but the perception of spatial separation is overcome.[28] Although Yahweh is frequently depicted as the "God of heaven" for the reasons suggested above, the spatial difference between Yahweh and the people can be minimized through the use of vivid metaphors such as the hand.

Within book 5 of the Psalter, the psalmists repeatedly make use of the terms יָד and יָמִין.[29] Although the image ("the hand") remains the same, it can connote a variety of meanings. For example, the "right hand" of Yahweh serves as a reminder of Yahweh's capacity to deliver. In Ps 108:6–7, the psalmist prays

> Be exalted, O God, above the heavens!
>   Let your glory be over all the earth.
> Save by your right hand (יָמִין) and answer me
>   so that your beloved ones may be liberated.

In a similar vein, in Ps 118 the psalmist draws heavily from Exod 15, borrowing as well the image of the hand as a metaphor for deliverance. The psalmist confesses

> The right hand (יָמִין) of Yahweh does mighty things;
> the right hand (יָמִין) of Yahweh is exalted;

---

respectively). See William P. Brown, *Seeing the Psalms: A Theology of Metaphor* (Louisville: Westminster John Knox, 2002), 175–78; J. J. M. Roberts, "The Hand of Yahweh," *VT* 21 (1971): 244–51.

27. Susan Gillmayr-Bucher, "Body Images in the Psalter," *JSOT* 28 (2004), 305.
28. Ibid., 305–6.
29. The image of the hand is not reserved for Yahweh alone. Note its usage in conjunction with the enemies in Pss 140:4 and 144:7, 8, 11 as well as its reference to idols in Ps 115:7.

the right hand (יָמִין) of Yahweh does mighty things. (118:15–16)

As Hossfeld and Zenger have suggested, "the right hand or the right arm is *pars pro toto* for Yahweh's saving action" especially in connection to the exodus (Ps 136:12–13), to deliverance from military occupation, and liberation from oppression at the hands of foreign nations (Pss 118:15–16; 138:7; 144:7).[30]

A second use of the image of the right hand also aids in closing the spatial gap. In selected uses, the image of the right hand has a spatial connotation. Rather than alluding to the hand or, more specifically, the right hand of Yahweh, the terms are used to refer to the position of one party in respect to the other. As suggested above (§3), Yahweh stands at the right hand of the poor and needy (109:31) to provide deliverance to those powerless and threatened. The location of Yahweh "at the right hand" suggests the sure presence of Yahweh with those suffering; such imagery implies a certain solidarity between deity and supplicant. Further, by standing at the right hand of the psalmist (121:5), Yahweh provides protection from "all evil" (121:7a). Finally, in a slight modification of the image, Yahweh invites the psalmist to sit at the right hand of Yahweh (110:1), in some sense ensuring that the psalmist enjoys the power of the Divine King.[31] The individual will sit at the right hand while Yahweh makes the foes a footstool.[32]

A striking use of hand imagery occurs in Ps 139:10. In the second strophe, the psalmist claims that

Even there your hand (יָד) shall lead me,
and your right hand (יָמִין) shall hold me.

This is the only location in the Hebrew Bible in which Yahweh leads (נָחָה) a person by the hand. This type of handholding scene appears regularly in ancient Near Eastern iconography and texts. In Egyptian and Mesopotamian iconography, in particular, two figures are depicted, with the first holding the hand (or often the wrist) of the second. Typically the scene reflects a religious context in which one person leads the other into the

---

30. Hossfeld and Zenger, *Psalms 3*, 120.
31. See Keel, *The Symbolism of the Biblical World*, 254–56.
32. Goldingay, *Psalms 90–150* (BCOT; Grand Rapids: Baker Academic, 2008), 293–94.

presence of a deity.[33] This is particularly true of Mesopotamian usages, including much earlier Neo-Sumerian seals that even appear to portray the actual deity leading the individual (as implied in Ps 139). Similar scenes in Egyptian art span the history of ancient Egyptian art from the Old Kingdom down through the Roman period.[34]

The image also makes its way into Persian iconography in the Apadana relief at Persepolis. In that context, the gift bearing delegates from the various vassal lands are led by the hand in a grand procession towards the center of the relief.[35] At the center is the king, the prince, and a royal entourage, with Ahuramazda appearing above the royal party.[36] Root contends that the Achaemenids *might* have drawn such an image from the iconographic symbolism present in the larger ancient Near Eastern context. She avers that the appropriation of such an image likely sought to cast the Achaemenid king (and Ahuramazda) symbolically as the center of the cosmos with the intent of reifying, in some sense, the notions of "imperial order and power."[37]

Whether the psalmist has drawn from the religious and political imagery culturally present, or whether the appearance of such hand imagery is mere happenstance cannot be proven conclusively, but the similarities are intriguing. The use of the imagery by the psalmist does prove significant in attempting to construct the notion of power in book 5. In Ps 139, the poet imagines a cosmos in which the God of Israel alone guides his people. As Gönke Eberhardt has noted,

> Psalm 139 does not propose a cosmology for its own sake; instead all the statements in verses 7–12 about Yhwh's presence in the cosmos serve to … determine the relationship between God and the human being.… Here we find no assertion about the place where Yhwh dwells, but instead a description of his guidance of the human being.[38]

---

33. Margaret C. Root, *King and Kingship in Achaemenid Art: Essays on the Creation of an Iconography of Empire* (AcIr 19; Leiden: Brill, 1979), 267–84; see also plates 62 and 63.
34. Ibid., 270–72; see also plates 64 and 65.
35. See Kuhrt, *The Persian Empire*, 522–26, figs. 11:22–23.
36. Ibid., 536, fig. 11.29.
37. Ibid., 283. See also fig. 11 for a proposed reconstruction of the Apadana relief.
38. Gönke Eberhardt, *JHWH und die Unterwelt: Spuren einer Kompetenzausweitung JHWHs im Alten Testament* (FAT 2/23; Tübingen: Mohr Siebeck, 2007), 153 (translation from Hossfeld and Zenger, *Psalms 3*, 546).

Whereas the use of hand imagery in other cultures suggests that the individual is being led *into* the presence of the deity, the psalmist implies something altogether different. Although Yahweh is the God of heaven and present in all of the cosmos, one need not be led into the presence of this deity. Instead, the psalmist claims that Yahweh himself, the God of Israel, holds the hands of his people, assuring them of his presence (139:7b), even as he is present in all of the cosmos (139:8–9). This imagery also has dramatic implications later in the psalm, as the psalmist seeks deliverance from the powers that surround him (139:19–20).

The use of hand imagery in the psalms proves critical in the construction of power in book 5. As noted above (§§2.0–2.3), the psalmists consistently portray Yahweh as the God of heaven, ensuring that Yahweh and no other reigns over all of creation. Yet the repeated use of hand imagery serves to provide Israel with a visual reminder of Yahweh's intervention, and by implication, God's presence. Although Yahweh is in heaven, his reach extends into the daily lives of his faithful, ensuring that despite a perceived spatial distance, the capacity for deliverance remains at hand.

5.4. The Role of Zion in Book 5

The emphasis on Yahweh as the God of heaven has implications for the perceived role of Zion. Within book 5, the role of Zion shifts noticeably, creating what Hossfeld and Zenger have labeled, "a new Zion theology."[39] The role of Zion in the latter books of the Psalter deserves a separate treatment entirely, one that is beyond the scope of this study. That said, however, a few brief comments related to the present line of inquiry are in order and may prove suggestive.

The majority of references to Jerusalem, Israel, and Zion in book 5 appear in the Psalms of Ascents and frequently are found in psalms that deal with a perceived or imminent threat.[40] In comparing this collection with another, albeit earlier pilgrimage collection, Hossfeld and Zenger

---

39. Hossfeld and Zenger, *Psalms 3*, 297. On the role of Zion in book 5, see also Erich Zenger, "The Composition and Theology of the Fifth Book of Psalms, Psalms 107–145," *JSOT* 80 (1998): 77–102.

40. See Derek Edward Wittman, "The Kingship of Yahweh and the Politics of Poverty and Oppression in the Hebrew Psalter," (PhD diss., Baylor University, 2010), 79. On the appropriation of Zion as symbol, see Robert D. Miller II, "The Zion Hymns as Instruments of Power," *ANES* 47 (2010): 218–40.

note that while both collections work with "creation-theological motifs" and both allude to Zion as "the sheltering center in the midst of a threatening world," there are substantial differences worth noting.[41] They explain

> In the Korah Psalter (Psalm 42–48), Yhwh is the "great king" enthroned on the divine mountain of Zion, who as the powerful Yhwh Sabaoth and in a spectacular theophany combats and disempowers the hostile kings who are representatives of chaos. This theophanic God-is-king theology is absent from the Pilgrim Psalter (Psalms 120–134). Here Yhwh is the creator God enthroned in heaven, who like a kind "household patron" provides for, protects, and saves his maidservants and man servants. Yhwh's divine capacity is now experienced especially in everyday and in very concrete blessings.[42]

Zion as the place of blessing appears repeatedly in the second half of the Psalms of Ascents collection (128:4, 5; 129:8; 132:15; 133:3; and 134:3). The mention of blessing in these psalms functions as a response of sorts to the earlier psalms in the collection and their reference to the numerous threats facing the community (121:7; 122:6–7; 123:3; 124:2–5; 125:3; 126:4).[43] The blessings named however refer to the more mundane aspects of life and certainly are absent of the mythopoeic and paradisiacal images employed in texts such as Ezekiel, and in particular, the earlier Psalms of Zion.[44] In the midst of a "threatening world," the blessings of Yahweh include sufficient food (128:2; 132:15), a family (128:2–4), and a long life (128:6; 133:3). But these blessing are not just found *in* Jerusalem, they flow out *from* Jerusalem.[45]

---

41. Hossfeld and Zenger, *Psalms 3*, 297. See also, Philip E. Satterthwaite, "Zion in the Songs of Ascents," in *Zion, City of our God* (ed. Richard S. Hess and Gordon J. Wenhem; Grand Rapids: Eerdmans, 1999), 105–28.

42. Ibid. On the shift in emphasis from "king and state" to that of family as the primary place of solidarity and blessing, see especially Erich Zenger, "'Es segne dich JHWH vom Zion aus … ' (Ps 134,3): Die Gottesmetaphorik in den Wallfahrtpsalmen Pss 120–134," in *Gott und Mensch im Dialog: Festschrift für Otto Kaiser zum 80. Geburtstag* (ed. Markus Witte; Berlin: de Gruyter, 2004), 601–21.

43. See Matthias Millard's assessment of the compositional arc involving Psalms 120–124 and the need for deliverance expressed therein (*Die Komposition des Psalters: Ein formgeschichtlicher Ansatz* [FAT 1/9; Tübingen: Mohr Siebeck, 1994], 76–77).

44. Körting, *Zion in den Psalmen*, 135–36.

45. As Erich Zenger contends, these psalms "bind temple liturgy and everyday reality together so that both, as two sides, represent one and the same reality" ("Der

The affirmation that the blessings of Yahweh come from Zion may appear at first glance to have little in common with the earlier observations related to Yahweh as the God of heaven. Yet, as Körting has rightly suggested, Zion possesses an intermediary function in the psalms. Zion serves as "the dispenser (*Spender*) of the good gifts of God to Israel, [that being] his presence and his blessings."[46] These psalms suggest that although Yahweh is the heavenly enthroned king, his blessings are made manifest through Zion. And as mundane as they may appear, these blessings, similar to the imagery of the hand, reinforce the nearness of God despite the cognitive dissonance created by living under foreign rule. These psalms imply that the community can never be too far removed from the view of Yahweh despite the perceived spatial distance.[47]

Further, this new Zion theology also reinterprets the notion of Zion's inviolability. In the earlier Psalms of Zion, the city itself remained central to the notion of inviolability. In Ps 46 for example, the psalmist boldly asserts

> God is in the midst of her [Jerusalem]; she shall not be moved.
> God will help her when the morning comes. (46:5)

In somewhat more mythopoeic language, the psalmist declares in Ps 48

> Great is the Lord and greatly to be praised in the city of our God,
> his holy mountain, beautiful in elevation,
>   is the joy of the earth,
> Mount Zion, in the far north,
>   the city of the Great King.
> With its citadels, God has shown himself a sure defense. (48:1–3)

Zion als Ort der Gottesnähe: Beobachtungen zum Weltbild des Wallfahrtspsalters Ps 120–134" in *Gottes Nähe im Alten Testament* [ed. Gönke Eberhardt and Kathrin Liess; SBS 202; Stuttgart: Katholische Bibelwerk, 2004], 111). Satterthwaite notes how consistently the Psalms of Ascents link the welfare of Zion with the welfare of the individual ("Zion in the Songs of Ascents," 128). On the centrality of Jerusalem and its implications for social and religious practices in the Persian period, see Melody D. Knowles, *Centrality Practiced: Jerusalem in the Religious Practice of Yehud and the Diaspora in the Persian Period* (SBLABS 16; Atlanta: Society of Biblical Literature, 2006).

46. Körting, *Zion in den Psalmen*, 144.

47. Ibid. See also, Millard, *Die Komposition des Psalters*, 228–29; Jerome Creach, *The Destiny of the Righteous in the Psalms* (St. Louis: Chalice Press, 2008), 131–33.

The association in these two psalms is clear. Yahweh is in Zion; the city is inviolable. Yet, in book 5 of the Psalter, the traditional association between Zion and inviolability appears to have shifted. Although the connection between Zion and inviolability appears to have receded from its prominence in earlier psalms, the stress on security remains consistent. Even though these psalms shift the notion of inviolability to the God of heaven, Zion nonetheless plays an important role within the larger collection. By emphasizing Zion as the "dispenser" of God's good gifts, the psalmists reinforce the role of Zion in sustaining the people of God amid a hostile environment. Further, by casting Zion in this role, the city serves as another indicator of the nearness of God to his people.

In summary then, while there is a new Zion theology of sorts in book 5, the tenets of such a theology remain largely in place. Zion remains central to the identity and survival of the people of God in a hostile world. Yet security and blessings are not guaranteed because of the inviolability of Zion; they are guaranteed because the God of heaven remains impervious to the threats of human power and their attempts to mimic the divine (cf. 115:3–8).

5.5. Psalm 145 and the Kingship of Yahweh

The final psalm in book 5 serves in part as a recapitulation of the themes outlined above and articulated throughout the collection, reinforcing Gerald Wilson's claim that Ps 145 functions as the "climax" of the fifth book.[48] Although an acrostic poem, the form should not "be understood as a playful pastime only; it served a communal purpose."[49] The psalm, which is an individual psalm of praise, alludes to the relationship between Yahweh and the community throughout (cf. 145:4, 6, 7, 9, 10, 14–15, 18–20), culminating in the call for "all flesh to bless [Yahweh's] holy name forever and ever" (145:21). In this grand call to praise, the psalmist highlights the claims mentioned earlier (i.e., the heavenly location of Yahweh coupled with the claim of the nearness of Yahweh), yet places such claims under the larger rubric of the kingship of Yahweh, a theme once located

---

48. Gerald Wilson, *The Editing of the Hebrew Psalter* (SBLDS 76; Chico, Calif.: Scholars Press, 1985), 225.

49. Erhard S. Gerstenberger, *Psalms, Part 2, and Lamentations* (FOTL 15; Grand Rapids: Eerdmans, 2001), 433. On the absence of the נ-line in the acrostic, see the discussion in Hossfeld and Zenger, *Psalms 3*, 592–93.

squarely within Zion theology, but here apparently detached to some degree.[50]

5.5.1. The Kingship of Yahweh

In the opening line of Ps 145, the psalmist announces the kingship of Yahweh in unqualified terms.

> I will exalt you my God the king (אֱלוֹהַי הַמֶּלֶךְ).

Egbert Ballhorn suggests that the "meta-thesis" of the psalm is captured in the expression אֱלוֹהַי הַמֶּלֶךְ. Elsewhere in the Psalter the terms are usually reversed (מַלְכִּי אלהִים) as evident in Ps 44:5 (cf. 5:3; 84:4). Ballhorn contends, however, that the absolute form used in Ps 145 may in fact be a prelude to the universalistic tenor expressed throughout the psalm.[51] The psalmist declares emphatically that this God is in fact the king, and that there is no other, human or divine. Although earlier psalms in book 5 have referred to the kingship of Yahweh through the use of metaphors, metonymy, and spatial imagery, Ps 145 concludes the collection with an overt claim to the kingship of Yahweh.[52]

The focus on Yahweh as king reappears later in the psalm in verses 11–13. Just prior to these verses, the psalmist explains in verse 10b that all the "faithful ones" (חֲסִידִים) will bless Yahweh. He then announces

---

50. Erich Zenger suggests that Ps 145 should be understood, compositionally, as the concluding psalm of book 5, and moreover, that it was likely created for this very purpose. ("Das Buch der Psalmen," in *Einleitung in das Alte Testament* [ed. Erich Zenger; 6th ed.; Stuttgart: Kohlhammer, 2006], 355). Whether the psalm was created for this location in the collection is ultimately unverifiable, but Zenger's stress on the psalm's function within the larger composition (Pss 107–145) remains tenable and corresponds to the argument being made here.

51. Egbert Ballhorn, *Zum Telos des Psalters: Der Textzusammenhang des Vierten und Fünften Psalmenbuches (Ps 90–150)* (BBB 138. Berlin: Philo, 2004), 288.

52. Reinhard G. Kratz argues more forcefully, "Nowhere else is the theme of the reign of God placed in the foreground to such an extent" ("Das *Schema* des Psalters: Die Botschaft vom Reich Gottes nach Psalm 145," in *Gott und Mensch im Dialog: Festschrift für Otto Kaiser zum 80. Geburtstag* [ed. Markus Witte; BZAW 345; 2 vols.; Berlin: de Gruyter, 2004]), 628. On role of the chiasm in vv. 11–13 and its contribution to the theme of the reign of God, see p. 629.

> Let them tell of the glory of your kingdom (מַלְכוּת),
>   and let them speak of your might,
> to make known to the children of humanity your mighty acts,
>   and the glory of the splendor of his kingdom (מַלְכוּת).
> Your kingdom (מַלְכוּת) is an everlasting kingdom (מַלְכוּת),
>   and your dominion endures from generation to generation.
> (145:11–13)

The emphasis on the kingship of Yahweh is evidenced with the four-fold repetition of מַלְכוּת in verses 11–13.[53] Wilfred G. E. Watson, in his analysis of acrostic poetry, attempts to further this point, noting that the verses that reinforce the reign of God appear in lines that begin with כ, ל, and מ, which in reverse form the root מלך.[54] A number of scholars including Adele Berlin, Ballhorn, and Hossfeld and Zenger appear unconvinced by the claims of Watson, claiming instead that the use of מַלְכוּת within this section of the acrostic is simply "the nature of the alphabet."[55] Whether the appearance of these verses in this section of the psalm was mere happenstance or part of the artistry of the psalmist cannot be determined conclusively, but as Martin Leuenberger has noted, the fact remains that these verses form "the conceptual basis of book 5 of the Psalter."[56]

If part of the function of book 5 was to challenge the role of human power, and particularly that of imperial power, then the absolute claims to Yahweh's kingship in Ps 145 most certainly contribute to that notion.[57] In the Aramaic portions of Daniel, the themes found in Ps 145:13 play an

---

53. Barnabas Lindars, "The Structure of Psalm CXLV," *VT* 29 (1989), 26–28.

54. Wilfred G. E. Watson, "Reversed Rootplay in Psalm 145," *Bib* 62 (1981): 101–2. See also his brief comments on the issue in *Classical Hebrew Poetry: A Guide to Its Techniques* (New York: T&T Clark, 2005), 193.

55. Ballhorn, *Zum Telos des Psalters*, 286; Adele Berlin, "Rhetoric of Psalm 145," in *Biblical and Related Studies Presented to Samuel Iwry* (ed. Ann Kort and Scott Morschauser; Winona Lake, Ind.: Eisenbrauns, 1985), 19; Hossfeld and Zenger, *Psalms 3*, 594.

56. Martin Leuenberger, *Konzeptionen des Königtums Gottes im Psalter: Untersuchungen zu Komposition und Redaktion der theokratischen Bücher IV–V im Psalter* (ATANT 83; Zürich: Theologischer, 2004), 387.

57. Erich Zenger, "Der jüdische Psalter—ein anti-imperiales Buch?" in *Religion und Gesellschaft: Studien zu ihrer Wechselbeziehung in den Kulturen des Antiken Vorderen Orients* (ed. Rainer Albertz; AZERKAVO 1/AOAT 248; Münster: Ugarit, 1997), 99. Zenger contends that Psalm 145 creates a "new model" of the kingdom, which means the overturning of all imperial models of rule.

important role in light of the imperial threats outlined in that book. In Dan 3:33, as the three young men sit inside the furnace, having been condemned to die there by the sentence of King Nebuchadnezzar, the youths acknowledge the universal kingship of Yahweh by invoking portions of Ps 145:13. Following Daniel's interpretation of Nebuchadnezzar's dream in ch. 4 and his subsequent humiliation, Nebuchadnezzar himself professes

> For [Yahweh's] dominion is an everlasting dominion
>   and his kingdom endures from generation to generation. (Dan 4:31 [Eng. 34])

In the last instance (Dan 6:27 [Eng. 26]), King Darius declares Yahweh's rule has no end, once again seemingly borrowing from the language and thought of Ps 145.[58]

5.5.2. The Location of Yahweh in Psalm 145

Psalm 145 can be divided thematically in half, creating two sections of near equal length (145:1–13; 14–21). The content of the two sections corresponds nicely to the earlier discussion related to the location of Yahweh in book 5. As Hossfeld and Zenger explain,

> The first half concentrates on human praise of the majesty and the transcendence of Yhwh, while the second half describes his imminence, and lists the divine deeds of devotion to the created world.[59]

In addition to proclaiming the kingship of Yahweh and his enduring rule (145:1, 13), the psalmist acknowledges the greatness of Yahweh (145:3) in the first section, concluding that his "greatness is not fathomable (חֵקֶר)." The accolade in this context suggests that no one can grasp fully the rule of Yahweh over the entire world order.[60] The emphasis in the first sec-

---

58. Ballhorn, *Zum Telos des Psalter*, 288; Hossfeld and Zenger, *Psalms 3*, 599. Goldingay seems to imply that the line of influence went in the reverse, with the text in Psalm 145 "a variant" on the Daniel texts (*Psalms 90–150*, 702). Leslie Allen contends instead that Ps 145:13 and the Daniel texts likely borrowed from a stylized formula or poem to which both had access (*Psalms 101–150* [WBC 21; Waco, Tex.: Word Books, 1983], 297).

59. Hossfeld and Zenger, *Psalms 3*, 594.

60. Gordon H. Matties and Richard D. Patterson, "חֵקֶר," *NIDOTTE* 2:254.

tion of the psalm pertains to the greatness of Yahweh's rule rather than simply an abstract characterization of Yahweh as "great." The emphasis on his capacity as an unfathomable ruler appears in the following verses. For example, the lofty description of Yahweh continues in verse 5a with the use of a double genitive, employing "three traditional insignia of divine and human royal dignity."[61] The psalmist reflects "on the splendor of the glory of your majesty," piling up terms that reflect the lofty status assigned to Yahweh the divine king.

In addition to these images, the psalmist refers to the "works" of Yahweh in verse 4a, the "mighty acts" (גְּבוּרָה) in verse 4b, the "wondrous works" (נִפְלְאוֹת) in verse 5b, and the power of Yahweh's "awe-inspiring deeds" (נוֹרָאֹת) in verse 6a. In truncated fashion, these terms invoke images of Yahweh's royal deeds of power throughout history, once again establishing Yahweh as the unfathomable king who sits over the cosmos executing his rule. So great is this testimony that one generation shall praise these works to the next (145:4a).

These images, coupled with the repeated claims concerning the kingdom of Yahweh in verses 11–13, reinforce the notion of Yahweh as the cosmic ruler, one whose renown shall be recognized by all the "children of humanity" (145:12). While Ps 145 does not invoke heavenly imagery in an attempt to locate Yahweh, through the various images and language employed, the psalm does in fact proclaim Yahweh as the one true king, unfathomable in his rule over all of creation (145:9).[62]

Even as the first half of the psalm recounts the transcendence of Yahweh, the second half affirms the nearness of God. The psalmist announces

> Yahweh upholds all who are falling,
> > and raises up those who are bowed down in distress.
> The eyes of all look to you,
> > and you give them their food in its season.
> You open your hand
> > and you satisfy the desire of every living thing....
> Yahweh is near to all who call upon him,
> > to all who call upon him in truth.
> He fulfills the desire of all who fear him,

---

61. Hossfeld and Zenger, *Psalms 3*, 598.
62. Zenger, "Der jüdischer Psalter—ein anti-imperiales Buch," 98–99.

> he also hears their cry and saves them.
> Yahweh preserves all who love him;
>> but he destroys all the wicked ones. (145:14–16, 18–20)

Whereas the first portion of the psalm went to great lengths to establish Yahweh as the cosmic king, the second half goes to equal lengths in affirming the nearness of God to those who love him. Repeatedly, the psalmist depicts Yahweh in highly personified language in an effort to reinforce the nearness of Yahweh. Yahweh holds up those who are falling and lifts up those already bent over in distress and humiliation (145:14). In verse 16, the psalmist invokes the image of the hand once more, signaling the nearness of God and his capacity for meeting the needs of the people. And lest the reader or hearer fail to recognize the claim being outlined in the second half of the psalm, the psalmist simply acknowledges

> Yahweh is near (קָרוֹב) to all who call upon him. (145:17)[63]

And because Yahweh remains near, he also hears their cry and saves them (145:19b).

In short, the very structure of Ps 145 itself acknowledges and confesses the spatial tension created throughout book 5. The psalmist proclaims Yahweh as the cosmic King, yet in so doing, reinforces Yahweh's commitment to remain near to those who love him (145:17, 20).

5.6. Conclusion

As suggested earlier, the notion of Yahweh as the God of heaven cannot be assigned solely to the theological constructs developed during the Persian period. The move from Yahweh as "king of Zion" to Yahweh as "God of heaven" does not follow a strict linear path of development. That said, however, the literature from the Persian period does shift its rhetoric decidedly in one direction. Repeatedly in book 5 of the Psalter, for example, through varying images, metaphors, and verbiage, the psalmists assert that Yahweh is in fact the "God of heaven."[64] In asserting that Yahweh, the God of those

---

63. See Christoph Buysch, *Der letzte Davidpsalter: Interpretation, Komposition und Funktion der Psalmengruppe Ps 138–145* (SBB 63; Stuttgart: Katholisches Bibelwerk, 2009), 338.

64. The importance of this theme and its influence is evident in the prevalence

in Yehud, is in fact the God of heaven, the psalmists and the community that appropriated these psalms, attempted to make two fundamental theological statements. In some sense, these psalms, *and the process involved*, serve as witness to the robust theological imagination of these poets.

The claim that Yahweh is the God of heaven is likely a response in part to the earlier claims of the inviolability of Zion. Despite the events associated with the Babylonian exile and the continued Persian rule, the community apparently refused to jettison the idea of inviolability entirely. Admittedly, the realities associated with exile and the subsequent colonialism under Persian rule made the claim regarding *Zion's* inviolability no longer tenable. As a result, the theological affirmations articulated in the Persian period confess that it was no longer Jerusalem itself that appears inviolable, but rather Yahweh, the one who creates the heavens and the earth, the one enthroned in the heavens, who is inviolable.[65] By placing Yahweh in the heavens, the psalmists do more than simply remove Yahweh from the social, political, and militaristic machinations to which Zion remains susceptible, but instead, by placing Yahweh in the heavens, the psalmists actually place Yahweh *over* all of creation, making those same social, political, and militaristic machinations subject to the watchful eye of the Divine King (cf. 123:1, 3–4; 144:5–11). And because Yahweh is the Divine King who stands over all of creation, no power within that creation can thwart the power of its Creator. Despite the events associated with Zion, it is Yahweh himself that remains inviolable.

This leads to the second claim. Although the psalmists assert that Yahweh is the God of heaven, they remain undeterred in their confession concerning the nearness of God. Despite the cognitive dissonance created by the spatial imagery employed in declaring God as the "God of heaven," the psalmists appreciate the theological importance of the nearness of God.[66] As noted above, the claim that Yahweh is the God of heaven appears in psalms that also refer to the threatening presence of nations and enemy powers. The hope confessed in these psalms is that Yahweh, the one who made heaven and earth, will "look down" (113:6), "have mercy" (123:3), "remember" (136:23), and "bend the heavens and

---

of its usage in the concluding run of Hallel psalms. See 146:6; 147:8, 15–18; 148:1, 4, 13; 150:1.

65. Ego, "Der Herr blickt herab von der Höhe seines Heiligtums," 556–57.

66. As Schmid explains, "by virtue of his inviolable, powerful position in the heavens, God can help and deliver," ("Himmelsgott, Weltgott, und Schöpfer," 35).

come down" (144:5). The placement of Yahweh in the heavens in no way removes Yahweh from the plight of his people, but rather, emphatically suggests that the full power of the heavenly enthroned Divine King will intervene into the history of his threatened people to bring deliverance.[67] This intervention is seen most clearly through the metaphor of the hand, as Yahweh reaches into the lives of those who love him to provide deliverance (145:20).

The shifts in the spatial location of Yahweh and the somewhat altered role of Zion in book 5 of the Psalter suggest the theological elasticity of these concepts in varying historical periods amid varying political circumstances. Yet despite such shifts, these psalms bear witness to Israel's fundamental theological claims concerning Yahweh and Yahweh's role in the world. Despite the shifts in imagery and spatial location, these psalms reinforce the claim of the kingship of Yahweh. Together these theological tenets reject the claims of imperial rule and instead reconstruct power according to the claims of Yahweh, the Divine King. Power does not reside in human kingship, despite appearances to the contrary, but instead rests fully with the God of heaven, the one who remains inviolable, yet ever present.

---

67. Ego notes, "God's heavenly sanctuary is thus not only the throne room of his lofty and unattainable transcendence, but is a sign of his universal justice-giving action, which finds its expression in the salvation and preservation of the poor and needy" ("Der Herr blickt herab von der Höhe seines Heiligtums," 569).

6
THE IDENTITY OF THE PEOPLE OF GOD: DECONSTRUCTED AND CONSTRUCTED POWER

6.0. INTRODUCTION

In response to the Persian claims of world dominance, the psalmists countered by reasserting Yahweh's role as cosmic ruler in an effort to construct an image of power that was consonant with their covenantal commitments. In addition to constructing an idea of Yahweh as cosmic ruler, the psalms in book 5 also appear to construct, or reconstruct, the identity of the people of God. As discussed above (§2), the Persians depicted their subjects as joyous participants in the empire. The various scenes, most notably the socle figurines in selected iconography, portray the captives with outstretched arms, bearing the full weight of the empire as embodied in the Achaemenid ruler (§2.2.2). The position of these subjects (directly beneath the king) portrays at once both their joyous support of the empire, but also their willing subjugation to the same.

In an attempt to deconstruct the kind of ideology of power initially promulgated in the Persian iconography, the psalms in book 5 attempt to construct an identity of the people of God that appears to undercut the larger claims associated with empire. While the Persians constructed such images primarily through iconography, such work in Yehud was primarily textual and requires a somewhat different interpretive approach. In her book, *The Self as Symbolic Space: Constructing Identity and Community at Qumran*, Carol Newsom explores how the Qumran community shaped the identity and ideology of its community in creating a "figured world" through texts.[1] In analyzing the *Serek ha-Yahad* and the *Hodayot* texts

---

1. Carol A. Newsom, *The Self as Symbolic Space: Constructing Identity and Community at Qumran* (STDJ 52; Leiden: Brill, 2004).

from Qumran, she explores both the nature and function of the language employed in two texts. According to Newsom, such an inquiry is "essential for understanding the way in which the Qumran community used language to constitute a world of meaning, a distinctive identity, a community of values, and a structure of selfhood."[2] Perhaps most instructive for the present study is Newsom's claim that such discursive language must be understood within its broader historical, socio-political, and cultural context.[3] She contends

> The words they used, the forms of speech, the content of their prayers, and the claims they made about themselves were always in part *replies, responses, and counter-claims* to utterances made by others within a broader cultural context.[4]

In other words, the claims made in *Serek ha-Yahad* and the *Hodayot* texts are in fact "replies, responses, and counter-claims" articulated amid a larger cultural conversation.[5] These claims however are only discoverable through the words employed within the text.

Through the "words they used, the forms of speech, the content of their prayers, and the claims they made about themselves," the psalms in book 5 construct an identity for the people of God. As suggested below, this identity centers on several ideas present elsewhere in the Hebrew Bible, but particularly concentrated in this portion of the Psalter. The language of the poor plays a significant role in the Psalter and particularly in book 5. The same can also be said about the language and imagery associated with the servant(s). Although earlier studies attempted to identify the poor as a group within Ancient Israel through sociological and historical analysis, with such analyses also alluding to the servants, this chapter will move in a

---

2. Ibid., 2.

3. Newsom surmises "not every society is so preoccupied with a discourse of identity, but the peculiar historical circumstances of Second Temple Judaism brought this issue to the fore. Even when not explicitly engaged in responding to one another, the literary works, religious movements, new social institutions, emerging symbols, and so forth, ceaselessly suggested alternative ways of answering that question" (ibid., 4). See also the work on identity, and in particular collective identity, by David Goodblatt (*Elements of Ancient Jewish Nationalism* [Cambridge: Cambridge University Press, 2006]).

4. Ibid., 3, emphasis added.

5. Ibid., 347.

6. THE IDENTITY OF THE PEOPLE OF GOD   167

different direction.⁶ The overarching question throughout this volume has focused on how power has been deconstructed and constructed throughout book 5 of the Psalter. Consequently, the driving question for this chapter is not who *were* the servants or the poor, but rather, how did these images construct an identity for those seeking to deconstruct power.

The structure of book 5, as a whole, suggests that among its other functions, the construction of identity was paramount. In the final verses of Ps 107, the psalmist acknowledges

> Let the upright see this and be glad,
>   and all the wicked ones shut their mouth.
> Whoever is wise, let him give heed to these things.
>   Let them understand the proofs of Yahweh's love. (107:42–43)⁷

The wisdom elements that conclude Ps 107 are found similarly in the final psalm in the collection (Ps 145), particularly the juxtaposition of the way of the upright and the way of the wicked ones (Ps 145:19–20).⁸ These texts, both at the beginning and the end of book 5, along with

---

6. Among the earlier studies that adopted such a position, see Hermann Hupfeld, *Die Psalmen* (Gotha: Perthes, 1855), 189–191; Heinrich Graetz, *Kritischer Kommentar zu den Psalmen: Nebts Text und Übersetzung* (Breslau: Schottländer, 1882), 20–37; Ernest Renan, *Histoire du peuple d'Israël* (Paris: Calmany-Levy, 1893), 3:37–50, 3:113–40; Alfred Rahlfs, עֲנִי und עָנָו in den Psalmen (Göttingen: Dieterische, 1892), 80–88. See also Norbert Lohfink, "Von der 'Anawim-Partei' zur 'Kirche der Armen.' Die bibelwissenschaftliche Ahentafel eines Hauptbegriffs der 'Theologie der Befreiung,'" *Bib* 67 (1986): 153–75). More recently, in his work *A History of Israelite Religion in the Old Testament Period* (trans. John Bowden; Louisville: Westminster John Knox, 1994), Rainer Albertz rejects the earlier claims that the poor were a specified group within Yehud and suggests instead that a "piety of the poor" emerged in the postexilic period more broadly among the lower class citizenry, primarily as a response to their "aristocratic colleagues who demonstrated no solidarity" with the poor in the face of growing social and economic challenges (2:518–22).

7. On the jussive rendering of vv. 42–43, see Frank Lothar Hossfeld and Erich Zenger, *Psalms 3: A Commentary on Psalms 101–150*. (ed. Klaus Baltzer; trans. Linda Maloney; Hermeneia; Minneapolis: Fortress Press, 2011), 98–99.

8. The terms utilized in Ps 145:19–20 differ from those employed in Ps 107:42–43. In Ps 107, the psalmist speaks of the "upright," יְשָׁרִים, and the "wicked ones," עַוְלָה, whereas the psalmist in Ps 145 refers to those that "fear" Yahweh, יְרֵאָיו, and those who "love" Yahweh, אֹהֲבָיו, while referring to the wicked as the הָרְשָׁעִים. Broadly speaking, these terms reflect a wisdom influence on both psalms. On the wisdom character of Ps 145 and its significance for the book, see Beat Weber, *Werkbuch Psalmen III: The-*

other wisdom texts throughout the book (cf. Pss 111; 112; 119; 128; 139) suggest that the collection as a whole has an identity shaping function.[9] Anthony Ceresko has aptly explained that the psalms and wisdom literature "intersect in their common enterprise of maintaining and/or reshaping this world inhabited by the community of Israel, particularly in the question of the individual and his or her role, comportment, and place in this world."[10] The images employed in book 5 do in fact "reshape the world" in their declaration of Yahweh's kingship, but the collection of psalms proves equally instructive in determining the role and identity of the faithful within such a "figured world."

As noted in the previous chapter, the psalmists deconstructed imperial claims of world dominance and concomitantly the dominance of Ahuramazda asserted by the Persians by constructing an image of Yahweh as the God of Heaven. In attempting to deconstruct the imperial claims concerning those under its subjugation, one might expect a similar move to be made. To cast off the Persian claims of dominance and the willing acquiescence of its subjects the psalmist could have constructed an identity of the people of God that highlights strength, power, and independence. Such an idea was not lost on the Persians as they sought to portray such an image of its young. Strabo recounts the schooling the Persian youth received

> From age five to twenty-five, they are trained to shoot with the bow, handle the spear, ride on the horseback, and speak the truth. And as teachers of learning they use the wisest men, who weave in the legendary element in order to make it useful. Both without and with song they

---

ologie und Spiritualität des Psalters und seiner Psalmen (Stuttgart: Kohlhammer, 2010), 197–99.

9. On the role of the wisdom influence in book 5, see Gerald Wilson, "Shaping the Psalter: A Consideration of Editorial Linkage in the Book of Psalms," in *The Shape and Shaping of the Psalter* (ed. J. Clinton McCann Jr.; JSOTSup 159; Sheffield: JSOT Press, 1993), 72–82. Wilson concludes that "wisdom has the last word" in book 5 and notes well the wisdom connections present between Pss 1 and 145 and Pss 2 and 144 (80). See also the observations of Erich Zenger on book 5 in "The Composition and Theology of the Fifth Book of Psalms, Psalms 107–145," *JSOT* 89 (1998): 77–102.

10. Anthony Ceresko, "The Sage in the Psalms," in *The Sage in Israel and the Ancient Near East* (ed. John Gammie and Leo Perdue; Winona Lake, Ind.: Eisenbrauns, 1990), 217–30. See also Nancy deClaissé-Walford, *Reading from the Beginning: The Shaping of the Hebrew Psalter* (Macon, Ga.: Mercer University Press, 1997), 93–99.

recite the deeds of the gods and the noblest men. They gather the boys in one place, after rousing them before dawn with the noise of a bronze instrument, as though for arming or the hunt.... They demand that they give an account of each lesson. At the same time they train them in speaking loudly, how to breathe and use their lungs, and to endure heat and cold and rain and to cross torrents, so that their weapons and clothes remain dry; and also to herd flocks and live outdoors, surviving on wild fruit. (Strabo 15:3.18–19)[11]

Although the wisdom literature in the Hebrew Bible, and Proverbs in particular, does offer similar thoughts concerning the training of the youth, such an image is absent in the final book of the Psalter. Rather than positing an identity of strength and power that could overcome a similar Persian ideology, the psalmists make a countermove, invoking those who read the psalms to adopt the posture of a poor servant of Yahweh. The ramifications of this somewhat surprising move are suggested below.

6.1. Rejection of Human Power as Source of Deliverance

In response to the shame of the Babylonian exile and the continued struggle under Persian rule, certain claims were made throughout the literature associated with the postexilic period.[12] Although the composition of the Psalter both diachronically and synchronically remains a matter of some debate, the Psalter does make certain claims, it appears, in light of these experiences.[13] As has often been noted, the kingship of Yahweh remains

---

11. See Amélie Kuhrt, *The Persian Empire: A Corpus of Sources from the Achaemenid Period* (London: Routledge, 2007), 629. As Kuhrt suggests, this appears to imply a *rite de passage* for boys seeking to enter manhood, but the requirements for making the passage are suggestive more generally for a Persian anthropology of the ideal human.

12. See for example, the sweeping assessment of the biblical literature in Erhard Gerstenberger, *Israel in the Persian Period: The Fifth and Fourth Centuries B.C.E.* (trans. Siegfried Schatzmann; BE 18; Atlanta: Society of Biblical Literature, 2011), esp. 142–426. See also Konrad Schmid, *The Old Testament: A Literary History* (trans. Linda Maloney; Minneapolis: Fortress Press, 2012). For a cursory treatment of the biblical texts and related themes from the period, see Lester L. Grabbe, *Judaic Religion in the Second Temple Period: Belief and Practice from the Exile to Yavneh* (London: Routledge, 2000), esp. 13–36.

13. For a suggested outline of the composition history of the Psalter, see Erich Zenger, "Das Buch der Psalmen," in *Einleitung in das Alte Testament* (ed. Erich Zenger;

the fundamental claim in the Psalter, as is especially evident in Pss 90–150. In making this claim in book 5, however, the psalmists also confess in varying ways the inefficacy of human power to deliver amid oppression and distress. Three texts, in particular, emphasize this point. While such a claim is clearly not the dominant theme of book 5, the claim does prove pivotal in the overall thesis of book 5 in that it undercuts any hope in human power to provide deliverance.

The first overt critique of human power and its capacity to deliver those in distress occurs in Ps 108. In the last strophe of the psalm, the first-person language used earlier in the psalm gives way to a communal orientation. In verse 12, the psalmist alludes to a potential battle scene, inquiring as to whether Yahweh will go into battle with his people or if he has rejected them altogether. The community then implores Yahweh in verses 13–14

> O grant us help against the foe (צָר),
>> for worthless (שָׁוְא) is the help of humans.
> With God, we shall do mighty things;
>> it is he who will tread down our foes (צָר).

The psalmist critiques human help, suggesting that it is שָׁוְא. Although the term is used sparingly in the Hebrew Bible (fifty-three times), שָׁוְא is frequently rendered as "ineffectiveness" or "fraudulence." Human help, then, is שָׁוְא or "worthless" because it is unreliable.[14] In the face of enemies, the psalmist acknowledges that "human rescue is an illusion."[15] Consequently, the community must abandon any hope of deliverance from humans and instead, assert that their hope resides in Yahweh alone. The juxtaposition of both ideas, the failure of humans to deliver and the belief that Yahweh

---

6th ed.; Stuttgart: Kohlhammer, 2006), 364–67. See also Schmid's claims concerning the various elements of the Psalter during the overall growth of the Hebrew Bible (*The Old Testament: A Literary History*, 69–71, 113–15, 152–54, 192–194, 214–16). For a different rendering of the composition history, see, for example, Gerald Wilson, "The Structure of the Psalter," in *Interpreting the Psalms: Issues and Approaches* (ed. David Firth and Philip S. Johnston; Downers Grove, Ill.: InterVarsity Press, 2005), 230–34. For a synchronic reading of the Psalter and the theological claims therein, see Jerome F. D. Creach, *The Destiny of the Righteous in the Psalms* (St. Louis: Chalice Press, 2008).

14. Jerry Shepherd, "שָׁוְא," *NIDOTTE* 4:53–55.
15. Hossfeld and Zenger, *Psalms 3*, 113.

will, becomes what Phil Botha labels "a well-known theme" in book 5.[16] The appearance of this theme in the opening Davidic collection in book 5 likely signals the importance of this theme in all that is to follow.

The second critique of human power appears in Ps 116. There the psalmist confesses

> I kept my faith, even when I said
>   "I am greatly afflicted."
> I said in my consternation,
>   "All humans (אָדָם) are deceivers (כֹּזֵב)." (116:10–11)

The psalmist asserted earlier in the psalm that the "cords of death" (116:3a) had wrapped about him, that the torments of Sheol had found him (116:3b), and consequently, that the psalmist "had found distress and anguish" (116:3c). Yet, it was Yahweh who saved him from death (116:8). In verses 10–11, the psalmist pauses to confess his relentless faith in Yahweh as the sole deliverer from a circumstance of great affliction (עָנָה).[17] In his treatment of Ps 116, Thijs Booij, however, challenges the notion that the psalmist retains his faith in verse 10a. To the contrary, he suggests that verse 10a should be rendered "I trusted that I could speak" rather than "I believed even when I spoke," and that verse10a, in fact, is not about the maintenance of faith amid crisis but about the possible loss of faith.[18] He cites the "consternation" mentioned in verse 11a as creating "obvious incongruity" with the notion that the psalmist retained his faith. Yet, Booij's argument fails because the comparison is not between verses 10a and 11a (between faith and consternation), but between verses

---

16. Phil J. Botha, "Psalm 108 and the Quest for the Closure to the Exile," *OTE* 23 (2010), 591. Botha notes that although Ps 108 is comprised of two earlier psalms, the new poetic construction shares numerous parallels to Ps 2 (2:1 // 108:4; 2:4 // 108:5,6; 2:7 // 108:8; 2:8 // 108:6; 2:9 // 108:9), in effect linking the beginning of book 1 with the beginning of book 5. Yet, as Botha contends, Ps 108 "is not for an earthly king; it is the divine ruler himself who will partition his kingdom and take control of it. This provides a new perspective and a way of looking beyond human rule, since 'vain is the help of man' (v. 13b)."

17. Booij contends that the two verses point out the "hardship caused by some form of ill-treatment" by humans that has led to the suffering of the psalmist (Thijs Booij, "Psalm 116:10–11: The Account of an Inner Crisis," *Bib* 76 [1995], 392). See also John Goldingay, *Psalms 90–150* (BCOT; Grand Rapids: Baker Academic, 2008), 344.

18. Ibid.

10a (belief in the power of Yahweh) and 11b (refusal to believe in human power). In contrast to his "belief" in the faithfulness of Yahweh to deliver, the psalmist concludes that "all humans deceive" (116:10b). Although this assessment of all humans may appear rather innocuous in its claim, the evaluation proves damning in the psalmist's assessment of human power. The verb in verse 11b, כזב, carries with it a strong connotation. As Hossfeld and Zenger have explained, the claim in verse 11b "is not primarily an ethical qualification, but a metaphysical one.... כזב, 'deception,' describes human 'nothingness' and 'worthlessness' for others, that is, the unreliability that comes from human nature."[19] Similar to the claim in Ps 108 that help from humans is worthless (שָׁוְא), Ps 116 asserts that humans deceive, implying that reliance upon human power is deceptive because ultimately it is worthless in the face of great affliction. In such circumstances, the psalmist is left to rely upon Yahweh and Yahweh's ability to deliver his people from death (116:8).[20]

The futility of trusting in humans for deliverance appears as well in Ps 118:8-9. In that context, the psalm recalls a time of distress (הַמֵּצַר; 118:5) in which "all the nations (גּוֹיִם) surrounded" the psalmist (118:10). Yet the use of the phrase יֹאמַר־נָא יִשְׂרָאֵל, "let Israel now say," in verse 2, followed in verses 3 and 4 with a similar injunction for the house of Aaron and those who fear Yahweh, implies that the psalm in its final form "transfers the hard experiences described in the prayer [of the individual] to the experiences of Israel."[21] The individual psalmist's confession concerning the inefficacy of human power becomes, in essence, the confession of the community. In the face of external threats, the psalmist instructs in 118:8-9 that

> It is better to take refuge in Yahweh
> than to trust in humans (אָדָם).

---

19. Hossfeld and Zenger, *Psalms 3*, 218.
20. Goldingay, *Psalms 90–150*, 344.
21. Marko Marttila, *Collective Reinterpretation in the Psalms: A Study of the Redaction History of the Psalter* (FAT 2/13; Tübingen: Mohr Siebeck, 2006), 170. See also Christoph Levin, "Psalm 136 als zeitweilige Schlussdoxologie des Psalters," *SJOT* 14 (2000): 17–27. Levin contends that the similar collective statements found in Pss 124 and 129 were derived from Ps 118 when the Psalms of Ascents were placed in relation to Ps 118. Whether one agrees with the diachronic model suggested by Levin, the point remains valid that in several places in book 5, subsequent redactors sought to shape or reshape earlier psalms to influence the identity of the entire community.

6. THE IDENTITY OF THE PEOPLE OF GOD

> It is better to take refuge in Yahweh
> than to trust in princes (נְדִיבִים).

The "better ... than" sayings (טוֹב ... מִן) appear regularly in wisdom literature, adding an educative element to the psalm and supporting further the earlier claim (§6.1) that one of the functions of book 5 is to shape the identity of those that pray these psalms.[22] The primary issue at stake concerns the refuge sought when the individual or community is under duress.[23] According to the psalmist, one cannot trust in humans in general (118:8b) because, similar to the claim established in Pss 108 and 116, humans are fallible and unreliable in such circumstances.[24] The second wisdom saying (118:9) narrows the claim by suggesting that one cannot trust in the princes (נְדִיבִים), the wealthy and powerful elite. The term נְדִיבִים occurs in five other texts within the Psalter (47:10; 83:12; 107:40; 113:8; and 146:3) and in each instance, the נְדִיבִים do not appear as those capable of delivering people in need.[25] Further, while the term may suggest a position of power or status, such power is denuded when compared with that of Yahweh. As the psalmist claims, the נְדִיבִים offer no real sense of protection; that task resides fully with Yahweh, the God who provides refuge.

Attempts to identify the נְדִיבִים have resulted in various options,[26] including foreign leaders, as observed in Ezra 1–6 or Neh 2–6, or per-

---

22. On the association with wisdom literature in vv. 8–9, see Erhard Gerstenberger, *Psalms, Part 2, and Lamentations* (FOTL 15; Grand Rapids: Eerdmans, 2001), 303.

23. On the role of חסה as a central organizational feature in the Psalter as a whole, see Jerome F. D. Creach, *Yahweh as Refuge and the Editing of the Hebrew Psalter* (JSOTSup 217; Sheffield: Sheffield Academic Press, 1996). Creach contends that previous collections of psalms were edited and combined with the "effect of encouraging readers to seek refuge in Yahweh, that is to choose the eternal king as a source of protection and sustenance vis-a-vis human power" (18). While the verb חסה does not play a dominant role in the present study, the conclusions reached by Creach support those being argued here.

24. Hossfeld and Zenger, *Psalms 3*, 238.

25. The adjectival form also appears in Pss 51:14 and 110:3 but both are better rendered as "a noble spirit" (51:14) and "your noble people" (110:3), respectively. In Ps 47:10, the "princes of the peoples" stream to Jerusalem to acknowledge that Yahweh alone is the king of the earth, while in Ps 113, the poor are placed alongside the princes, but the psalm is clear that this is the work of the God of heaven (vv. 4–6) and not that of the princes.

26. On the various interpretations proposed for the socio-political context in

haps those within their own community who were elevated to positions of power.[27] Regardless of the precise identity of the נְדִיבִים, the point remains that "recourse to human allies and counselors comes a poor second" to faith in Yahweh.[28]

6.2. A Theology of the Poor in Book 5

Having recognized that human power, whether from within their own community or without, is ultimately ineffectual, the psalmists in book 5 adopt a different posture and instead invoke language associated with the theology of the poor.[29] Berges and Hoppe rightly note the significance of such language in the Psalter and observe that "in no other book is the terminology of the poor represented so heavily" as in the Psalter.[30] For example, the term אֶבְיוֹן appears twenty-eight times in the Psalter (and only thirty times in the remainder of the Hebrew Bible). Similarly, the term עָנִי appears seventy-eight times throughout the Hebrew Bible with more than one-third of the occurrences in the Psalter (twenty-nine times). Admittedly, while statistics such as these are nothing more than numbers, they do offer evidence that suggests the language of the poor occupied an unusually significant role in psalmic material. This has led to the suggestion by Rainer Albertz, among others, that a "piety of the poor" developed among the lower class circles in the postexilic period.[31] While there was no doubt a religious connotation to the language, Albertz contends nevertheless that a social connotation remains clearly in view. As suggested in the present volume, the lack of power (social connotation) experienced by

---

Yehud, see Jeremiah W. Cataldo, *A Theocratic Yehud? Issues of Government in a Persian Province* (LHBOTS 498; New York: T&T Clark, 2009), 12–32.

27. Goldingay, *Psalms 90–150*, 359.

28. Leslie C. Allen, *Psalms 101–150* (WBC 21; Waco, Tex.: Word, 1983), 124.

29. On the place of the theology of the poor in postexilic psalmody, see Norbert Lohfink, *Lobgesänge der Armen: Studien zum Magnifikat, den Hodajot von Qumran, und einigen späten Psalmen* (SBS 143; Stuttgart: Katholisches Bibelwerk, 1990). See also the summary review of the language of the poor in Ulrich Berges and Rudolf Hoppe, *Arm und Reich* (Würzburg: Echter, 2009), 49–56.

30. Berges and Hoppe, *Arm und Reich*, 49. See also my earlier study, W. Dennis Tucker Jr., "A Polysemiotic Approach to the Poor in the Psalms," *PRSt* 31 (2004): 425–39.

31. Rainer Albertz, *A History of Israelite Religion in the Old Testament Period* (trans. John Bowden; OTL; Louisville: Westminster John Knox, 1994), 2:518–22.

those who prayed the psalms no doubt generated a religious and theological connotation as well.

In his assessment of the material, Albertz limits his understanding of such a movement ("piety of the poor") to the "religious outsider groups" who sought to resist the dominant social circles and their official theology.[32] The struggle, so it seems from Albertz's assessment, is an internal struggle between those with power and those without. Interestingly, however, in his treatment of the psalms, he fails to mention the pressures that were being exerted upon the community by Persia and the complicating factors that this would have generated upon the social structure in Yehud and its impact upon the theology expressed in the Psalter.[33] Such a view seems to support Pierre Briant's claim that Yehud experienced an internal autonomy under Persian rule. Lisbeth Fried, however, has dismissed that notion as overly generalized, suggesting instead that as long as Yehud remained in the hands of the Persian imperial government, the local officials had little if any real power.[34] Fried's explanation of the social situation may shed additional light upon the theology of the poor in book 5. As noted above, human power was dismissed as illusory and ineffectual. This assessment of human power may have reflected the view that in reality those with *presumed* power in that society did not possess the *actual* power necessary to deliver those in need, and perhaps more sinisterly, those with *presumed* power had no interest in delivering those in need. Because the psalmists could not rely upon human power to deliver those in need, they utilized themes from the theology of the poor to suggest that ultimately

---

32. Ibid., 2:522.

33. This is not to suggest, however, that Albertz fails to recognize the Persian influence more broadly on postexilic literature—see *A History of Israelite Religion in the Old Testament Period*, 2:464–70, for example. For a more extensive analysis of the Persian influence, see Kenneth Hoglund, *Achaemenid Imperial Administration in Syria-Palestine and the Missions of Ezra and Nehemiah* (SBLDS 125; Atlanta: Scholars Press, 1992), 207–40 and Jon L. Berquist, *Judaism in Persia's Shadow: A Social and Historical Approach* (Minneapolis: Fortress Press, 1995), 131–46, and their assessment of the impact of Persian political and economic pressures upon Yehud and the literature of the postexilic literature.

34. Lisbeth S. Fried, *Priest and the Great King: Temple-Palace Relations in the Persian Empire* (BJSUCSD 10; Winona Lake, Ind.: Eisenbrauns, 2004), 233. As Fried explains, "Persian period Judah was not self-governing: There were no assemblies, no Jewish lay bodies to advise the governor, no sanhedrins. There was no vehicle for local control. ... Local officials, whether priest or lay, held little real power."

Yahweh will deliver the poor from the kings and external people groups that oppress them (Ps 144:11) as well as the princes and those internal groups who appear to have failed the poor as well (Ps 107:40).

6.2.1. SELF-DESCRIBING AS ONE OF THE POOR

In a recent study Johannes Bremer tracked the language of the poor in the Psalter, with particular interest in its function within book 5.[35] Beyond simply identifying the "poor" semantic domain and the number of occurrences of each term, Bremer tracks Yahweh's dealings and interactions with the poor. Critical to his observations is Bremer's claim that "God reacts at no point in the Psalter to poverty as such, but to one or more persons who are characterized or who characterize themselves as 'poor.'"[36] This self-characterization by the psalmist as "poor" functions to create the kind of "figured world" mentioned above by Newsom. Such language enables the psalmist "to constitute a world of meaning, a distinctive identity, a community of values, and a structure of selfhood."[37] In self-describing as one of the poor, the psalmist restructures the identity of himself and those who also identify as the poor. They are no longer simply the ones without power, but instead, the ones to whom God responds.

At times, the psalmists make general claims about the poor and Yahweh's response to their plight. The appearance of these verses in book 5 buttresses the assertion that a theology of the poor pervades much of the final book in the Psalter. In Ps 113:7, for example, the psalmist contends

> He raises the poor (דָּל) from the dust
> and lifts the needy (אֶבְיוֹן) from the ash heap.[38]

---

35. Johannes Bremer, "'Doch den אֶבְיוֹן hob er aus dem עוֹנִי empor' (Ps 107:41a): Eine synchrone Analyse des Umgangs Gottes mit den Armen im Psalter und diachrone Verortung im 5. Psalmenbuch (Ps 107–145) und im Schluss Hallel (Ps 146–150). Frank-Lothar Hossfeld zur Vollendung des 70. Lebensjahres," *BN* 158 (2013): 55–84. See also Johannes Bremer, "Developments of the 'Theology of the Poor' in the Psalter," in *The Psalter as Witness: The Theology and Theologies of the Book of Psalms* (ed. W. Dennis Tucker Jr.; Waco, Tex.: Baylor University Press, forthcoming).

36. Ibid., 60. Bremer notes that it may be difficult at times to differentiate between a material or spiritual form of poverty being experienced by the psalmist, but he suggests that while the *Selbstprädikation* may carry a spiritual connotation, the material aspect cannot be denied (60n16).

37. Newsom, *The Self as Symbolic Space*, 2.

38. The subsequent verses include statements about the poor man and the barren

Similarly, in Ps 138:6, the psalmist claims

> For though Yahweh is high,
>> he regards the lowly (שָׁפָל).[39]

Then in perhaps somewhat less dramatic fashion, Yahweh announces in Ps 132:15b, "I will satisfy her poor (אֶבְיוֹן) with bread."[40] These claims, while not necessarily self-referential, do support the claim that Yahweh responds to the poor. Further, because the psalmist self-describes as one of the poor in other psalms (see below), these larger claims from the theology of the poor do in fact become self-referential to some degree and likely are meant to form the identity of the community.

In other places in book 5, however, the psalmist employs first-person language, and in so doing, explicitly self-identifies as one of the poor. In such contexts, the psalmist not only draws from the vocabulary of the theology of the poor, the psalmist seeks to portray himself as one who is poor, one in need of the action of Yahweh. In Ps 109:22, under great duress, the psalmist announces, "I am poor (עָנִי) and needy (אֶבְיוֹן)," and in the final verse of the psalm, he claims that Yahweh "stands at the right hand of the needy (אֶבְיוֹן)" (109:31). Although this final claim appears in the third person, the earlier self-description of the psalmist as one of the needy (אֶבְיוֹן) in verse 22 extends to the final verse, implying that Yahweh stands at the right hand of the psalmist as well.

Similar instances appear elsewhere in book 5. In Ps 116, the psalmist declares that he was "greatly afflicted" (עָנָה) and "brought low" (דָּלַל). Although the terms could imply a spiritual attitude of humility, the terms also carry with them a sense of "concrete pressure or oppression."[41] Likewise, in Ps 118, the psalmist acknowledges "out of my distress (הַמֵּצַר) I

---

women, who serve as metaphors for all those who suffer. As Prinsloo and Breukelman suggest, these figures serve as representatives for God's people. See Gert T. M. Prinsloo, "Yahweh and the Poor in Psalm 113: Literary Motif and/or Theological Reality?" *OTE* 9 (1996), 477; Frans Breukelman, "Psalm 113 oder die Struktur der biblischen Theologie," *T&K* 53 (1992), 16.

39. Bremer does not include שָׁפָל in his list of terms associated with the poor. Obviously the term is not linguistically related to the dominant terms in the semantic domain (the terms עָנִי and אֶבְיוֹן), but its imagery and usage remain consistent; the שָׁפָל are those who have been brought low by others and to whom Yahweh responds.

40. Bremer, "Doch den אֶבְיוֹן hob er aus dem עוֹנִי empor," 62.

41. Hossfeld and Zenger, *Psalms 3*, 218.

called upon Yahweh." Although the specific language of the poor is absent in Ps 118, the psalmist alludes to having been "pushed down" (118:13) by the nations that had surrounded him. According to the psalmist, his only strength was that of Yahweh's (118:14).[42]

A similar declaration appears in Ps 142:7.

> Listen attentively to my cry,
>   for I am very powerless (דַּלּוֹתִי).

Although דַּלּוֹתִי is often rendered as "low," the subsequent verse in Ps 142 offers some justification for understanding the meaning as "powerless." In verse 7b, the psalmist asked to be delivered from his persecutors because "they are too strong (אָמְצוּ) for me." In this sense, the psalmist aligns himself with the poor as he confesses his inability to redeem his present circumstance. This inability to change the present circumstance due to powerlessness is reinforced in verse 8 with the image of the "dungeon." As Christoph Buysch has suggested, מַסְגֵּר may serve as another image of death, thus reinforcing the psalmist's desperate plight and his inability to redeem himself from it.[43]

In these and similar texts in book 5, the psalmists have not only reiterated the claims associated with the theology of the poor, but more

---

42. See Frank Lothar Hossfeld, "Der gnädige Gott und der arme Gerechte: Anthropologische Akzente in der Psalmengruppe 111–118," in *Kircheneinheit und Weltverantwortung: Festscrift für Peter Neuner* (ed. Christoph Böttigheimer and Hubert Filser; Regensburg: Pustet, 2006), 51–63. Hossfeld suggests that within Pss 111–118, two images of the psalmist emerge: the royal depiction of a person (Pss 112 and 115) and the image of a person shaped by the theology of the poor (Pss 113; 116; 118). He rightly notes that these two images are meant to mirror the images of David in the first two books of the Psalter, but in their present literary context, the images function as descriptors of "the common person" (62).

43. Christoph Buysch, *Der letzte Davidpsalter: Interpretation, Komposition und Funktion der Psalmengruppe Ps 138–145* (SBB 63; Stuttgart: Katholisches Bibelwerk, 2009), 248. Gerstenberger suggests that with the verb יָצָא the psalmist may have been invoking the image of being "brought out" of Egypt or Babylon. In that case, according to Gerstenberger, the psalmist may have attempted to highlight the weakness of the supplicant and the power of the oppressor by recalling previous moments in which the weak supplicant was utterly dependent upon deliverance by Yahweh (*Psalms, Part 2, and Lamentations*, 420). Even if one follows the suggestion of Gerstenberger, the image of the dungeon retains its force as a place of death.

importantly, the psalmists have self-described *as* one of the poor and, in so doing, placed their trust in Yahweh alone for a remedy to their plight.

6.2.2. Self-Describing as a Servant of Yahweh

In addition to self-describing as one of the poor, the psalmist also self-describes as a servant of Yahweh throughout the Psalter. Although the role of the servant and servants in the Book of Isaiah has garnered significant attention, the role of the same in the book of Psalms has gone relatively untreated.[44] Ulrich Berges, perhaps more than any other, has examined the role of the servants in the Psalter in light of similar usage in Isaiah.[45] Berges argues that the "servants" played a central role in the *Kompositionsgeschichte* of both Isaiah and the Psalter, with the servants accomplishing the final composition of Isaiah. Because the last appearance of עֲבָדִים occurs in Ps 135, however, Berges concludes that the group was responsible for the "next to last" stage in the composition of the Psalter, with a subsequent group responsible for Pss 138–145 and the final Hallel.[46]

While Berges' insights are instructive, the primary focus of the present study, however, does not concern the *Kompositionsgeschichte* of the Psalter nor does the validity of this study depend upon the ability to correctly identify those termed עֲבָדִים or עֶבֶד. Rather the primary focus remains on how images and language construct identity and deconstruct power in the Psalter. In several instances עֲבָדִים or עֶבֶד appears alongside psalms in

---

44. On the role of the servants in Isaiah, see in particular, Joseph Blenkinsopp, *The "Servants of the Lord" in Third Isaiah: Profile of a Pietistic Group in the Persian Period* (PIBA 7; Dublin: Irish Bible Association, 1983): 1–23; idem, "A Jewish Sect of the Persian Period," *CBQ* 52 (1990): 5–20; and Ulrich Berges, *The Book of Isaiah: Its Composition and Final Form* (trans. Millard Lind; HBM 46; Sheffield: Sheffield Phoenix, 2012), esp. 451–501.

45. Ulrich Berges, "Die Knechte im Psalter. Ein Beitrag zu seiner Kompositionsgeschichte," *Bib* 81 (2000): 153–78. See also his shorter analysis in "Who Were the Servants? A Comparative Inquiry in the Book of Isaiah and the Psalms," in *Past, Present, Future: The Deuteronomistic History and the Prophets* (ed. Johannes C. de Moor and Harry F. van Rooy; OtSt 44; Leiden: Brill, 2000), 1–18.

46. Berges, "Who were the Servants," 15. Christoph Levin suggests, based on the appearance of חֲסִידִים in Psalm 149, that the final redaction of the Psalter was carried out by this group sometime in the second century B.C.E. ("Das Gebetbuch der Gerechten: Literargeschichtliche Beobachtungen am Psalter," *ZTK* 90 [1993]: 355–81), see especially 375–79.

which the psalmist alludes to a theology of the poor, or in psalms in which the psalmist self-describes as one of the poor. As noted above, the psalmist self-describes in Ps 109:22 as poor (עָנִי) and needy (אֶבְיוֹן), but later in 109:28 the psalmist prays

> Let them curse, but you bless.
>> They have arisen and will be put to shame,
>
> but your servant (עֶבֶד) will rejoice.

The psalm concludes with the claim that Yahweh stands at the right hand of the needy (אֶבְיוֹן), the same term for "poor" that was used earlier in self-describing. This association appears elsewhere in the Psalter, but with particular regularity in book 5.[47] In such psalms the image of a servant or servants cannot be separated from that of the poor. Similar to Ps 109, Ps 116 employs both terms in close proximity. In Ps 116, for example, the psalmist self-describes as one who was "brought low" (דָּלַל) and "greatly afflicted" (עָנָה). In addition, the psalmist also self-describes by declaring, "I am your servant (עֶבֶד)" not once, but twice (116:16). The language and imagery used in these psalms, and those similar to them, reinforce the connection between the theology of the poor and that of servant imagery.

Because Ps 119 is a תּוֹרָה psalm, attention is frequently and rightly given to the multiple terms used in reference to the תּוֹרָה. Yet this psalm also makes repeated use of the term "servant" while also invoking themes and images associated with a theology of the poor. In Ps 119, the term עֶבֶד appears thirteen times (with only twenty-five appearances elsewhere in the Psalter) and the language of affliction appears with similar regularity in the psalm (e.g. 119:23, 50, 67, 71, 107, 134, 153, 161).[48] Strikingly, there are a number of instances in which both images occur within the same verse or adjacent verses, creating a connection between the language of the servant and the theology of the poor. In 119:49–50, for example, the psalmist prays

---

47. See additional pairings of servant(s) imagery and the language and imagery of the poor in Pss 113; 123; 136; 143. On the use of דְּכָא in 143:1 and its relation to the theology of the poor, see Egbert Ballhorn, *Zum Telos des Psalters: Der Textzusammenhang des Vierten und Fünften Psalmenbuches (Ps 90–150)* (BBB 138; Berlin: Philo, 2004), 275.

48. Bremer, "Doch den אֶבְיוֹן hob er aus dem עוֹנִי empor," 74.

6. THE IDENTITY OF THE PEOPLE OF GOD

> Remember your word to your servant (עֶבֶד),
>   for which you have made me wait.
> This is my consolation in my affliction (עֳנִי),
>   that your word will give me life.

Or in 119:134–135

> Redeem me from the oppression (עֹשֶׁק) of humans
>   that I may keep your precepts.
> Make your face to shine upon your servant (עֶבֶד)
>   and teach me your statutes.

There are additional examples in Ps 119 that reflect this pairing of images.[49] Although the rhetoric in Ps 119 appears focused on intracommunal tensions, particularly the princes and the godless and their treatment of the psalmist, the psalmist nevertheless seeks to construct an identity rooted in torah obedience, but born out amid oppression and godless action as one of the poor servants of Yahweh.

6.2.3. David as Poor Servant

The connection between a theology of the poor and servant language is extended in the image of David, with David becoming emblematic of the poor servant who depends entirely upon Yahweh for deliverance.[50] The structure of book 5 appears to give attention to David, and the psalms within book 5 frequently allude to texts from the previous David collections. Book 5 opens and closes with a Davidic collection (Pss 108–110; 138–145) and the intertextual connections in book 5 frequently refer back to books 1 and 2 in the Psalter—the books most associated with David.[51]

---

49. Other explicit examples include 119:23, 84–85, 121–122, 140–141.

50. Egbert Ballhorn, "'Um deines Knechtes David willen' (Ps 132:10): Die Gestalt Davids im Psalter," *BN* 76 (1995), 16–31, esp. 29–30; idem, "Der Davidbund in Ps 132 und im Kontext des Psalters," in *Für immer verbündet: Studien zur Bundestheologie der Bibel* (ed. Christoph Dohmen and Christian Frevel; SB 211; Stuttgart: Katholisches Bibelwerk, 2007), 11–18.

51. Harm van Grol, "David and his *Chasidim*: Place and Function of Psalms 138–145," in *The Composition of the Book of Psalms* (ed. Erich Zenger; BETL 238; Leuven: Peeters, 2010), 309–37. See also Ballhorn's brief assessment (*Zum Telos des Psalters*, 379–81).

Yet these subtle references in book 5 fail to portray David as a king, full of power and might, capable of delivering his people from oppression.[52] To the contrary, these psalms frequently depict David as one without power and in need of Yahweh's might in overcoming the enemy.[53]

In Ps 144, for example, David is no longer referred to as "anointed," but as "servant." Arguably with the shift in language, David functions paradigmatically. The designation "servant" in Ps 144 may seem inconsequential except for the fact that the language of "servant" or "servants" has appeared throughout book 5, as noted above. Ballhorn contends that while the phrase "servant of Yahweh" can indeed be a kingly title, as often seen in the prophetic literature, in book 5 it appears to serve as a collective reference to Israel (136:22) or to an individual petitioner (Ps 116:16; 119:176).[54]

---

52. Ballhorn contends that in Pss 108–110, the first Davidic collection in book 5, David appears as a "powerful king upon whom God confers blessings and surrounds him with the wealth of nations" (*Zum Telos des Psalters*, 379). But as suggested above (§§3.2.1–3), these psalms are insistent upon their claim that Yahweh and no other has the power to withstand the onslaught of those threatening his people. Although David appears in the superscription of each psalm, he does not appear as the one prepared to deliver his people.

53. The precise function of the Psalter and David's place within the collection remains a matter of scholarly debate. In his work, David Mitchell has forcefully claimed that the book of Psalms has an eschatological-messianic orientation rather than a sapiential focus as argued by Gerald Wilson and others. See David Mitchell, "Lord, Remember David: G. H. Wilson and the Message of the Psalter," *VT* 56 (2006): 526–48, esp. 537, and Mitchell's earlier work, *The Message of the Psalter: An Eschatological Programme in the Book of Psalms* (JSOT Sup 252; Sheffield: Sheffield Academic Press, 1997). See also Gerald Wilson, *The Editing of the Hebrew Psalter* (SBLDS 76; Chico, Calif.: Scholars Press, 1985). Wilson modified his perspective somewhat in "King, Messiah, and the Reign of God: Revisiting the Royal Psalms and the Shape of the Psalter," in *The Book of Psalms: Composition and Reception* (ed. Peter Flint and Patrick D. Miller; VTSup 99; Leiden: Brill, 2005), 391–406, see especially pages 403–4. More likely, the Psalter had a sapiential orientation in its final form, as suggested by Wilson, but, as a more robust messianism developed in later Second Temple literature, the Psalter was reread with eschatological-messianic overtones, likely explaining the use of selected psalms in the New Testament. On messianism more generally in the Second Temple period, see John J. Collins, *The Scepter and the Star: The Messiahs of the Dead Sea Scrolls and Other Ancient Literature* (ABRL; New York: Doubleday, 1995).

54. Ballhorn, *Zum Telos des Psalters*, 281. Likewise, citing Ps 89, Zenger contends for a collective reading in Ps 144 (Erich Zenger, "Der jüdischer Psalter—ein antiimperiales Buch?" in *Religion und Gesellschaft: Studien zu ihrer Wechselbeziehung in*

Such a reading of the term is evident in Ps 143:12. The psalmist concludes Ps 143 by pleading

> And in your steadfast love cut off my enemies,
>   and destroy all my adversaries (צֹרְרֵי),
>   for I am your servant (עַבְדֶּךָ).

Thus in Ps 143, the psalmist self-describes as a servant, but more importantly, as a servant who has been crushed (143:3) and stands in need of deliverance from the adversaries. עַבְדֶּךָ appears as the last word in the psalm linking the image of the psalmist as servant in Ps 143 with that of David as servant in the subsequent psalm.[55] The praying servant in Ps 143 is aligned with the royal servant David in Ps 144, both incapable of delivering themselves, needing instead the work of the Divine King, the dominant claim of the subsequent psalm (Ps 145).

The psalmist in Ps 144 has clearly appropriated royal psalms and royal imagery, and while the royal theme is diminished, as Ballhorn has opined, it is not altogether erased.[56] Rather, as Zenger suggests, the psalmist has characterized David "not as a powerful, imperial king, but as a weak character (*Gestalt*) that needs the deliverance of Yahweh."[57] Thus the royal language and its related imagery do not serve as a sign of the psalmist's own power in Ps 144 (*contra* Ps 18) nor the longing for a renewed Davidic power (*contra* Booij), but instead such language of power and position has been transformed as David becomes the symbol of the poor servant.[58] The psalmist who employs royal imagery does so not to invoke power, but to align himself with the one (David) who has been redeemed from the cruel sword as the servant of Yahweh, with the hope that Yahweh will do the same for another servant, the psalmist, in his present circumstance.

---

den Kulturen des Antiken Vorderen Orients [ed. Rainer Albertz; AZERKAVO 1/AOAT 248; Münster: Ugarit, 1997], 98). On collective reinterpretation in the Psalter more generally, see Marttila, *Collective Reinterpretation in the Psalms*.

55. Ballhorn, *Zum Telos des Psalters*, 281.
56. Ibid., 280. For additional comments on Ps 144, see §4.3.2 in the present study.
57. Zenger, "Der jüdischer Psalter—ein anti-imperiales Buch," 98.
58. Thijs Booij, "Psalm 144: Hope of Davidic Welfare," *VT* 59 (2009): 173–80.

6.3. Conclusion: The Poor Servant and Its Implications

As suggested above, the psalmists' construction of identity sought both to construct and deconstruct power. In his analysis of the poor in the Psalter, Bremer posits a possible social context for those seeking to construct an identity of the poor in the Persian period.[59] He recalls Neh 5 and suggests that the taxation exacted upon those in Yehud resulted in a sense of oppression particularly for the poor. This was only exacerbated by the fact that the elite of the community exploited and enslaved many within the community of Yehud in order to carry out the Persian mandates, leaving the poor with no real hope for deliverance. This image of those in Yehud stands in stark contrast to the Persian iconography and political propaganda that sought to portray all inhabitants in the empire as joyful participants under Achaemenid rule—instead of self-describing as joyful participants, the psalmists self-describe as poor servants.

In the psalmists' attempt to deconstruct power, they refused to acknowledge human agency, and particularly that of political power, as a means for deliverance out of their circumstances. According to the psalms in book 5 all human power is illusory and vain, and in the face of oppression, such power is worthless. As a result, the psalmists self-describe as poor servants of Yahweh. But as noted above, Bremer contends that the primary concern of the psalmists was not simply self-describing as the poor, but recognizing that Yahweh responds to those declared among the poor. Strikingly, the language of the poor and Yahweh's interaction with the poor shifts as one reads the Psalter synchronically. The first two books in the Psalter contain a heavy concentration of poor language and the various reactions of Yahweh to those self-described as the poor. In book 3, such language appears only in Psalms 74, 76 and 86. In book 4, however, such language is absent altogether, save two examples, and certainly does not constitute a resounding theme within that collection.[60] Yet within book 5, the language and imagery of the poor moves to the fore again, signaling

---

59. Bremer, "Doch den אֶבְיוֹן hob er aus dem עוֹנִי empor," 76.

60. Bremer's analysis of the "poor" semantic domain includes a rather expansive list of terms but fails to include the term עֲשׁוּקִים, "oppressed" (ibid., 56). The absence of power for the עֲשׁוּקִים appears to make it synonymous with the more traditional terms associated with a theology of the poor. Within book 4, עֲשׁוּקִים does occur once (103:6), but beyond that the only other appearance of a "poor" term is in the superscription in Ps 102:1 (עָנִי).

a renewed interest in a theology of the poor and its implications for their current social and political context. Bremer explains that

> The cooperation of a part of the Jewish population [in the exploitation] may have led to the modification of the ancient Near Eastern motif of the king's concern for justice for the poor. No Persian kings, no satraps, and no governors will take on these statements regarding the poor. Yahweh assumes this responsibility.[61]

In self-describing as the poor servants of Yahweh, the psalmists yearned for the intervention of the Divine King not only to serve as refuge for the oppressed (140:14), but also to provide relief from the political forces that threatened them (144:7). The image of a world rightly ordered under the Achaemenid Empire is altogether absent in these psalms. Rather than recognizing Ahuramazda or any one of the Achaemenid kings (or their representatives) as the source of hope, the psalmists turned their gaze to Yahweh, the Divine King. In this figured world, the only hope of deliverance was to self-describe as one who was utterly powerless, and in so doing, trust in Yahweh's faithful response to them.

---

61. Ibid., 77.

7
CONCLUSION: BOOK 5 AND IMPERIAL IDEOLOGY

7.0. INTRODUCTION

Throughout this study, the notion of power has remained at the fore. The psalmists have repeatedly assailed the power of the other, while concomitantly affirming the power of their covenant God. As noted in the opening chapter, Erich Zenger has suggested that the Psalter functioned in part as an anti-imperial book of sorts.[1] In explaining the rationale for such nomenclature, Zenger contends that

> One reads the book of Psalms as a mirror to the experiences of the world. It is the history of a dramatic altercation between the righteous and the evildoers, but also between the people of God and the idolatrous nations of the earth ... The Psalter constructs Yahweh poetically not only as the warrior for justice and righteousness, but above all, as the warrior against the mythic chaos which has been articulated in the enemies of the individuals, *but also in the political systems, and especially in the kings and princes of historically hostile nations*. In the individual and structural "enemies," the creation-averse and life-threatening forces of Chaos break through, to which the warring of Yahweh is called upon in the psalms. From this dynamic of prayer, the Psalter is an anti-imperial book. It denounces the destructive imperial structures and systems and holds firmly that the biblical God will put an end to these systems.[2]

---

1. Erich Zenger, "Der jüdische Psalter—ein anti-imperiales Buch?" in *Religion und Gesellschaft: Studien zu ihrer Wechselbeziehung in den Kulturen des Antiken Vorderen Orients* (ed. Rainer Albertz; AZERKAVO 1/AOAT 248; Münster: Ugarit, 1997), 95–105.
2. Ibid., 97, emphasis added.

188   CONSTRUCTING AND DECONSTRUCTING POWER

In chapters 3 and 4 of the present study, numerous psalms in book 5 were considered, each illustrating the various responses to the kinds of powers mentioned by Zenger. Through metaphorical and image-laden language, these psalms challenge a number of assumptions related to institutional power and seek to deconstruct the power traditionally associated with empires, nations, and peoples. If, like much of the literature in the Hebrew Bible, the Psalter began to take its shape in the Persian period, then the social and historical events, as well as the ideological claims of that period must be considered when reading these texts. Moreover these texts should be understood in part as "*replies, responses, and counter-claims* to utterances made by others within a broader cultural context" as Newsom has suggested.[3] Despite the strident claims of the Achaemenid dynasty and their claims to universal rule, selected psalms in book 5 provide a resounding rejection of human power, especially the kind embodied in empires and nations. Egbert Ballhorn, among others, has correctly observed that there are significant political dynamics at work in the Psalter.[4] Amid the praise of Yahweh as the God of Yehud there is a secondary claim meant to discredit the power associated with other nations and peoples.

The psalmists challenge the Persian notion of a worldwide empire governed by an Achaemenid ruler under the watchful eye of Ahuramazda and instead assert that kingship belongs to Yahweh alone (108:4–7) and that his "glory is over the whole earth" (108:6). The political powers that surround those in Yehud cannot match the power of Yahweh and will be shattered utterly by the Divine King as he stands alongside his people (e.g., 109:31; 110:5; 124:6–8).

The psalms also discredit any claim that those subjugated to the Persian Empire do so in joyous participation. To the contrary, the psalmists employ vivid imagery that reflects the toll that such subjugation has taken upon the people. The result of unchecked power is compared to a warrior's sharp arrows (120:4) or deep furrows plowed upon their backs (129:3). Even more emphatically, the psalmist in Ps 125:3 refers to the political enemies as "the scepter of wickedness," suggesting a thoroughly negative critique of their rule. Throughout the various psalms, the depiction of

---

3. Carol A. Newsom, *The Self as Symbolic Space: Constructing Identity and Community at Qumran* (STDJ 52; Leiden: Brill, 2004), 3, emphasis added.

4. Egbert Ballhorn, *Zum Telos des Psalters: Der Textzusammenhang des Vierten und Fünften Psalmenbuches* (BBB 138; Berlin: Philo, 2004), 147.

7. CONCLUSION

empires and enemies remains unflattering, and subjugation to such enemies is never perceived as beneficial or welcome.

Although the Persians claimed that their empire created cosmic order, the psalms in book 5 undercut any such notion, offering instead a vision of chaos and cosmic disorder in reference to the nations and enemies. Drawing on the classic images of a watery abyss as an image of chaos, the psalmist notes that had Yahweh not been on the side of Israel when she was attacked

> they would have swallowed us up alive,
>   when their anger was kindled against us
> then the flood would have swept us away,
>   the torrent would have gone over us;
> then over us would have gone the raging waters. (124:3b–5 NRSV)

Even at the close of book 5, the psalmist alludes to the disorder created by those that have ruled over them. As noted in chapter 4, the psalmist longs for a time when their sons and daughters shall grow strong (144:12), when the storehouses will be full (144:13), and perhaps most telling, when "there is no cry of distress" in the streets (144:14). By virtue of this request, the psalmist implies such is not the case under the "hands of the foreigner" (144:7, 11). In short, throughout book 5, not a single psalm provides a positive assessment of the nations as political powers but instead understands the foe (צָר) as that which must be thwarted and overcome so that "all flesh can bless his holy name" (145:21).

The threat of the foe (צָר) and its potential to wreak havoc upon those in Yehud did not dampen the community's allegiance to Yahweh, however. As explained in chapter 5, following a similar move in other biblical literature from the Persian period, the psalmists constructed an image of God that stressed Yahweh's preeminence because of the deity's rightful place in the heavens. By emphasizing Yahweh's position over the heavens and the earth, the community envisioned a deity that remained above the political machinations of the day. There was one God and one God alone according to the psalmists (cf. Ps 115). This construal of the deity however was buttressed further by the notion of Yahweh's outstretched hand, an image meant to convey Yahweh's capacity to deliver despite his heavenly location. Although the psalmists dismiss the efficacy of human power to deliver those in Yehud from the threats of unchecked power, they retained hope because the God who created the heavens and the earth is the same

God who "raises the poor from the dust and lifts the needy from the ash heap" (113:7).

7.1. Psalms 146–150: An Extension of Themes

The claims found in book 5 (Pss 107–145) that deconstruct human power, preferring instead to acknowledge Yahweh as the sole source of deliverance, continue in the concluding collection of psalms (146–150).[5] Zenger has argued that the concluding Hallel "builds to a grandiose anti-imperial finale".[6] What he fails to notice in his earlier article is the continuity that exists between selected psalms in book 5 and those in Pss 146–150 as it pertains to their anti-imperial bent. Hossfeld and Zenger have suggested that

> the composition in Psalms 146–150 is inspired primarily by the Yahweh-is-king Psalms 96, 98, and 100, but now in adapting them and taking them further, profiles Yahweh's kingship much more strongly as care for the suffering, the weak, the poor, as well as the disempowerment of all imperial regimes.[7]

While the psalms in the concluding Hallel are certainly inspired by the psalms from book 4, as Hossfeld and Zenger suggest, these psalms share much in common with book 5, particularly the rhetoric employed regarding empires and those who suffer under them. As outlined below, there are at least three themes from book 5 that show a certain continuity with the theology in Pss 146–150. While an extensive analysis of the final Hallel remains the task of a subsequent study, a brief review does reveal certain connections between the final book in the Psalter and the concluding Hallel.[8]

---

5. Donatella Scaiola notes that relatively little attention has been given to the conclusion to the Psalter and its implications for the interpretation of the entire Psalter, particularly in comparison to the attention give to Pss 1–2 ("The End of the Psalter," in *The Composition of the Psalter* [ed. Erich Zenger; BETL 238; Leuven: Peeters, 2010], 701–710).

6. Zenger, "Der jüdische Psalter—ein anti-imperiales Buch," 99.

7. Frank Lothar Hossfeld and Erich Zenger, *Psalms 3: A Commentary on Psalms 101–150* (ed. Klaus Baltzer; trans. Linda Maloney; Hermeneia; Minneapolis: Fortress Press, 2011), 606.

8. So Kun Ahn contends that the concluding Hallel psalms may provide some

7.1.1. A Political Critique

The political critique that started in book 5 continues in the conclusion to the Psalter. Similar to the critique mentioned in selected psalms in book 5, the psalmists deconstruct the power associated with nations and their human kings. In fact, the first four psalms of the concluding Hallel contain a political critique of some sort. Despite their appearances of power, these earthly rulers will not thwart the power that belongs to Yahweh nor can such rulers replicate that power. In Ps 146:3–4, the psalmist implores

> Do not trust in princes (נְדִיבִים),
>   in a human (בֶן־אָדָם) in whom there is no deliverance.
> When his breath departs, he returns to the earth;
>   on that day, his plans perish.

Similar to the claims made in Pss 108 and 116 regarding the trustworthiness of human power, the psalmist confesses in Ps 146 that such power cannot be trusted due to its ephemeral nature. While there are certainly religious dimensions to this confession (e.g., one should trust in Yahweh alone), Ballhorn is surely correct in his assessment that there is also a "sharp political statement" which provides a strong critique of human power.[9]

A more explicit critique of human power appears in Ps 147:10. There the psalmist acknowledges of Yahweh that

> His delight is not in the strength of the horse
>   nor his pleasure in the legs of a man.

Whereas the language in Ps 146 referred specifically to human leaders with power, the language in Ps 147 is more opaque in its reference due to its use of synecdoche. According to Hossfeld and Zenger, "Yahweh takes no pleasure in the arrogant, terrorizing power, the paradigms for which

---

insight into the overall composition history of the Psalter ("I Salmi 146–150 come conclusione del Salterio" [PhD diss., Pontifical Biblical Institute, 2008]). Ahn contends, "From these psalms—from the single psalms, from the composition of the group and from their position in the Psalter—it is possible to grasp the characteristics of the final version of the book, which originated in its present form. The study of the last part of the Psalter will enable us to grasp the principles which orient the unity of the book" (3, quoted in Scaiola, "The End of the Psalter," 704).

9. Ballhorn, *Zum Telos des Psalters*, 305.

are the war steed ... and the handsomely armed soldiers."[10] While such images of war steeds and armored foot soldiers can be found in Assyrian reliefs, the Persians were well known for their use of horsemen and foot soldiers to quell uprisings and to expand their territorial holdings.[11] According to Briant, at one point, Artaxerxes II employed 20,000 horses and riders along with another 100,000 foot soldiers of Persian nationality along with tens of thousands of Greek mercenaries. With the language in Ps 147:10, the psalmist conjures up impressive, if not terrorizing images, of imperial war machines. Such empires should rightfully be recognized by humans and deities alike, but the psalmist rebuffs such a claim, suggesting that Yahweh takes neither enjoyment nor delight in such images of power, preferring instead one "who fears Yahweh" (147:11).

In Ps 148, the psalmist celebrates the kingship of Yahweh (see §7.1.2) and in so doing, creates an onomasticon of sorts, listing out the various elements within creation that are to praise Yahweh. Alongside the mountains and hills, and the beasts and cattle, are the "kings of the earth and all peoples, princes and all rulers of the earth" (148:11). In this subtle move, the psalmist has stripped human power of any hierarchical place within creation. Despite the grand claims of human kingship and its power to lord over its subjugated peoples, the psalmist redraws the line of power in creation. Before Yahweh, human kings and rulers of the earth are simply part of the created order and they will ultimately give praise to the Divine King.

The fourth, and perhaps most explicit example of Yahweh's rule over human power appears in Ps 149. The psalmist envisions a coming day in which Yahweh and the humble (עֲנָוִים) will act.

> Let the high praises of God be in their throats
>   and two-edged swords in their hands.
> To wreak vengeance on the nations,
>   and chastisement on peoples,
> to bind the kings with shackles,
>   and their nobles with iron chains. (149:6–8)

---

10. Hossfeld and Zenger, *Psalms 3*, 625. Othmar Keel notes that admiration for the horse "was based primarily on its military capabilities" (*The Symbolism of the Biblical World: Ancient Near Eastern Iconography and the Book of Psalms* [Winona Lake, Ind.: Eisenbrauns, 1997], 239.

11. Pierre Briant, *From Cyrus to Alexander: A History of the Persian Empire* (trans. Peter T. Daniels; Winona Lake, Ind.: Eisenbrauns, 2002), 796–97.

The precise meaning of verse 6 and its allusion to a two-edged sword in the hands of the faithful remains the *crux interpretum* for this psalm. Some have opted to understand the term metaphorically, suggesting that the two-edged sword refers to the songs of praise uttered by the worshipping community. To the sword the psalmist "attributes such effective power to Israel's praise that it sets in motion the accomplishment of Yhwh's order of justice."[12] Others have suggested that the term refers to a "sword dance" carried by the faithful in hopes of invoking Yahweh's action, despite any firm evidence to validate the claim.[13] Yet beyond these metaphorical understandings, a more literal reading may be understood. While theologically and ideologically more challenging to some, a literal reading may in fact be the intended meaning. As Erhard Gerstenberger has reminded, "Considering the real situation of early Jewish communities lost in the jungle of vast empires, there is little reason to be surprised at the propagation of violence and revenge, which are at the forefront of our psalm's concerns."[14] A further justification of a more literal reading includes the binding of kings and noble persons in 149:8. The image of fettered kings and leaders processing before the conquering king represents a common ancient Near Eastern motif.[15] With this image, the psalmist deconstructs the power associated with the nations and their kings, suggesting that such power cannot withstand the judgment of God to be exacted by his people.

---

12. Hossfeld and Zenger, *Psalms 3*, 651.

13. See most recently, Michael D. Goulder, *The Psalms of the Return (Book V, Psalms 107–150): Studies in the Psalter, IV* (JSOTSup 258; Sheffield: Sheffield Academic Press, 1998), 299.

14. Erhard S. Gerstenberger, *Psalms, Part 2, and Lamentations* (FOTL 15; Grand Rapids: Eerdmans, 2001), 457. Similarly, John Goldingay argues for a more literal reading of v. 6, "The exile meant that Yhwh turned back the edge of the king's sword … but after the exile, the community learned how to use its sword again" (*Psalms 90–150* [BCOT; Grand Rapids: Baker Academic, 2008], 740).

15. See the image on the Behistun inscription in which numerous kings and leaders appear before Darius I bound to one another in chains. This is not to suggest that the image in Ps 149 was influenced by the Behistun inscription as much as it is to note the widespread use of such imagery (both in iconography and textual witnesses) in the ancient Near East. On the association of this theme with the larger ancient Near East, see Hossfeld and Zenger, *Psalms 3*, 652.

7.1.2. THE GOD OF HEAVEN AND THE HOPE OF THE POOR

The final two themes can be addressed together. Similar to the psalms in book 5, the psalms in the concluding Hallel psalms depict Yahweh as the God of Heaven. The spatial imagery and language employed in Pss 146–150 resonates with that found in book 5. Further, the political critique mentioned above in these psalms rests upon such a claim, as does the claims involving the theology of the poor (see below). In Ps 146, Yahweh is praised as the "one who made the heavens and the earth" (עֹשֶׂה שָׁמַיִם וָאָרֶץ). As noted in §5.2.3, this phrase occurs only five times in the Psalter, four times in book 5 and here in Ps 146. The attribution of Yahweh as the creator God establishes or "constructs" an image of Yahweh as the one with power who is capable of creating life anew for those in need. The creator God, by virtue of his creative activity then and now is the king. Within this psalm, Yahweh's concern for the poor and needy remains paramount. According to Ps 146, Yahweh is

> the one who executes justice for the oppressed (עֲשׁוּקִים)
>   the one who gives food to the hungry.
> Yahweh sets the prisoners free;
>   Yahweh opens the eyes of the blind.
> Yahweh lifts up those who are bowed down....
> Yahweh watches over the sojourners;
>   he upholds the widow and the fatherless. (146:7–9a).

The God of heaven remains intimately aware of and concerned for the oppressed, but more suggestive, the creator God still acts on behalf of those without power.

A similar portrayal appears in Ps 147. The spatial imagery in Ps 146 continues in Ps 147 with the image of Yahweh as the creator God who resides in the heavens. Yahweh is praised because he covers the heavens with clouds. He orders the rain (147:8) and ensures that the grass grows on the hills (147:8). Because of his position in the heavens, the psalmist attributes to Yahweh an array of meteorological phenomena (e.g., snow, ice, and wind). Yet all of this is meant to reinforce the claim made in verse 4 that "Great is our Lord, abundant in power." From the psalmist's perspective the one who rules in the heavens oversees all of creation and consequently is the one who possesses great power. And like Ps 146, this psalm invokes themes associated with the theology of the poor. Yahweh gathers the outcasts of Israel (147:2), but even more

7. CONCLUSION

> He heals the brokenhearted
> and binds up their wounds. ...
> Yahweh lifts up the poor;
> he brings down the wicked to the ground. (147:3, 6)

Yahweh, the one abundant in power, rules over the earth, lifting up the poor and disempowering the wicked.[16]

As noted in chapter 6, the psalmists acknowledge the nearness of the God of Heaven with an allusion to the outstretched arm of Yahweh. The lifting of the poor in verse 6 invites a similar image. Elsewhere in Ps 147, the image shifts. Yahweh no longer stretches out his arm to overcome the perceived chasm between heaven and the earthly affairs of the psalmist, Yahweh is said to "send forth his command to the earth; his word runs swiftly" (147:15), and again, in verse 18, the psalmist indicates that Yahweh sends forth his word. This thought culminates with the claim in verse 19 that Yahweh has declared his "word" to Jacob and he has given his statutes and ordinances, the Torah, to Israel. These laws come to symbolize the "judging and saving power of the creator God and world king Yahweh to create order" throughout all of creation.[17]

Psalms 148 and 149 each give attention to a different element within this theology. Psalm 148 stands at the center of the five psalm collection signaling Yahweh's "cosmic royal rule."[18] Yahweh is the God of the heavens because his majesty (הוֹדוֹ) is above the earth and the heaven. All of creation, from the highest of the heavens (148:4a) to the depths of the earth (148:7a), is called to give praise to the Divine King. As noted above, even the kings of the earth and the rulers shall join in giving praise to Yahweh and acknowledging that he alone is the king (148:13b). Psalm 148 reinforces the larger claim that all of creation stands under the power and authority of the Divine King. Psalm 149, on the other hand, emphasizes Yahweh's action amid the political dynamics associated with kings and rulers. Psalm 149 does refer to Yahweh both as Israel's creator and king, reinforcing the claims of Yahweh's cosmic rule, but this claim serves as a

---

16. Hossfeld and Zenger argue that the imagery in v. 6 has "primarily economic, social, and political connotations, although religious connotations are not to be excluded to the extent that these 'poor' are the subjects of Yahweh's special concern" (ibid., 624).
17. Ibid., 626.
18. Ibid., 635.

rationale for that which follows. Yahweh will join with the poor in exacting judgment on the nations and their kings even as he "adorns the עֲנָוִים with saving victory."

Psalm 150 concludes the last collection of Hallel psalms with a view of the heavenly king being celebrated. So great is his power and so impressive is his greatness that "all that has breath will praise Yah."

7.1.3. Summary

This brief, and albeit cursory, review of Pss 146–150 proves instructive for the larger study at hand. These psalms illustrate well the continued emphasis on the deconstruction and construction of power identified in book 5. Had these themes been absent from the concluding psalms, one could have argued that perhaps such ideas fell out of use within the community in Yehud. Given that Pss 146–150 were likely part of the final composition of the Psalter, and that the themes identified within Pss 107–145 continued to play a significant role within the psalmody of Israel, suggests that the anti-imperial bent in book 5 manifested itself in the literature and ideologies of subsequent periods.

7.2. Conclusion

Throughout this study, the emphasis has remained on the various ways in which the psalms in book 5 have sought to both deconstruct and construct power. Through various means, the Persians sought to create a political ideology that reinforced a sense of imperial power. While the Psalter's resistance to such claims to power may have been subtle at times, there is an unmistakable rhetoric within book 5 that "denounces the destructive, imperial structures and systems, and holds firmly that the biblical God will put an end to these systems."[19] These same claims appear in the concluding Hallel psalms as well, suggesting the significance of these themes for the Psalter more generally. In the face of destructive powers and systems, the psalmists are clear in their confession: it is Yahweh who will tread down their foes (108:14). And for those beaten down by such forces, their hope resides in the Divine King, the one capable of "raising up all who are bowed down" (145:14).

---

19. Ibid., 97.

Bibliography

Ackroyd, Peter R. *Exile and Restoration: A Study of Hebrew Thought of the Sixth Century B.C.* OTL. Philadelphia: Westminster, 1968

Ahn, Gregor. *Religiöse Herrscherlegitimation im achämendischen Iran: Die Voraussetzungen und die Struktur ihrer Argumentation.* AcIr 31. Leiden: Brill, 1992.

Ahn, John J. *Exile as Forced Migrations: A Sociological, Literary, and Theological Approach of the Displacement and Resettlement of the Southern Kingdom of Judah.* BZAW 417. Berlin: de Gruyter, 2011.

Ahn, So Kun. "I Salmi 146–150 come conclusione del Salterio." PhD diss., Pontifical Biblical Institute, 2008.

Albertz, Rainer. "Darius in Place of Cyrus: The First Edition of Deutero-Isaiah (Isaiah 40:1–52:12) in 521 B.C.E." *JSOT* 27 (2003): 371–83.

———. *A History of Israelite Religion in the Old Testament Period.* Translated by John Bowden. 2 vols. Louisville: Westminster John Knox, 1994.

———. *Israel in Exile: The History and Literature of the Sixth Century B.C.E.* Translated by David Green. Atlanta: Society of Biblical Literature, 2003.

Allen, Leslie C. *Psalms 101–150.* WBC 21. Waco, Tex.: Word Books, 1983.

Balcer, Jack Martin. *Herodotus and Bisitun: Problems in Ancient Persian Historiography.* Historia Einzelschriften 49. Stuttgart: Schreiner, 1987.

Baltzer, Klaus. *Deutero-Isaiah: A Commentary on Isaiah 40–55.* Edited by Peter Machinist. Translated by Margaret Kohl. Hermeneia. Minneapolis: Fortress Press, 2001.

Ballhorn, Egbert. "Der Davidbund in Ps 132 und im Kontext des Psalters." Pages 11–18 in *Für immer verbündet: Studien zur Bundestheologie der Bibel.* Edited by Christoph Dohmen and Christian Frevel. SB 211. Stuttgart: Katholisches Bibelwerk, 2007.

———. "'Um deines Knechtes David willen' (Ps 132:10): Die Gestalt Davids im Psalter." *BN* 76 (1995): 16–31.

———. *Zum Telos des Psalters: Der Textzusammenhang des Vierten und Fünften Psalmenbuches (Ps 90–150)*. BBB 138. Berlin: Philo, 2004.

Barstad, Hans M. "On the So-called Babylonian Literary Influence in Second Isaiah." *SJOT* 2 (1987): 90–110.

———. *The Babylonian Captivity of the Book of Isaiah: 'Exilic' Judah and the Provenance of Isaiah 40–55*. Institute for the Comparative Research in Human Culture, Series B, 102. Oslo: Novus, 1997.

Becker, Joachim. *Israel deutet seine Psalmen*. SB 18. Stuttgart: Katholisches Bibelwerk, 1966.

Becking, Bob. "Does Exile Equal Suffering: A Fresh Look at Psalm 137." Pages 181–202 in *Exile and Suffering: A Selection of Papers Read at the 50th Anniversary Meeting of the Old Testament Society of South Africa OTWSA/OTSSA, Pretoria August 2007*. Edited by Bob Becking and Dirk Human. OTS 50. Leiden: Brill, 2009.

———. *Ezra, Nehemiah, and the Construction of Early Jewish Identity*. FAT. First series 80. Tübingen: Mohr Siebeck, 2011.

Berges, Ulrich. *The Book of Isaiah: Its Composition and Final Form*. Translated by Millard Lind. HBM 46. Sheffield: Sheffield Phoenix, 2012.

———. "Die Knechte im Psalter: Ein Beitrag zu seiner Kompositionsgeschichte." *Bib* 81 (2000): 153–78.

———. "Who Were the Servants? A Comparative Inquiry in the Book of Isaiah and the Psalms." Pages 1–18 in *Past, Present, Future: The Deuteronomistic History and the Prophets*. Edited by Johannes C. de Moor and Harry F. van Rooy. OtSt 44. Leiden: Brill, 2000.

Berges, Ulrich, and Rudolf Hoppe. *Arm und Reich*. Würzburg: Echter, 2009.

Berlin, Adele. "Rhetoric of Psalm 145." Pages 17–22 in *Biblical and Related Studies Presented to Samuel Iwry*. Edited by Ann Kort and Scott Morschauser. Winona Lake, Ind.: Eisenbrauns, 1985.

Berquist, Jon L. "Approaching Yehud." Pages 1–6 in *Approaching Yehud: New Approaches to the Study of the Persian Period*. Edited by Jon L. Berquist. SemeiaSt 50. Atlanta: Society of Biblical Literature, 2007.

———, ed. *Approaching Yehud: New Approaches to the Study of the Persian Period*. SemeiaSt 50. Atlanta: Society of Biblical Literature, 2007.

———. "Constructions of Identity in Postcolonial Yehud." Pages 53–66 in *Judah and the Judeans in the Persian Period*. Edited by Oded Lipschits and Manfred Oeming. Winona Lake, Ind.: Eisenbrauns, 2006.

———. *Judaism in Persia's Shadow: A Social and Historical Approach*. Minneapolis: Fortress Press, 1995.

———. "Postcolonialism and Imperial Motives for Canonization." *Semeia* 75 (1996): 15–35.

———. "Psalms, Postcolonialism, and the Construction of the Self." Pages 195–202 in *Approaching Yehud: New Approaches to the Study of the Persian Period*. Edited by Jon L. Berquist. SemeiaSt 50. Atlanta: Society of Biblical Literature, 2007.

———. "Resistance and Accommodation in the Persian Empire." Pages 41–58 in *In the Shadow of the Empire: Reclaiming the Bible as a History of Faithful Resistance*. Edited by Richard Horsley. Louisville: Westminster John Knox, 2008.

Berquist, Jon L., and Claudia V. Camp, eds. *Constructions of Space I: Theory, Geography, and Narrative*. LHBOTS 481. New York: T&T Clark, 2007.

———, eds. *Constructions of Space II: The Biblical City and Other Imagined Spaces*. LHBOTS 490. New York: T&T Clark, 2008.

Beyerlin, Walter. *Im Licht der Traditionen: Psalm LXVII und CXV: Ein Entwicklungszusammenhang*. VTSup 45. Leiden: Brill, 1992.

———. *Werden und Wesen des 107. Psalms*. BZAW 153. Berlin: de Gruyter, 1979.

Birkeland, Harris. *The Evildoers in the Book of Psalms*. Oslo: Dybwad, 1955.

———. *Die Feinde des Individuums in der israelitischen Psalmenliteratur: Ein Beitrag zur Kenntnis der semitischen Literatur- und Religionsgeschichte*. Oslo: Grøndahl, 1933.

Blenkinsopp, Joseph. "The Cosmological and Protological Language of Deutero-Isaiah." *CBQ* 73 (2011): 493–510.

———. *Ezra, Nehemiah: A Commentary*. OTL. Louisville: Westminster, 1988.

———. "A Jewish Sect of the Persian Period." *CBQ* 52 (1990): 5–20.

———. "Second-Isaiah, Prophet of Universalism?" *JSOT* 41 (1988): 83–103.

———. *The "Servants of the Lord" in Third Isaiah: Profile of a Pietistic Group in the Persian Period*. PIBA 7. Dublin: Irish Bible Association, 1983.

Bonfante, Larissa. *Etruscan Dress*. Baltimore: Johns Hopkins University Press, 1975.

Booij, Thijs. "Psalm 110: Rule in the Midst of Your Foes." *VT* 41 (1991): 396–407.

———. "Psalm 116:10–11: The Account of an Inner Crisis." *Bib* 76 (1995): 388–95.

———. "Psalm 144: Hope of Davidic Welfare." *VT* 59 (2009): 173–80.

Botha, Phil J. "Psalm 108 and the Quest for the Closure to the Exile." *OTE* 23 (2010): 574–96.

Bowick, James. "Characters in Stone: Royal Ideology and Yehudite Identity in the Behistun Inscription and the Book of Haggai." Pages 87–117 in *Community Identity in Judean Historiography: Biblical and Comparative Perspectives*. Edited by Gary N. Knoppers and Kenneth A. Ristau. Winona Lake, Ind.: Eisenbrauns, 2009.

Bremer, Johannes. "Developments of the 'Theology of the Poor' in the Psalter." In *The Psalter as Witness: The Theology and Theologies of the Book of Psalms*. Edited by W. Dennis Tucker Jr. Waco, Tex.: Baylor University Press, forthcoming.

———. "'Doch den אֶבְיוֹן hob er aus dem עוֹנִי empor' (Ps 107:41a): Eine synchrone Analyse des Umgangs Gottes mit den Armen im Psalter und diachrone Verortung im 5. Psalmenbuch (Ps 107–145) und im Schluss Hallel (Ps 146–150) Frank-Lothar Hossfeld zur Vollendung des 70. Lebensjahres." *BN* 158 (2013): 55–84.

Breukelman, Frans. "Psalm 113 oder die Struktur der biblischen Theologie." *T&K* 53 (1992): 2–32.

Briant, Pierre. *From Cyrus to Alexander: A History of the Persian Empire*. Translated by Peter T. Daniels. Winona Lake, Ind.: Eisenbrauns, 2002.

Briggs, Charles A., and Emilie G. Briggs. *A Critical and Exegetical Commentary on the Book of Psalms*. 2 vols. ICC. Edinburgh: T&T Clark, 1909.

Bright, John. *A History of Israel*. 4th ed. Louisville: Westminster John Knox, 2000.

Brosius, Maria. "Ancient Archives and Concepts of Record Keeping: An Introduction." Pages 1–16 in *Ancient Archives and Archival Traditions: Concepts of Record-Keeping in the Ancient World*. Edited by Maria Brosius. Oxford: Oxford University Press, 2003.

Brown, William P. *Seeing the Psalms: A Theology of Metaphor*. Louisville: Westminster John Knox, 2002.

Broyles, Craig. *The Conflict of Faith and Experience in the Psalms: A Form-Critical and Theological Study of Selected Lament Psalms*. JSOTSup 52. Sheffield: JSOT Press, 1989.

Buysch, Christoph. *Der letzte Davidpsalter: Interpretation, Komposition und Funktion der Psalmengruppe Ps 138–145*. SBB 63. Stuttgart: Katholisches Bibelwerk, 2009.

Cameron, George C. *Persepolis Treasury Tablets*. OIP 65. Chicago: University of Chicago Press, 1948.

Carey, Greg. "Book of Revelation as Counter-Imperial Script." Pages 157–76 in *In the Shadow of the Empire: Reclaiming the Bible as a His-

tory of Faithful Resistance. Edited by Richard A. Horsley. Louisville: Westminster John Knox, 2008.

Carr, David. *Writing on the Tablet of the Heart: Origins of Scripture and Literature*. Oxford: Oxford University Press, 2005.

Cataldo, Jeremiah W. *A Theocratic Yehud? Issues of Government in a Persian Province*. LHBOTS 498. New York: T&T Clark, 2009.

Ceresko, Anthony. "The Sage in the Psalms." Pages 217–30 in *The Sage in Israel and the Ancient Near East*. Edited by John Gammie and Leo Perdue. Winona Lake, Ind.: Eisenbrauns, 1990.

Childs, Brevard S. "The Enemy from the North and the Chaos Tradition." *JBL* 78 (1959): 187–98.

Clements, Ronald E. *Isaiah and the Deliverance of Jerusalem: A Study in the Interpretation of Prophecy in the Old Testament*. JSOTSup 13. Sheffield: JSOT Press, 1980.

Collins, John J. *The Scepter and the Star: The Messiahs of the Dead Sea Scrolls and Other Ancient Literature*. ABRL. New York: Doubleday, 1995.

Coogan, Michael D. *The Old Testament: A Historical and Literary Introduction to the Hebrew Scriptures*. 2d ed. Oxford: Oxford University Press, 2010.

Cook, Stephen L. "Apocalypticism and the Psalter." *ZAW* 104 (1992): 82–99.

Cottrill, Amy. *Language, Power, and Identity in the Lament Psalms of the Individual*. LHBOTS 493. New York: T&T Clark, 2008.

Creach, Jerome F. D. *The Destiny of the Righteous in the Psalms*. St. Louis: Chalice Press, 2008.

———. *Yahweh as Refuge and the Editing of the Hebrew Psalter*. JSOTSup 217. Sheffield: Sheffield Academic Press, 1996.

Croft, Steven J. L. *The Identity of the Individual in the Psalms*. JSOTSup 14. Sheffield: JSOT Press, 1987.

Crow, Loren. *Songs of Ascents (Psalms 120–134): Their Place in Israelite History and Religion*. SBLDS 148. Atlanta: Scholars Press, 1996.

Crüsemann, Frank. *Studien zur Formgeschichte von Hymnus und Danklied in Israel*. WMANT 32. Neukirchen-Vluyn: Neukirchener 1969.

Dandamaev, Muhammed A. *A Political History of the Achaemenid Empire*. Translated by Willem J. Vogelsang. Leiden: Brill, 1989.

Dahood, Mitchell. *Psalms III: 101–150; Introduction, Translation, and Notes with an Appendix; The Grammar of the Psalter*. AB 17A. New York: Doubleday, 1970.

Davidson, Steed V. *Empire and Exile: Postcolonial Readings of the Book of Jeremiah*. LHBOTS 542. New York: T&T Clark, 2011.

Davies, Philip R. "God of Cyrus, God of Israel: Some Religio-historical Reflections on Isaiah 40–55." Pages 207–25 in *Words Remembered, Texts Renewed: Essays in Honor of John F. A. Sawyer*. Edited by Jon Davies, Graham Harvey, John F. A. Sawyer, and Wilfred G. E. Watson. JSOTSup 195. Sheffield: Sheffield Academic Press, 1995.

DeClaissé-Walford, Nancy. *Reading from the Beginning: The Shaping of the Hebrew Psalter*. Macon, Ga.: Mercer University Press, 1997.

Dhanaraj, Dharmakkan. *Theological Significance of the Motif of Enemies in Selected Psalms of Individual Lament*. Glückstadt: Augustin, 1992.

Duhm, Berhard. *Die Psalmen erklärt*. KHC 14. Freiburg: Mohr, 1899.

Dussaud, René. *Les Découvertes de Ras Shamra (Ugarit) et l'Ancien Testament*. Paris: Geuthner, 1941.

Eaton, John. *Kingship and the Psalms*. The Biblical Seminar 3. Sheffield: JSOT Press, 1980.

Eberhardt, Gönke. *JHWH und die Unterwelt: Spuren einer Kompetenzausweitung JHWHs im Alten Testament*. FAT. Second series 23. Tübingen: Mohr Siebeck, 2007.

Ego, Beate. "'Der Herr blickt herab von der Höhe seines Heiligtums': Zur Vorstellung von Gottes himmlischen Thronen in exilisch-nachexilischer Zeit." *ZAW* 110 (1998): 556–69.

Eidevall, Göran. *Prophecy and Propaganda: Images of Enemies in the Book of Isaiah*. ConBOT 46. Winona Lake, Ind.: Eisenbrauns, 2009.

Elliger, Karl, and Wilhelm Rudolph. *Biblia Hebraica Stuttgartensia*. 5th ed. Stuttgart: Deutsche Bibelgesellschaft, 1997.

Ephʻal, Israel, and Joseph Naveh. *Aramaic Ostraca of the Fourth Century B.C. from Idumaea*. Jerusalem: Magnes, 1996.

Franke, Sabine. *Königsinschriften und Königsideologie: die Könige von Akkade zwischen Tradition und Neuerung*. Altorientalistik 1. Münich: LIT, 1995.

Freedman, David N. "The Structure of Psalm 137." Pages 187–205 in *Near Eastern Studies in Honor of W. F. Albright*. Edited by Hans Goedicke. Baltimore: Johns Hopkins University Press, 1971.

Frei, Peter, and Klaus Koch. *Reichsidee und Reichsorganisation im Perserreich*. OBO 55. Göttingen: Vandenhoeck & Ruprecht, 1984.

Fried, Lisbeth S. "The *ʻam hāʼāreṣ* in Ezra 4:4 and Persian Imperial Administration." Pages 123–45 in *Judah and the Judeans in the Persian Period*.

Edited by Oded Lipschits and Manfred Oeming. Winona Lake, Ind.: Eisenbrauns, 2006.

———. "Cyrus the Messiah? The Historical Background to Isaiah 45:1." *HTR* 95 (2002): 373–93.

———. *Priest and the Great King: Temple-Palace Relations in the Persian Empire.* BJSUCSD 10. Winona Lake, Ind.: Eisenbrauns, 2004.

Frye, Richard N. *The History of Ancient Iran.* München: Beck, 1984.

Garrison, Mark B., and Margaret C. Root with Charles E. Jones. *Seals on the Persepolis Fortification Tablets Volume I: Images of the Heroic Encounter.* OIP 117. Chicago: Oriental Institute of the University of Chicago, 2001.

Gärtner, Judith. "The Torah in Psalm 106." Pages 479–88 in *The Composition of the Book of Psalms.* Edited by Erich Zenger. BETL 238. Leuven: Peeters, 2010.

Gerstenberger, Erhard. "'World Dominion' in Yahweh-Kinghip Psalms. *HBT* 23 (2001): 192–210.

———. *Israel in the Persian Period: The Fifth and Fourth Centuries B.C.E.* Translated by Siegfried Schatzmann. BE 8. Atlanta: Society of Biblical Literature, 2011.

———. *Psalms, Part 2, and Lamentations.* FOTL 15. Grand Rapids: Eerdmans, 2001.

Gillmayr-Bucher, Susanne. "Body Images in the Psalter." *JSOT* 28 (2004): 301–26.

———. "Images of Space in the Psalms of Ascents." Pages 489–500 in *The Composition of the Book of Psalms.* Edited by Erich Zenger. BETL 238. Leuven: Peeters, 2010.

Goldingay, John. *Psalms 90–150.* BCOT. Grand Rapids: Baker Academic, 2008.

Goldingay, John, and David Payne. *A Critical and Exegetical Commentary on Isaiah 40–55: Volume 2.* ICC. New York: T&T Clark, 2006.

Goodblatt, David. *Elements of Ancient Jewish Nationalism.* Cambridge: Cambridge University Press, 2006.

Gottwald, Norman. *The Hebrew Bible: A Brief Socio-Literary Introduction.* Abridged by Rebecca J. Kruger Gaudino. Minneapolis: Fortress Press, 2009.

Goulder, Michael D. *The Psalms of the Return (Book V, Psalms 107–150): Studies in the Psalter, IV.* JSOTSup 258. Sheffield: Sheffield Academic Press, 1998.

Grabbe, Lester L. *Judaic Religion in the Second Temple Period: Belief and Practice from the Exile to Yavneh.* London: Routledge, 2000.

———. "The 'Persian Documents' in the Book of Ezra." Pages 531–70 in *Judah and Judeans in the Persian Period.* Edited by Oded Lipschits and Manfred Oeming. Winona Lake, Ind.: Eisenbrauns, 2006.

———. *Yehud: A History of the Persian Province of Judah.* Vol. 1 of *A History of the Jews and Judaism in the Second Temple Period.* LSTS 47:1. New York: T&T Clark, 2004.

Graetz, Heinrich. *Kritischer Commentar zu den Psalmen: Nebts Text und Übersetzung.* Breslau: Schottländer, 1882.

Greenfield Jonas C., Bezalel Porten, and Ada Yardeni. *The Bisitun Inscription of Darius the Great: Aramaic Version.* Corpus Inscriptonium Iranicarum, Part I. Inscriptions of Ancient Iran, Vol. 5. London: Humphries, 1982.

Grol, Harm van. "David and his *Chasidim*: Place and Function of Psalms 138–145." Pages 309–37 in *The Composition of the Book of Psalms.* Edited by Erich Zenger. BETL 238. Leuven: Peeters, 2010.

Guillaume, Alfred. "The Meaning of *twll* in Psalm 137:3." *JBL* 75 (1956): 143–44.

Gunkel, Herman. *An Introduction to the Psalms: The Genres of the Religious Lyric of Israel.* Translated by James D. Nogalski. MLBS. Macon, Ga.: Mercer University Press, 1998.

Gunneweg, Antonius H. J. *Esra.* KAT 19/1. Gütersloh: Mohn, 1985.

Habel, Norman. "Yahweh Maker of Heaven and Earth: A Study of Tradition Criticism." *JBL* 91 (1972): 321–37.

Hallock, Richard T. *Persepolis Fortification Tablets.* OIP 92. Chicago: University of Chicago Press, 1969.

Hallo, William W., and K. Lawson Younger, eds. *The Context of Scripture.* 3 vols. Leiden: Brill, 1997–2002.

Hartberger, Birgit. *"An den Wassern von Babylon ...": Psalm 137 auf dem Hintergrund von Jeremia 51, der biblischen Edom-traditionen, und babylonischer Originalquellen.* BBB 63. Frankfurt am Main: Hanstein, 1986.

Hayes, Elizabeth. "The Unity of the Egyptian Hallel: Psalms 113–118." *BBR* 9 (1999): 145–56.

———. "'Where is the Lord?' The Extended Great Chain of Being as a Source Domain for Conceptual Metaphor in the Egyptian Hallel, Psalms 113–118." Pages 55–69 in *Metaphors in the Psalms.* Edited by Pierre van Hecke and Antje Labahn. BETL 231. Leuven: Peeters, 2010.

Herodotus. *The Histories*. Translated by Robin Waterfield. Edited by Carolyn Dewald. Oxford World Classics. Oxford: Oxford University Press, 2008.
Herrenschmidt, Clarisse. "Désignation de l'empire et concepts politiques de Darius 1er d'après ses inscriptions en vieux perse." *StIr* 6 (1976): 17–58.
Herrenschmidt, Clarisse, and Bruce Lincoln. "Healing and Salt Waters: The Bifurcated Cosmos of Mazdean Religion." *HR* 43 (2004): 269–83.
Hobbs, T. R., and P. K. Jackson. "The Enemy in the Psalms." *BTB* 21 (1991): 22–29.
Hoglund, Kenneth. *Achaemenid Imperial Administration in Syria-Palestine and the Missions of Ezra and Nehemiah*. SBLDS 125. Atlanta: Scholars Press, 1992.
Holtz, Shalom E. "The Thematic Unity of Psalm cxliv in Light of Mesopotamian Royal Ideology." *VT* 58 (2008): 367–80.
Hossfeld, Frank Lothar. "Der gnädige Gott und der arme Gerechte: Anthropologische Akzente in der Psalmengruppe 111–118." Pages 51–63 in *Kircheneinheit und Weltverantwortung: Festscrift für Peter Neuner*. Edited by Christoph Böttigheimer and Hubert Filser. Regensburg: Pustet, 2006.
Hossfeld, Frank Lothar, and Erich Zenger. *Psalmen 101–150*. HTKAT. Freiburg: Herders, 2008.
——— . *Psalms 3: A Commentary on Psalms 101–150*. Edited by Klaus Baltzer. Translated by Linda Maloney. Hermeneia. Minneapolis: Fortress Press, 2011.
Houtman, Cornelius. *Der Himmel im Alten Testament: Israel's Weltbild und Weltanschauung*. OtSt 30. Leiden: Brill, 1993.
Howard, Cameron B. R. "Writing Yehud: Textuality and Power under Persian Rule." PhD diss., Emory University, 2010.
Human, Dirk J. "Psalm 136: A Liturgy with Reference to Creation and History." Pages 73–88 in *Psalms and Liturgy*. Edited by Dirk J. Human and Cas J. A. Vos. LHBOTS 410. New York: T&T Clark, 2004.
Hupfeld, Hermann. *Die Psalmen*. Gotha: Perthes, 1855.
Hurvitz, Avi. "Originals and Imitations in Biblical Poetry: A Comparative Examination of 1 Sam 2:1–10 and Ps 113:5–9." Pages 115–21 in *Biblical and Related Studies Presented to Samuel Iwry*. Edited by Ann Kort and Scott Morschauser. Winona Lake, Ind.: Eisenbrauns, 1985.
Jacobson, Rolf. *'Many Are Saying': The Function of Direct Discourse in the Hebrew Psalter*. LHBOTS 397. New York: T&T Clark, 2004.

Janowski, Bernd. "Die heilige Wohnung des Höchsten: Kosmologische Implikationen der Jerusalemer Tempeltheologie." Pages 24–68 in *Gottesstadt und Gottesgarten: Zu Geschichte und Theologie des Jerusalemer Tempels.* Edited by Othmar Keel and Erich Zenger. QD 191. Freiburg: Herder, 2002.

———. "Dem Löwen gleich, gierig nach Raub: Zum Feindbild in den Psalmen." *EvT* 55 (1995): 155–73.

Janzen, David. "The 'Mission' of Ezra and the Persian-Period Temple Community." *JBL* 119 (2000): 619–43.

Jarick, John. "The Four Corners of Psalms 107." *CBQ* 59 (1997): 270–87.

Jenni, Ernst, with the assistance of Claus Westermann. *Theological Lexicon of the Old Testament.* Translated by Mark E. Biddle. 3 vols. Peabody, Mass.: Hendrickson, 1997.

Jones, Charles E. and Matthew W. Stolper. "How Many Persepolis Fortification Tablets are There?" Pages 37–44 in *L'archive des fortifications de Persépolis: état des questions et perspectives de recherches.* Edited by Pierre Briant, Wouter F. M. Henkelman, and Matthew W. Stolper. Persika 12. Paris: De Boccard, 2008.

Jursa, Michael. "Accounting in Neo-Babylonian Institutional Archives: Structure, Usage, and Implications." Pages 145–98 in *Creating Economic Order: Record-Keeping, Standardization, and the Development of Accounting in the Ancient Near East.* Edited by Michael Hudson and Cornelia Wunsch. International Scholars Conference on Ancient Near Eastern Economics 4. Bethesda, Md.: CDL Press, 2004.

Keel, Othmar. *Feinde und Gottesleugner: Studien zum Image der Widersacher in den Individualpsalmen.* SBM 7. Stuttgart: Katholisches Bibelwerk, 1969.

———. *The Symbolism of the Biblical World: Ancient Near Eastern Iconography and the Book of Psalms.* Winona Lake, Ind.: Eisenbrauns, 1997.

Keet, Cuthbert C. *A Study of the Psalms of Ascents: A Critical and Exegetical Commentary upon Psalms CXX to CXXXIV.* London: Mitre, 1969.

Kellerman, Ulrich. "Psalm 137." *ZAW* 90 (1978): 43–58.

Kent, Roland G. *Old Persian: Grammar, Texts, Lexicon.* New Haven, Conn.: American Oriental Society, 1953.

Kirkpatrick, Alexander F. *The Book of Psalms 3.* The Cambridge Bible for Schools and Colleges 16. Cambridge: Cambridge University Press, 1903.

Kittel, Rudolph. "Cyrus und Deuterojesaja." *ZAW* (1898): 149–62.

Klingbeil, Martin. *Yahweh Fighting from Heaven: God as Warrior and as God of Heaven in the Hebrew Psalter and Ancient Near Eastern Iconography.* OBO 169. Göttingen: Vandenhoeck & Ruprecht, 1999.
Knauf, Ernst Axel. "Psalm LX und Psalm CVIII." *VT* 50 (2000): 55–65.
Knowles, Melody D. *Centrality Practiced: Jerusalem in the Religious Practice of Yehud and the Diaspora in the Persian Period.* SBLABS 16. Atlanta: Society of Biblical Literature, 2006.
Koehler, Ludwig, Walter Baumgartner, and Johann Jakob Stamm. *The Hebrew and Aramaic Lexicon of the Old Testament.* Translated and edited by M. E. J. Richardson. 2 vols. Leiden: Brill, 2001.
Körting, Corinna. *Zion in den Psalmen.* FAT. First series 48. Tübingen: Mohr Siebeck, 2006.
Kraabal, Thomas. "The God-fearers Meet the Beloved Disciple." Pages 276–84 in *The Future of Early Christianity: Essays in Honor of Helmut Koester.* Edited by Birger A. Pearson, A. Thomas Kraabel, George W. E. Nickelsburg, and Norman R. Petersen. Minneapolis: Fortress Press, 1991.
Kratz, Reinhard. "Das *Schema* des Psalters: Die Botschaft vom Reich Gottes nach Psalm 145." Pages 624–38 in *Gott und Mensch im Dialog: Festschrift für Otto Kaiser zum 80. Geburtstag.* Edited by Markus Witte. BZAW 345. 2 vols. Berlin: de Gruyter, 2004.
Kraus, Hans Joachim. *Psalms 60–150: A Commentary.* Translated by Hilton Oswald. CC. Minneapolis: Fortress Press, 1993.
———. *Theology of the Psalms.* Translated by Keith Crim. CC. Minneapolis: Fortress Press, 1992.
Kuhrt, Amélie. "The Cyrus Cylinder and the Achaemenid Imperial Policy." *JSOT* 25 (1983): 83–97.
———. *The Persian Empire: A Corpus of Sources from the Achaemenid Empire.* London: Routledge, 2007.
Lang, Mabel. "Prexaspes and Usurper Smerdis." *JNES* 51 (1992): 201–7.
Lefebvre, Henri. *The Production of Space.* Translated by Donald Nicholson-Smith. Oxford: Blackwell, 1996.
———. *Postmodern Geographies: The Reassertion of Space in Critical Space Theory.* London: Verso, 1989.
Leuenberger, Martin. *Konzeptionen des Königtums Gottes im Psalter: Untersuchungen zu Komposition und Redaktion der theokratischen Bücher IV–V im Psalter.* ATANT 83. Zürich: Theologischer, 2004.
Levin, Christoph. "Das Gebetbuch der Gerechten: Literargeschichtliche Beobachtungen am Psalter." *ZTK* 90 (1993): 355–81.

———. "Psalm 136 als zeitweilige Schlussdoxologie des Psalters." *SJOT* 14 (2000): 17–27.
Lichtheim, Mariam. *Ancient Egyptian Literature: Volume 3; The Late Period.* Berkeley: University of California Press, 1980.
Lincoln, Bruce. *Religion, Empire, and Torture: The Case of Achaemenian Persia with a Postscript on Abu Ghraib.* Chicago: University of Chicago Press, 2007.
———. *'Happiness for Mankind': Achaemenian Religion and the Imperial Project.* AcIr 53. Leuven: Peeters, 2012.
Lindars, Barnabas. "The Structure of Psalm CXLV." *VT* 29 (1989): 23–30.
Liverani, Mario. "The Ideology of the Assyrian Empire." Pages 297–371 in *Power and Propaganda: A Symposium on Ancient Empires.* Edited by Mogens Trolle Larsen. Mesopotamia: Copenhagen Studies in Assyriology 7. Copenhagen: Akademisk, 1979.
———. "Akkad: An Introduction." Pages 1–10 in *Akkad: The First World Empire: Structure, Ideology, Traditions.* Edited by Mario Liverani. HANES 5. Padova: Sargon, 1993.
Lohfink, Norbert. *Lobgesänge der Armen: Studien zum Magnifikat, den Hodajot von Qumran und einigen späten Psalmen.* SBS 143. Stuttgart: Katholisches Bibelwerk, 1990.
———. "Three Ways to Talk About Poverty: Psalm 109." Pages 120–35 in *In the Shadow of Your Wings: New Readings of Great Texts from the Bible.* Edited by Norbert Lohfink. Collegeville, Minn.: Liturgical Press, 2003.
———. "Von der 'Anawim-Partei' zur 'Kirche der Armen': Die bibelwissenschaftliche Ahnentafel eines Hauptbegriffs der 'Theologie der Befreiung.'" *Bib* 67 (1986): 153–75.
Magonet, Jonathan. "Convention and Creativity: The Phrase 'Maker of Heaven and Earth' in the Psalms." Pages 139–53 in *"Open thou mine eyes...": Essays on Aggadah and Judaica Presented to Rabbi William G. Braude on His Eightieth Birthday and Dedicated to His Memory.* Edited by H. Blumberg, Benjamin Braude, and Bernard Mehlman. Hoboken, N.J.: Ktav, 1992.
Maier, Christl M. *Daughter Zion, Mother Zion: Gender, Space, and the Sacred in Ancient Israel.* Minneapolis: Fortress Press, 2008.
Malandra, William W. *An Introduction to Ancient Iranian Religion: Readings from the Avesta and Achaemenid Inscriptions.* Minnesota Publications in the Humanities 2. Minneapolis: University of Minnesota Press, 1983.

Macholz, Christian. "Psalm 136: Exegetische Beobachtungen mit methodologischen Seitenblicken." Pages 177–86 in *Mincha: Festgabe für Rolf Rendtorff zum 75. Geburtstag*. Edited by Erhard Blum. Neukirchen-Vluyn: Neukirchener, 2000.

Martin-Achard, Robert. *Israël et les nations. La perspective missionaire de l'Ancien Testament*. CahT 42. Neuchâtel: Delachaux & Niestlé, 1959.

Marttila, Marko. *Collective Reinterpretation in the Psalms: A Study of the Redaction History of the Psalter*. FAT. Second series 13. Tübingen: Mohr Siebeck, 2006.

Mathys, Hans-Peter. *Dichter und Beter: Theologen aus spätalttestamentlicher Zeit*. OBO 132. Göttingen: Vandenhoeck & Ruprecht, 1994.

McCann, J. Clinton, Jr. "Psalms." *NIB* 4:641–1280.

Meer, Willem van der. "Psalm 110: A Psalm of Rehabilitation?" Pages 207–34 in *The Structural Analysis of Biblical and Canaanite Poetry*. Edited by Willem van der Meer and Johannes C. de Moor. JSOTSup 74. Sheffield: JSOT Press, 1988.

Millard, Matthias. *Die Komposition des Psalters: Ein formgeschichtlicher Ansatz*. FAT. First series 9. Tübingen: Mohr Siebeck, 1994.

Miller, Robert D., II. "The Zion Hymns as Instruments of Power." *ANES* 47 (2010): 218–40.

Mitchell, David C. "Lord, Remember David: G. H. Wilson and the Message of the Psalter," *VT* 56 (2006): 526–48.

———. *The Message of the Psalter: An Eschatological Programme in the Book of Psalms*. JSOTSup 252. Sheffield: Sheffield Academic Press, 1997.

Mowinckel, Sigmund. "Psalm Criticism between 1900 and 1935," *VT* 5 (1955): 13–33.

———. *The Psalms in Israel's Worship*. 2 vols. Oxford: Blackwell, 1962.

Newsom, Carol A. *The Self as Symbolic Space: Constructing Identity and Community at Qumran*. STDJ 52. Leiden: Brill, 2004.

Nordheim, Mariam von. *Geboren von der Morgenröte? Psalm 110 in Tradition, Redaktion und Rezeption*. WMANT 117. Neukirchen-Vluyn: Neukirchener, 2008.

O'Brien, Julia M. "From Exile to Empire: A Response." Pages 209–14 in *Approaching Yehud: New Approaches to the Study of the Persian Period*. Edited by Jon L. Berquist. SemeiaSt 50. Atlanta: Society of Biblical Literature, 2007.

Olmstead, Albert Ten Eyck. "Darius and his Behistun Inscription." *AJSL* 55 (1938): 392–416.

Ollenburger, Ben C. *Zion the City of the Great King: A Theological Symbol of the Jerusalem Cult.* JSOTSup 41. Sheffield: JSOT Press, 1987.
Poebel, Arno. "Chronology of Darius' First Year of Reign." *AJSL* 55 (1938): 142–65.
Prinsloo, Gert T. M. "Historical Reality and Mythological Metaphor in Psalm 124." Pages 181–203 in *Psalms and Mythology*. Edited by Dirk J. Human. LHBOTS 462. New York: T&T Clark, 2007.
———. "Šĕ'ôl→Yĕrûšālayim→Šamayim: Spatial Orientation in the Egyptian Hallel (Psalms 113–118)." *OTE* 19 (2006): 739–60.
———. "Yahweh and the Poor in Psalm 113: Literary Motif and/or Theological Reality." *OTE* 9 (1996): 465–85.
Rabe, Norbert. "'Tochter Babel, die verwüstete!' (Psalm 137,8)—textkritisch betrachtet," *BN* 78 (1995): 84–103.
Rahlfs, Alfred. עָנִי und עָנָו *in den Psalmen*. Göttingen: Dieterische, 1892.
Renan, Ernest. *Histoire du peuple d'Israël*. 5 vols. Paris: Calmann-Lévy, 1893.
Rensburg, J. F. J. van. "History as Poetry: A Study of Psalm 136." Pages 80–90 in *Exodus 1–15, Text and Context: Proceedings of the 29th Annual Congress of the Old Testament Society of South Africa (OTSSA)*. Edited by J. J. Burden. Pretoria: OTWSA/OTSSA, 1987.
Riede, Peter. *Im Netz des Jägers: Studien zur Feindmetaphorik der Individualpsalmen*. WMANT 85. Neukirchen-Vluyn: Neukirchener, 2000.
Roberts, J. J. M. "God's Imperial Reign According to the Psalter," *HBT* 23 (2001): 211–21.
———. "The Hand of Yahweh." *VT* 21 (1971): 244–51.
———. "Zion in the Theology of the Davidic-Solomonic Empire." Pages 93–108 in *Studies in the Period of David and Solomon and Other Essays: Papers Read at the International Symposium for Biblical Studies, Tokyo, 5-7 December, 1979*. Edited by Tomoo Ishida. Winona Lake, Ind.: Eisenbrauns, 1982.
Rohland, Edzard. "Die Bedeutung der Erwählungstraditionen Israels für die Eschatologie der alttestamentliche Propheten." DTheol diss., University of Heidelberg, 1956.
Root, Margaret C. *The King and Kingship in Achaemenid Art: Essays on the Creation of an Iconography of Empire*. AcIr 19. Leiden: Brill, 1979.
Rösel, Christoph. *Die messianische Redaktion des Psalters: Studien zu Entstehung und Theologie der Sammlung Psalm 2–89*. Calwer theologische Monographien Bibelwissenschaft 19. Stuttgart: Calwer, 1999.

Sancisi-Weerdenburg, Heleen. "Darius I and the Persian Empire." *CANE* 2:1035–50.
Satterthwaite, Philip E. "Zion in the Songs of Ascents." Pages 105–28 in *Zion, City of our God*. Edited by Richard S. Hess and Gordon J. Wenham. Grand Rapids: Eerdmans, 1999.
Saur, Markus. *Die Königspsalmen: Studien zur Entstehung und Theologie*. BZAW 340. Berlin: de Gruyter, 2004.
Scaiola, Donatella. "The End of the Psalter." Pages 701–10 in *The Composition of the Book of Psalms*. Edited by Erich Zenger. BETL 238. Leuven: Peeters, 2010.
Schmid, Konrad. "Himmelsgott, Weltgott, und Schöpfer: 'Gott' und der 'Himmel' in der Literatur der Zeit des Zweiten Tempels." Pages 111–48 in *Der Himmel*. Edited by Martin Ebner and Irmtraud Fischer. JBT 20. Neukirchen-Vluyn: Neukirchener, 2005.
———. *The Old Testament: A Literary History*. Translated by Linda Maloney. Minneapolis: Fortress Press, 2012.
Schmidt, Hans. *Das Gebet der Angeklagten im Alten Testament*. BZAW 49. Giessen: Töpelmann, 1928.
Schmitt, Rüdiger. "Bisotun iii: Darius's Inscriptions." *Encyclopædia Iranica*. Online: http://www.iranicaonline.org/articles/bisotun-iii.
Schniedewind, William M. *How the Bible Became a Book: The Textualization of Ancient Israel*. Cambridge: Cambridge University Press, 2004.
Scoralick, Ruth. "Hallelujah für einen gewalttätigen Gott? Zur Theologie von Psalm 135 und 136." *BZ* 46 (2002): 253–72.
Seidl, Ursula. "Ein Relief Dareios I. in Babylon." *AMI* 9 (1976): 125–30.
Seitz, Christopher R. *Zion's Final Destiny: The Development of the Book of Isaiah; A Reassessment of Isaiah 36–39*. Minneapolis: Fortress Press, 1991.
Segovia, Fernando. *Decolonizing Biblical Studies: A View from the Margins*. Maryknoll, N.Y.: Orbis Books, 2000.
Seybold, Klaus. *Introducing the Psalms*. Edinburgh: T&T Clark, 1990.
———. *Die Psalmen*. HAT. First series 15. Tübingen: Mohr Siebeck, 1996.
———. *Die Wallfahrtspsalmen: Studien zur Entstehungsgeschichte von Psalm 120–34*. Biblisch-theologische Studien 3. Neukirchen-Vluyn: Neukirchener, 1978.
Sheppard, Gerald. "'Enemies' and the Politics of Prayer in the Book of Psalms." Pages 61–82 in *The Bible and the Politics of Exegesis: Essays in Honor of Norman K. Gottwald on his Sixty-Fifth Birthday*. Edited

by David Jobling, Peggy Day, and Gerald Sheppard. Cleveland, Ohio: Pilgrim Press, 1991.

Silverman, Jason M. *Persepolis and Jerusalem: Iranian Influence on the Apocalyptic Hermeneutic.* LHBOTS 558. New York: T&T Clark, 2012.

Soja, Edward W. *Postmodern Geographies: The Reassertion of Space in Critical Space Theory.* London: Verso, 1989.

———. *Thirdspace: Journeys to Los Angeles and other Real-and-Imagined Places.* Cambridge, Mass.: Blackwell, 1996.

Starbuck, Scott R. A. *Court Oracles in the Psalms: The So-Called Royal Psalms in Their Ancient Near Eastern Context.* SBLDS 172. Atlanta: Scholars Press, 1999.

Steck, Odil Hannes. *Friedensvorstellung im alten Jerusalem: Psalmen, Jesaja, Deuterojesaja.* Theologischen Studien 111. Zürich: Theologischer, 1972.

Steiner, Till Magnus. "Perceived and Narrated Space in Psalm 48." *OTE* 25 (2012): 685–704.

Strawn, Brent, "'A World under Control': Isaiah 60 and the Apadana Reliefs from Persepolis." Pages 85–116 in *Approaching Yehud: New Approaches to the Study of the Persian Period.* Edited by Jon L. Berquist. SemeiaSt 50. Atlanta: Society of Biblical Literature, 2007.

Sugirtharajah, Rasaiah S. *Exploring Postcolonial Biblical Criticism: History, Method, Practice.* Malden, Mass.: Wiley-Blackwell, 2012.

———. *Postcolonial Criticism and Biblical Interpretation.* Oxford: Oxford University Press, 2002.

Tavernier, Jan. "An Achaemenid Royal Inscription: The Text of Paragraph 13 of the Aramaic Version of the Bisitun Inscription." *JNES* 60 (2001): 161–76.

Tiemeyer, Lena-Sofia. *For the Comfort of Zion: The Geographical and Theological Location of Isaiah 40–55.* VTSup 139. Leiden: Brill, 2011.

———. "Geography and Textual Allusions in Interpreting Isaiah XL–LV and Lamentations in Judahite Texts." *VT* 57 (2007): 367–85.

Tournay, Raymond J. *Seeing and Hearing God with the Psalms: the Prophetic Liturgy of the Second Temple in Jerusalem.* JSOTSup 118. Sheffield: JSOT Press, 1991.

Trebilco, Paul R. *Jewish Communities in Asia Minor.* SNTSMS 69. Cambridge: Cambridge University Press, 1991.

Trublet, Jaques. "Approche Canonique des Psaumes du Hallel." Pages 339–76 in *The Composition of the Book of Psalms.* Edited by Erich Zenger. BETL 238. Leuven: Peeters, 2010.

Tucker, W. Dennis, Jr. "Democratization and the Language of the Poor in Psalms 2–89." *HBT* 25 (2003): 161–78.

———. "Is Shame a Matter of Patronage in the Communal Laments?" *JSOT* 31 (2007): 465–80.

———. "A Polysemiotic Approach to the Poor in the Psalms." *PRSt* 31 (2004): 425–39.

Valeta, David M. *Lions and Ovens and Visions: A Satirical Reading of Daniel 1–6.* HBM 12. Sheffield: Sheffield Phoenix, 2008.

VanGemeren, Willem A., ed. *New International Dictionary of Old Testament Theology and Exegesis.* 5 vols. Grand Rapids: Zondervan, 1997.

Vanderhooft, David. "Cyrus II, Liberator or Conquerer?" Pages 351–72 in *Judah and the Judeans in the Persian Period.* Edited by Oded Lipschits and Manfred Oeming. Winona Lake, Ind.: Eisenbrauns, 2006.

Velden, Frank van der. *Psalm 109 und die Aussagen zur Feindschädigung in den Psalmen.* Stuttgart: Katholisches Bibelwerk, 1997.

Wallace, Howard N. *Psalms.* Readings: A New Biblical Commentary. Sheffield: Sheffield Phoenix, 2009.

Wanke, Gunther. "Prophecy and Psalms in the Persian Period." *CHJ* 1:162–88.

Watson, Rebecca. *Chaos Uncreated: A Reassessment of the Theme of 'Chaos' in the Hebrew Bible.* BZAW 341. Berlin: de Gruyter, 2005.

Watson, Wilfred G. E. *Classical Hebrew Poetry: A Guide to Its Techniques.* New York: T&T Clark, 2005.

———. "Reversed Rootplay in Psalm 145." *Bib* 62 (1981): 101–2.

Watts, John W., ed. *Persia and Torah: The Theory of Imperial Authorization of the Pentateuch.* SBLSymS 17. Atlanta: Society of Biblical Literature, 2001.

Weber, Beat. *Werkbuch Psalmen III: Theologie und Spiritualität des Psalters und seiner Psalmen.* Stuttgart: Kohlhammer, 2010.

Weiser, Artur. *The Psalms: A Commentary.* OTL. Philadelphia: Westminster, 1962.

Westermann, Claus. *The Praise of God in the Psalms.* Translated by Keith R. Crim. Richmond, Va.: John Knox, 1965.

Wittman, Derek Edward. "The Kingship of Yahweh and the Politics of Poverty and Oppression in the Hebrew Psalter." PhD diss., Baylor University, 2010.

Whybray, R. Norman. *The Second Isaiah.* OTG. Sheffield: JSOT Press, 1983.

Wilcox, Max. "'The God-Fearers' in Acts: A Reconsideration." *JSNT* 13 (1981): 102–22.

Williamson, Hugh G. M. *Ezra, Nehemiah*. WBC 16. Waco, Tex.: Word, 1985.

Willis, John T. "The Song of Hannah and Psalm 113." *CBQ* 35 (1973): 139–54.

Wilson, Gerald. *The Editing of the Hebrew Psalter*. SBLDS 76. Chico, Calif.: Scholars Press, 1985.

———. "King, Messiah, and the Reign of God: Revisiting the Royal Psalms and the Shape of the Psalter." Pages 391–406 in *The Book of Psalms: Composition and Reception*. Edited by Peter Flint and Patrick D. Miller. VTSup 99. Leiden: Brill, 2005.

———. "The Shape of the Book of Psalms." *Int* 46 (1992): 129–42.

———. "Shaping the Psalter: A Consideration of Editorial Linkage in the Book of Psalms." Pages 72–82 in *The Shape and Shaping of the Psalter*. Edited by J. Clinton McCann Jr. JSOTSup 159. Sheffield: JSOT Press, 1993.

———. "The Structure of the Psalter." Pages 229–46 in *Interpreting the Psalms: Issues and Approaches*. Edited by David Firth and Philip S. Johnston. Downers Grove, Ill.: InterVarsity Press, 2005.

———. "The Use of Royal Psalms in the 'Seams' of the Hebrew Psalter." *JSOT* 35 (1986): 85–94.

Windfuhr, Gernot L. "'Saith Darius': Dialectic, Numbers, Time and Space at Behistun (DB, Old Persian Version, 520 BC)." Pages 265–81 in *Continuity and Change: Proceedings of the Last Achaemenid Workshop, April 6–8, 1990, Ann Arbor, Michigan*. Edited by Heleen Sancisi-Weerdenburg, Amélie Kuhrt, and Margeret C. Root. AH 8. Leiden: Nederlands Instituut voor het Nabije Oosten, 1994.

Wright, David P. "Ritual Analogy in Psalm 109." *JBL* 113 (1994): 385–404.

Zakovitch, Yair. "The Interpretive Significance of the Sequence of Psalms 111–112, 113–118, 119." Pages 215–27 in *The Composition of the Book of Psalms*. Edited by Erich Zenger. BETL 238. Leuven: Peeters, 2010.

Zenger, Erich. "Das Buch der Psalmen." Pages 348–70 in *Einleitung in das Alte Testament*. Edited by Erich Zenger. 6th ed. Stuttgart: Kohlhammer, 2006.

———. "The Composition and Theology of the Fifth Book of Psalms, Psalms 107–145." *JSOT* 80 (1998): 77–102.

———. "'Es segne dich JHWH vom Zion aus … ' (Ps 134,3): Die Gottesmetaphorik in den Wallfahrtpsalmen Ps 120–134." Pages 601–21 in

Gott und Mensch im Dialog: Festschrift für Otto Kaiser zum 80. Geburtstag. Edited by Markus Witte. BZAW 345. 2 vols. Berlin: de Gruyter, 2004.

———. "The God of Israel's Reign over the World (Psalms 90–106)." Pages 161–90 in *The God of Israel and the Nations: Studies in Isaiah and the Psalms.* Edited by Norbert Lohfink and Erich Zenger. Translated by Everett R. Kalin. Collegeville, Minn.: Liturgical Press, 2000.

———. "Der jüdische Psalter—ein anti-imperiales Buch?" Pages 95–108 in *Religion und Gesellschaft: Studien zu ihrer Wechselbeziehung in den Kulturen des Antiken Vorderen Orients.* Edited by Rainer Albertz. AZERKAVO 1/AOAT 248. Münster: Ugarit, 1997.

———. "Der Zion als Ort der Gottesnähe: Beobachtungen zum Weltbild des Wallfahrtspsalters Ps 120–134." Pages 84–114 in *Gottes Nähe im Alten Testament.* Edited by Gönke Eberhardt and Kathrin Liess. SBS 202. Stuttgart: Katholische Bibelwerk, 2004.

Index of Ancient Sources

Hebrew Bible

Genesis
1–2	27

Exodus
6:6	60
14:22	85
14:27	85
15	150
15:6	91
15:11	91
15:12	91
15:13	60
18:11	113

Leviticus
25:48–49	60

Numbers
22:23	110
22:31	110

Deuteronomy
7:6	112
10:12	90
13:4	90
14:2	112
26:18	112
28:49	84
31:12	90
32:40–42	113

Joshua
5:13	110
10:24	80
12:24	117

Judges
1:6–7	108
3:22	110
8:10	110
9:54	110

1 Samuel
17:51	110
18:25–27	92
31:4	110

2 Samuel
4:12	108
22	129
24:9	110

1 Kings
5:2	120

2 Kings
3:26	110
18:30	102
18:34–35	86
19:10	102
19:26	110

Isaiah
8:7–8	101
9:3	105
14:5	105
24:11	134
28:11	84

Isaiah (cont.)

33:19	84	63:16	60
37:27	110	66:18	70
40–48	56		
40:2	56	**Jeremiah**	
40:10–20	85	5:15	84
41:4	147	14:2	134
41:6–7	85	20:4–5	102
41:14	60	26:18	107
41:20	147	34:20–21	102
41:29	126	41:10	120
42:5–13	56	41:14	120
42:17	23	46:12	134
43:7	147	50:29	102
43:14	60	50:34	60
44:6	60		
44:9–20	85, 126	**Ezekiel**	
44:23	60	3:5–6	84
44:24–28	56	22	102
44:28	57	26:16	124
45:1	58	36:20	86
45:2	64	38	99
45:4–5	57	38:15	62
45:7	147	39	99
45:11–13	56	39:2	62
45:13	64	39:2–4	99
46:10	147	47:2	101
47:1	124		
47:4	60	**Joel**	
47:6	56	2:17	86
48:12–15	56		
48:17	60	**Jonah**	
49:7	60	2:5	126
49:26	60	2:8	126
51:10	60		
51:23	80	**Micah**	
54:5	50	3:12	107
59:12	70		
59:20	60	**Zechariah**	
60	31	9–14	5
60:2	70	10:6	88
60:10	128	10:12	88
60:16	60		
61:5	129	**Psalms**	
62:12	60	1	3
		1–2	5

INDEX OF ANCIENT SOURCES

2	7	77:16	60
2:8–9	58	78	110
2:10	132	78:35	60
2–89	5, 9	79	13
2–106	9,	79:10	86
9–10	3	82:1	126
11:2	97	83:12	173
11:4	143	86	184
11:5	97	89	7, 8, 182
14:2	143	89:10	80
17:2–3	143	90	8
18	129, 130, 132, 134, 144	90–150	5
18:33–39	131	96	12
18:37–40	131	100	12
18:45–46	131	102:1	184
18:51	131, 132	102:23	132
32:4	150	103:6	184
33:7	62	103:17	90
35:15–16	102	104:1–4	146
38:2	150	105	110
40:3	90	105:45	111
42–48	154	106	110, 112
42:4	86	106:6	111
42:11	86	106:10	60, 61
44:5	157	106:41	61, 80, 102, 111
46	140	107	3, 8, 59, 76
46:5	155	107–110	10, 82
46:6–7	141	107–118	9,
47:2–3	86	107–145	17, 58, 190
47:10	173	107:2–3	60, 65, 113
48	140	107:4–9	63
48:1–3	155	107:4–32	62
48:5–7	141	107:6	63
51:14	173	107:7	64, 65
56	90	107:10–16	63
57:7–11	69	107:11	60
60:5–12	69	107:13	64
65:7	62	107:16	64
72	7, 66, 134	107:17	60
72:10	132	107:23–32	63
72:14	116	107:33–43	59, 65
74	13, 71, 184	107:39	66
74:2	60	107:40	173, 176
74:13	62	107:41	74, 83
76	140, 184	107:42	66, 67, 74, 167

Psalms (cont.)

107:43	59	114:1–2	84
108–110	8, 12, 68, 76, 182	114:3	85
108	10, 69, 123, 191	115	85, 178, 189
108:4	70, 86, 188	115:2	82, 85–86, 88
108:6	69, 188	115:3	144
108:6–7	150	115:3–8	156
108:8–10	70	115:5–8	86
108:10–11	74	115:7	150
108:11–14	71	115:11	87, 90, 144
108:12	170	115:11–13	157
108:13	72, 75, 76, 79	115:15	147, 148
108:13–14	170	116	177, 178, 191
108:14	196	116:3	171
109	72, 74, 75, 78	116:10–11	171, 172
109:1–3	74	116:16	182
109:6–19	76, 77	117	88, 125
109:8–13	77, 78	117:1	82, 86, 87
109:22	83, 177, 180	118	89, 150, 178
109:23	74	118:1	89
109:26–29	79	118:2–4	89, 172
109:28	180	118:4	87
109:29	75	118:5	90
109:30	74	118:8–9	172, 173
109:31	151, 177, 188	118:10	90, 91, 172
119–136	9	118:11	91
110	75, 76, 79	118:12	91
110:1	79, 80, 151	118:13	178
110:3	173	118:14	90, 178
110:5	76, 80, 188	118:15–16	90, 150–151
110:5–7	80	118:22	92
110:7	81	118:23	90
111	168	118:25	90, 93
112	168, 178	119	168, 180
112:1	90	119:13	127
113–118	82	119:23	180, 181
113	178	119:49–50	180
113:1	83	119:50	180
113:4	82, 83	119:67	180
113:5–6	143	119:71	180
113:6	83	119:72	127
113:7	176, 190	119:73–74	90
113:7–9	83	119:84–85	181
113:8	83, 173	119:88	127
114	82, 83, 85	119:107	180
		119:121–122	180

INDEX OF ANCIENT SOURCES

119:134	180	132–134	95
119:134–135	181	132:15	154, 177
119:140–141	181	133:3	154
119:153	180	134:3	147, 148, 154
119:161	180	135–136	110, 111
119:176	182	135:4	111
120	96, 97	135:5	112
120:1	97	135:5–7	114, 147
120:2	97	135:6	115
120:4	188	135:8	115
120:5–7	98	135:8–12	114
120:7	97, 99	135:10	112
121–122	95	135:12	135
121	148	135:14	113, 115
121:2	147	136	116
121:5	151	136:5–9	116, 118, 144
121:7	151, 154	136:10–22	116, 118, 119, 144
122:6–7	154	136:11	116
123:1	144, 162	136:12–13	151
123:3	154, 162	136:13	117
124	100, 148	136:17–20	117
124:1–2	100, 105	136:18–19	118
124:3–5	101, 102, 104, 135, 154, 189	136:21	118, 136
124:6	102, 104, 136	136:22	182
124:6–8	188	136:23	162
124:7	103	136:23–24	116, 118, 119
124:8	147	136:24	112, 118
125	3, 103	136:26	144
125:1–2	105	137	3, 10, 119, 135
125:3	154	137:1–3	120, 121, 122
125:3	105, 106, 136, 188	137:8	121, 122, 123
125:5	105	137:9	123
126:4	154	138–145	8
128	168	138	124, 125, 126
128:2	154	138:1	125, 128
128:4–5	154	138:2	126
128:6	154	138:4	125, 127, 128, 132
129	3, 106, 135	138:6	177
129:1–2	106, 109, 110, 135	138:7	144, 146, 151, 153
129:3	107, 108, 135, 188	139	168
129:4	108, 110	139:8	146, 153
129:5	109	139:9	146
129:5–8	108, 110	139:10	151
129:6	110	139:19	146, 153
129:8	154	139:19–22	146

Psalms (cont.)

140:2	124	147:4	194
140:4	150	147:8	194
140:14	185	147:10	191, 192
141	124	147:11	192
143:3	183	147:15	195
143:12	124, 183	147:19	195
144	3, 4, 12, 124, 128, 144, 182, 183	148	192, 195
144:1	130	148:4	195
144:2	130	148:7	195
144:5–6	130	148:11	192
144:5–7	144	148:13	195
144:5–11	162	149	195
144:7	128, 129, 130, 131, 150, 151, 185, 189	149:6	193
		149:6–8	192
144:10	130, 131, 132	149:8	193
144:11	128, 129, 130, 150, 176, 189	150	12, 196
144:12	189		
144:12–15	132–33, 136	Job	
144:13	189	2:8	124
144:14	128, 133, 135, 136, 189	12:12–35	66
145	3, 8, 9, 156, 183	12:21	66
145:1	157	20:25	110
145:1–13	159	21:28	67
145:3	159		
145:4	160	Qoheleth	
145:9	160	9:12	103
145:11–13	158		
145:13	158, 159	Lamentations	
145:14	196	5:2–5	77
145:14–16	161		
145:14–21	159	Esther	
145:17	161	1:20	45
145:19	161	6:1	45
145:19–20	167		
145:20	163	Daniel	
145:21	17, 156, 189	3:33	159
146	148	4:31	159
146:3	173, 195	6:8–9	45
146:3–4	191	6:11	126
146:5–9	148	6:27	159
146:7–9	194	8:24	115
146:10	148	11:10	101
146–150	5, 10, 190	11:24	115
147:2	194		

INDEX OF ANCIENT SOURCES

Ezra	
1:2–4	50
4:9–16	50
7:17–22	50
5:7–17	50
5:13	123
6:2–5	50
6:6–12	50
7:12–26	50

Nehemiah	
5	52, 106
5:2–5	51
13:6	123

1 Chronicles	
5:21	120

2 Chronicles	
2:11	147
6:36	120
8:17	62
19:9	90

Persian Sources

A?P	35

A2Hc	29

Behistun Inscription (DB)	
10–12	38
10–14	39
14	38
40–48	39
55	40
70	37, 42

Cyrus Cylinder	
5–7	23
8	23
11	23
15	24
19	24
22	25
24	25
28–29	25

DPd	28

DPh	29

DSab	29, 31, 32

DSe	
4	40
5	40

DZc	44

Nabonidus Chronicle	
2.1–4	22

Naqsh-I Rustam	33
1	27, 149
1–2	29
2c	34
2e	34
4	30

XPh	
4a	40
4b	41

Greco-Roman Sources

Herodotus, *Histories*	44
1.130	23
2.127	23
5.52–54	47
6.18–22	29
7.8	30

Justin	
1.6.16	23

Quintus Curtius Rufus, *Historiae Alexandri Magni*	
3.3.22–25	49

Strabo
    15:3.18–19   169

Xenophon, *Anabasis*
    3.4.31   48

Index of Modern Authors

Ackroyd, Peter R. 1
Ahn, Gregor 33
Ahn, John J. 121
Ahn, So Kun 190
Albertz, Ranier 56, 121, 174, 175
Allen, Leslie C. 59, 62, 65, 79, 84, 87, 106, 107, 112, 113, 132, 174
Balcer, Jack M. 39
Ballhorn, Egbert 7, 11, 12, 13, 16, 68, 69, 73, 80, 87, 89, 90, 101, 104, 112, 124, 128, 130, 134, 157, 158, 159, 180, 181, 182, 188
Baltzer, Klaus 58
Barstad, Hans 55, 57
Becking, Bob 51, 120
Berges, Ulrich 174, 179
Berquist, Jon L. 2, 3, 5, 13, 18, 19, 26, 133, 175
Beyerlin, Walter 60, 63, 65, 66, 86
Birkeland, Harris 12, 13, 14, 15, 75
Blenkinsopp, Joseph 52, 56, 179
Bonfante, Larissa 35
Booij, Thijs 79, 171, 183
Botha, Phil J. 171
Bremer, Johannes 176, 177, 180, 184, 185
Breukelman, Frans 177
Briant, Pierre 16, 20, 21, 24, 26, 31, 34, 35–36, 37, 38, 41, 47, 48, 52, 192
Briggs, Charles A. 87, 92, 121
Briggs, Emilie G. 87, 92, 121
Bright, John 1
Brown, William P. 91, 101, 102, 104, 150

Broyles, Craig 69
Buysch, Christopher 124, 125, 128, 161, 178
Cameron, George C. 46
Carey, Greg 16
Carr, David 16
Cataldo, Jeremiah W. 1, 174
Ceresko, Anthony 168
Childs, Brevard S. 101
Collins, John J. 182
Coogan, Michael D. 1
Cook, Stephen L. 69
Cottrill, Amy C. 12, 75, 77, 97, 113
Creach, Jerome F. D. 5, 70, 155, 170, 173
Croft, Steven J. L. 12, 76, 107
Crow, Loren 95, 99
Crüsemann, Frank 100, 107
Dahood, Mitchell 62, 67, 86
Dandamaev, Muhammed A. 21, 39, 78
Davidson, Steed V. 15
Davies, Philip R. 55, 58
deClaissé-Walford, Nancy 168
Duhm, Bernard 79
Eaton, John 76
Eberhardt, Gönke 152
Ego, Beate 142, 143, 162, 163
Eidevall, Göran 97
Franke, Sabine 25
Freedman, David N. 122
Fried, Lisbeth S. 58, 175
Frye, Richard N. 21
Garrison, Mark B. 47

Gärtner, Judith 111, 112
Gerstenberger, Erhard 19, 49, 50, 52, 77, 93, 100, 104, 105, 111, 117, 134, 156, 169, 173, 193
Gillmayer-Bucher, Susanne 99, 150
Goldingay, John 55, 83, 87, 93, 105, 109, 122, 123, 151, 159, 171, 174, 193
Goodblatt, David 166
Gottwald, Norman K. 1
Goulder, Michael D. 76, 93, 98, 100, 106, 122, 126, 130, 144, 193
Grabbe, Lester L. 21, 25, 29, 39, 50, 52, 169
Greenfield, Jonas C. 43
Grol, Harm van 124, 181
Guillaume, Alfred 120
Gunkel, Hermann 73, 110
Gunneweg, Antonius 50
Habel, Norman 147
Hayes, Elizabeth 82, 85
Herrenschmidt, Clarisse 29, 36. 39
Hallock, Richard T. 46
Hartberger, Brigitt 121
Hobbs, T. R. 12
Hoglund, Kenneth G. 2, 50, 175
Holtz, Shalom E. 134
Hossfeld, Frank L.
Hossfeld, Frank L. 61, 62, 63, 66, 69, 70, 71, 73, 76, 81, 83, 84, 86, 88, 92, 96, 105, 106, 108, 112, 116, 120, 126, 132, 135, 144, 146, 148, 151, 153, 154, 170, 178, 190, 192, 195
Houtmann, Cornelius 142, 145, 147, 148
Howard, Cameron B. R. 43
Human, Dirk J. 112, 116, 117, 118
Hupfeld, Hermann 167
Hurvitz, Avi 83
Jacobson, Rolf 70
Janowski, Bernd 4, 13, 141
Janzen, David 50
Jarick, John 62
Jursa, Michael 46
Keel, Othmar 79, 80, 117, 146, 151, 192
Keet, Cuthbert C. 98
Kellerman, Ulrich 122, 123, 124
Kent, Roland G. 29, 34, 38
Kessler, John 2
Kirkpatrick, Alexander F. 100
Klingbeil, Martin 148
Knauf, Ernst Axel 69
Knowles, Melody 2, 155
Körting, Corinna 140, 154, 155
Kratz, Reinhard G. 157
Kraus, Hans Joachim 12, 67, 69, 76, 85, 86, 88, 110, 111, 114, 116, 121, 132, 141
Kuhrt, Amélie 19, 21, 22, 25, 26, 34, 36, 38, 41, 45, 47, 57, 152
Lefebvre, Henri 143
Leuenberger, Martin 6, 7, 9, 10, 11, 16, 68, 72, 80, 85, 112, 123, 132, 158
Levin, Christoph 172, 179
Lincoln, Bruce 28, 36, 39, 149
Lindars, Barnabas 158
Lipschits, Oded 21
Liverani, Mario 19, 20, 21, 25
Lohfink, Norbert 174
Magonet, Jonathan 147, 148
Malandra, William 35
Malchoz, Christian 118, 119
Martilla, Marko 72, 96, 172, 183
Martin-Achard, Robert 88
Mathys, Hans-Peter 88, 144, 147
McCann, J. Clinton, Jr. 73, 79, 88, 126
Millard, Matthias 154, 155
Miller, Robert D., II 153
Mitchell, David C. 5, 98, 182
Mowinckel, Sigmund 12, 14, 75, 77, 86, 93
Newsom, Carol A. 165, 166, 176, 188
Nordheim, Miriam von 79, 81
O'Brien, Julia M. 2, 16, 19
Ollenberger, Ben C. 140
Olmstead, Ten Eyck 39
Poebel, Arno 39
Prinsloo, Gert T. M. 82, 83, 100, 177
Rensburg, J. F. J van 118
Riede, Peter 13, 92, 102
Roberts, J. J. M. 91, 129, 140, 141, 150

INDEX OF MODERN AUTHORS

Rohland, Edzard 140
Root, Margaret 20, 21, 30, 31, 32, 33, 34, 37, 152
Rösel, Christopher 5, 9, 132
Sancisi-Weedenburg, Heleen 26, 29, 39, 44
Satterthwaite, Philip E. 100, 107, 154
Saur, Markus 133
Scaioloa, Donatella 190
Schmid, Konrad 141, 142, 143, 145, 162, 169, 170
Schmidt, Hans 72
Schmitt, Rüdiger 43, 44
Schniedewind, William M. 19
Scoralick, Ruth 112, 115, 117
Segovia, Fernando 13
Seidl, Ursula 44
Seitz, Christopher R. 55
Seybold, Klaus 59, 65, 85, 87, 109, 119, 121, 122, 149
Sheppard, Gerald 12
Silverman, Jason M. 48
Starbuck, Scott R. A. 79, 80
Steiner, Till Magnus 143
Strawn, Brent 31
Sugirtharajah, Rasaiah S. 13
Tavernier, Jan 43
Tiemeyer, Lena-Sofia 56
Tournay, Raymond J. 71
Trublet, Jacque 82, 89
Tucker, W. Dennis, Jr. 5, 68, 75, 109, 113, 174
Valeta, David M. 45
Velden, Frank van der 70
Vanderhooft, David 23, 24
Wallace, Howard N. 68, 123
Wanke, Gunther 3
Watson, Rebecca 114
Watson, Wilfred G. E. 158
Watts, John W. 2
Weber, Beat 167
Weiser, Artur 87
Westermann, Claus 59
Whybry, R. Norman 55
Williamson, Hugh G. M. 50
Willis, John T. 83
Windfuhr, Gernot L. 39
Wilson, Gerald 6, 7, 8, 9, 16, 124, 156, 168, 170, 182
Wittman, Derek E. 153
Wright, David P. 74, 77
Zakovitch, Yair 82
Zenger, Erich 4, 5, 6, 10, 16, 61, 62, 63, 66, 68, 69, 70, 71, 73, 76, 81, 83, 84, 86, 88, 92, 96, 105, 106, 108, 112, 116, 120, 126, 132, 135, 144, 146, 148, 151, 153, 154, 157, 158, 160, 168, 169, 170, 182, 183, 187, 190, 192, 195

www.ingramcontent.com/pod-product-compliance
Lightning Source LLC
Chambersburg PA
CBHW032004220426
43664CB00005B/135